MOVING
from the
OUTSIDE, IN

One Woman's Transcendental Journey

Tracy Makarenko

BALBOA.
PRESS

A DIVISION OF HAY HOUSE

Balboa Press books may be ordered through booksellers or by contacting:

Balboa Press
A Division of Hay House
1663 Liberty Drive
Bloomington, IN 47403
www.balboapress.com
1-(877) 407-4847

Printed in the United States of America.

ISBN: 978-1-4525-7306-9 (sc)
ISBN: 978-1-4525-7308-3 (hc)
ISBN: 978-1-4525-7307-6 (e)

Library of Congress Control Number: 2013907403

Balboa Press rev. date: 6/17/2013

For my daughters
May the work I've done inspire you to find your
passion, your joy, and your happiness.

Mum
Thank you

Table of Contents

Disclaimer

I AM NOT A PHYSICIAN. I cannot and do not prescribe medical treatment. Therefore, the information provided in this book is for educational purposes only. Any decision on your part about how you use this information is your personal choice, and I am not liable or responsible in any way whatsoever for what you do with this material after reading it. The information in this book is not meant to diagnose, prescribe, or treat any disease. Please discuss any changes to your health with a qualified, licensed health care provider.

Introduction

AT THE AGE OF THIRTY-THREE I had been married for eight years. Notice that I did not say "happily married," although there were moments of pure joy. My husband and I had produced two beautiful daughters, then three and five years old. Since the age of six months I had moved fifteen times. I wasn't a military brat, but a child of a miner, and I had married a mining engineer. This last move had unhinged me. It had returned me to my past, the past I had put out of my mind because of all the emotions that surfaced and haunted me when I reflected backward in time. The return to my hometown, where I had lived between the ages of fifteen and twenty-five put me into enough of a tailspin that it wasn't a surprise when I found myself knee deep in an emotional quagmire. Or was it more of an identity crisis?

I had evolved into a different person. In fact every time I moved, I evolved into a different person. I adapted so often that perhaps the bigger problem was that I no longer knew who I was. That realization was just as scary as returning home. I hadn't meant to be difficult, but that persona had developed during my youth because I needed to protect myself. I wasn't one of those nasty girls; I just had a "didn't-care" attitude. No one was going to hurt me again, so I had used "the face" for a few years to protect myself. The result was that it was now necessary for me to reflect on my past to figure out who I had become. That is where my story begins, with me reflecting on the last time I needed my life to change, at the age of twenty years old.

I revisited the past to find the answers that would allow me to move forward into my future. My entire being needed to be rebuilt. The Gendron tarot cards say, "Castles built on sand crumble. Reassess your life and belief systems. Be prepared for rapid change." I was crumbling and needed a solid foundation if I was to move out of this mental and emotional hellhole. I had come to trust the cards and prepared for what was ahead. Okay, prepared as much as is possible.

Moving past the old into the new was a long and at times difficult journey. I turned to holistic health care and was surprised by its power. I had always been intuitive and never felt like I fit in anywhere. This place felt more like home. My intuition heightened, and the most unbelievable events took place as I moved forward. I share them so that if you are moving forward on your healing journey, you will know that you are not alone.

As I struggled with coming out of the closet with this new identity, I was also struggling with all my old relationships. Some needed to be severed; others it was possible to repair. All of it was part of the journey on which I had embarked.

Many moments left me feeling overwhelmed. But the reality was that each issue that was resolved offered another opportunity of freedom to my entire being! My head felt clearer, my body felt newer, my emotional state was more balanced, and I felt closer to God. I had gotten my life back.

Our world is changing and has been for a long time. Many of us are realizing there is more to life than what our parents or grandparents experienced. It isn't about what is right or wrong but what is inside us, what needs to be nourished. The bed we made no longer needs to be slept in; we are allowed to change our minds; we are allowed to release the bonds that society has placed on us for so long. Each and every day that I moved forward into my new life, things made more and more sense.

It is important that we live from our own truth, not one filled with lies, inconsistencies, or conditioning, but our real truth, the one we find when we fall in love with ourselves. Our body is a masterpiece, but we have never been given the tools to be the curators, the keepers of our own health.

You will journey with me into my forties, when I realized that my life on Earth was about helping others heal, and in doing so to share information, which led me to write this book. I have done my self-healing work to find many deeply hidden surprises. Take this journey with me and learn how to let go of your past and all the baggage attached to it. Learn tools that will allow you to work with your intuition in a healthy and grounding way. Heal your body physically, mentally, emotionally, and spiritually! Find your way to self-love and the surprises that are revealed beyond that! When you learn how to listen and speak from your heart chakra, life happens, miracles happen.

Take this journey with me. Transition from the outside in and then back out again!

What's Next?

CHAPTER 1

Change

It was time for a change. Not my huge hair or my trendy '80s clothes, but everything else. My name is Tracy, Tracy-Lynn to anyone who has known me since grammar school or is in my immediate family. My driver's licence states that I'm five feet, three inches, and since my nerves have recovered, slightly, I have gained some weight and sit at 105 pounds. I have red hair and freckles everywhere—the freckles, that is—and thankfully, at nearly twenty-one years of age can be called pretty. The days of being called Red-Headed Hamburger are long gone, thank God! The insecurities attached to all the name calling during my grammar school and junior high school years are not. It was necessary to change my mentality in order to survive their harmful effects. This came in handy when, during the last ten months of my senior year of high school, all the gossipmongers decided I was the perfect scapegoat for, well, everything. My reputation tanked! I put no energy into correcting their lies unless directly asked. Why should I feel bad for their behavior? What it did, however, was encrust me in an even thicker protective layer. Do I still trust? I trust only those I believe truly love me, which is what got me into this current mess. The facade I have carried around with me to show the world that everything in my life is perfect and that I am not damaged goods is starting to disintegrate. Therefore my world must change.

The guy sitting next to me, Peter, is the reason for this not-so-sudden decision. He is not much taller than I, has brown hair and brown eyes, and entered my life more than six years ago. Our turbulent relationship started when I was fourteen. Peter was the first boy to look at me. The first three months of our relationship were kind and loving. Then he cheated on me. For a multitude of reasons—insecurities at the top of that list—I was willing to continue our relationship. We worked though his cheating before we broke up as the result of a move. My parents wanted a new start in their own dysfunctional relationship and moved my younger sister, Jane; our dog, Skeeter; cat, Scruffy; and me twenty-four hundred kilometers across the Canadian countryside. Over the next two years, while we were apart, we both saw other people. I actually fell head over heels in love at one point, only to be dumped, painfully. It was after that incident that Peter and I reconnected. I realize now that he was a safer choice than putting my heart on the line again. Notice I didn't say "smarter choice."

My focus for the last two years of high school was friends and parties. When I received my high school transcripts, that was very apparent. Upgrading was necessary if I ever planned on attending a postsecondary school. It never crossed my mind that I wouldn't until I saw my transcript. Redoing the necessary high school classes to get a better grade with the same teachers seemed like an oxymoron, so I contacted Peter to see whether we could be roommates. That took three years of my life. One year of upgrading, bringing my marks up significantly, which allowed me to get into college. I was now a month away from receiving my two-year diploma in business administration, which I planned to transfer to the University of Winnipeg in the fall for another two years, finishing with a degree in human resources.

The last three years that Peter and I had been together make the word *dysfunctional* look functional! The three times we tried to live together maxed out at four months. I found the strength to make what I thought was the final break in January and was doing wonderfully until attending a party last month where Peter was in attendance. He acted like a jackass—nothing new, mind you—dragging me up a flight of stairs at one point to "get with me." Up until that point he had never actually laid a hand on me; he was more the mentally and emotionally abusive type of guy who only leaves internal bruising—stuff you can't see but that affects your self-esteem in a slower, more detrimental, way. If he had hit me, I would have left years ago. I'm pretty sure, anyway.

At the party I managed to get away, with no help from his friends, and I called a taxi. By the time my ride arrived, he was outside acting like an out-of-control delinquent again. *He is going to get his ass thrown in jail*, was the thought that raced through my mind. In the next instant I found myself grabbing his arm and throwing him into the taxi ahead of me and giving the driver my address. The next morning I looked over at him in my bed and thought, with much regret, *When will I ever learn? I should have left his sorry ass behind to deal with the consequences.* But I hadn't, and it was six weeks later that I found myself committed to change no matter what that looked like. I didn't know what was next, but I knew who was not.

The deciding factor had been a pregnancy scare. Moments before, we had been to the walk-in clinic, and thankfully, the results were negative. Negative. That always confused me, as in my mind I was taking a nonpregnancy test and wanted the answer to be positive. I questioned the nurse, and she confirmed that I was indeed not pregnant. "Thank God!"

Peter had been surprisingly disappointed by this news and mentioned to me how he had hoped I was pregnant so we could get married. There was no way I could conceal the amount of shock on my face at this statement. We had never, not ever, discussed a future together and now talk of marriage? I was still sitting in stunned disbelief half an hour later with Peter on my left side and half a dozen of his obnoxious male friends around a couple of tables in an Irish pub when I realized that the only way I could achieve separation from him and his friends was to return home, permanently. With a huge sigh, I realized this meant giving up school, at least for now.

Over the last three years—actually, six years—I had tried every scenario to be rid of Peter, but for whatever reason we were always thrown together again and again. I believe that things happen for a reason. What the reasoning was for this must be too close for me to understand. All I knew was that I couldn't continue living in the current turmoil that had become my life. The pattern that had presented itself showed that there was no way I could live in a city of six hundred thousand people and not in some way be connected to Peter and his insanity. I had tried really hard with no success. It was time to get off the hamster wheel and try something completely different. I hoped that having three provinces between us would give me what I was looking for—peace of mind.

Yellowknife, Northwest Territories, is located twenty-two hundred kilometers south of the magnetic North Pole and twenty-one hundred kilometers north of the Canada–United States border. It is located in the Canadian Shield, which is mostly made up of rock, with small pine and birch trees growing where possible. It is considered a desert, although there are numerous bodies of water, large and small. Yellowknife had been my home since the summer I turned sixteen, including every Christmas break and summer vacation for the last three years while I attended school. Currently the population was near twelve thousand. Yellowknifers mostly work for the government—territorial or federal—or one of the local gold mines. We enjoyed forty-four weeks of winter, one week of spring, one of fall, and six weeks of summer. Nowhere on earth could beat our summers, which featured twenty-four hours of sunlight a day. Walking out of the movie theater at eleven o'clock at night into daylight is magical. As a teenager walking home after a party or, now that I was of age, which is nineteen, the bar, I felt a sense of security having the sun still in the sky.

I had said good-bye to Peter at the airport as though it were any other departure. I hadn't had enough strength to tell him that I was not returning in the fall. I hadn't even tried to find the strength; leaving the news to a later date seemed simpler. I was too beaten down with all the changes I was making to bother having that long conversation where I would perhaps be persuaded to stay or return. He thought we were back together, and that made leaving easy. I was so exhausted and quite frankly, done, but it had all been about buying time.

It only took days for me to settle back into a routine once I had moved back in with my parents, whose relationship currently seemed fine. They had split up again the previous summer and reconciled that fall. That separation and reunion made three. My sister Jane would start her last year of high school in the fall. She was so grown up. When I had left for school three years ago she had still been so little. The four and a half years between us constantly left us on different pages of our lives. She was now a few inches taller than me and had blossomed into a woman. Her blonde—almost white—hair, perky nose, and inquisitive blue eyes turned heads, male and female. Her skin was beautifully tanned, not red and blotchy like mine when I spent too much time in the sun. Not that I would share my positive comments with her, ever. We didn't do that in my family. That whole "If you don't have anything nice to say, don't say anything at all," had been taken even further in our family. We just didn't say anything, nice or nasty. Don't get me wrong: my father's side of the family yelled when they spoke, and over the years Jane and I had learned that way of communicating. In those explosive moments we said things we regretted, which were never spoken about again.

For years I had perceived Jane as a troll who had taken the love of my mother away from me at the age of four when she showed up in my house. Those feelings of disdain developed because I saw love for Jane in my mother's eyes that I had never noticed when she looked at me. Over time my emotions had erupted, causing Jane physical pain in a number of ways. Even with the abuse at my hands, she returned love and compassion. That eventually won me over in my junior high years. I now loved her dearly and would protect her at all costs.

Since my return I had a full-time job with my previous employer. It was a government job that paid well for menial office tasks. Socially, a male friend I had met the previous summer had been popping by daily. Luke was a year older than I. What he did for work, I had no idea. Nothing, from what I could see. He was not much taller than I, but definitely taller than Peter. He had blond hair and blue eyes and a beach-bum tan. I had always been attracted to the tall, dark, and handsome type, but at no point did I seem to be dating that type.

Within weeks of my return, Luke and I were dating, I guess. I hadn't completely forgotten about Peter, but I hoped he had forgotten about me, which I knew was not true. My mum had given me a dozen phone messages from him.

I hadn't been able to keep anything down since the pregnancy scare. The years of living with Peter had done a number on my nerves, and the smallest thing seemed to throw my system out of whack. For that reason I should have just returned his calls. It took two weeks before he got me on the other end of the phone.

"Hello."

"Hi, I haven't heard from you."

As I held the receiver, I could feel my body shaking in fear at hearing his voice. *Here we go, be strong, Tracy.* "No, I've been busy with work and stuff."

I could feel that my standoffishness had caused tension on the other end of the phone, "Are you coming back in the fall?" It wasn't a question, but more of a demand.

"No." Yeah, I said it! Silently I kept repeating, *Stay strong, stay strong.*

"Have you met someone?" he questioned me.

This just brought out my anger. Did he really think that was the only reason I wouldn't return? What relationship had he been a part of? "Yes," I replied. If that was my way out, fine; I'd take it. He then hung up.

It was over.

Was it over? I wasn't crying. I was still shaking, and my stomach was tight. Where was the relief? *Enough is enough, Tracy! You have spent an abundant amount of time on this situation; it's time to move on.*

Telling my parents I wasn't returning to school was not any simpler. I fretted for a month before I finally told them in August. Their reply shocked me, "So what are you going to do?" I had expected a lecture about quitting school. Rather, they had posed a good question. My mind said, "Take it day by day," but I didn't dare express that out loud, for perhaps the lecture would then surface. I should have had a plan, but I didn't. My only plan had been to return home and away from Peter. With that accomplished, I would have to give my future some thought.

Luke was a great sounding board. He'd listen to me for hours, for days, which turned into months. To anyone else, perhaps, it would have seemed like complaining, but without my knowing, it was my therapy. Most of my verbal diarrhea was about Peter and his cheating nature. He had never stopped; I had just stopped noticing. When I did, it brought out a jealous side of me that made me cheat too. Now I was dealing with all the anger and guilt, never mind the recurring thought, *Could I be trusted in any relationship? Or was that just a reaction to being treated so badly?* I complained about the numerous weekends he never made it home because he was out on a drinking binge. What else, who knows? I unloaded about the night I spent in jail being questioned about the alleged assault Peter and his friends were being charged with. If I ever made plans with a girlfriend, something tragic would happen to Peter, and I would cancel my plans, to be with him. In the end he would never show up, leaving me home alone all night. He never once offered to drive me or loan me his car to go and visit my paternal grandmother, who lived only two and a half hours away. My aunt and favorite cousin were only five minutes away, and he had only visited once during those three years. Then there was an abundance of embarrassing parties where he would use information about me or our relationship to start conversations with various girls. One girl actually told me my boyfriend was a jerk. I nodded and agreed. What else could I do?

The previous year during one of our separations I had found the cutest little loft. Peter agreed to house-sit while I returned home to work over the summer. The day I returned to Winnipeg, ready to relax and get organized for school, I found out that we had been evicted. Peter had not paid the rent and had had one party after another. He had lost me my favorite apartment and my damage deposit. I was so devastated, and an apology was never forthcoming—only excuses. But the last straw came four months later when I found out that he was charging me more than my portion of the rent to cover his monthly parking space. How could he treat so badly someone he claimed to love? The answer could only be that he didn't love me, and if that was the answer then why treat me badly at all? That answer was easier, because I had allowed him to. I had put up with it for years. Time after time his sweet-talking nature lured me back in. He continued to have control over me even when I was in other relationships! Hating myself had come naturally. Did I deserve so little? I had considered suicide in March. Not to put myself out of my misery, but rather: "I'll show you, Peter! How would you feel if I was dead?" The scenario petered out quickly, as I had no idea where to get a gun, there was nowhere to hang a rope in my apartment, and the last time I accidently took too many pill I threw up for hours.

The fact that I never considered how my parents or sister would feel if I were dead spoke volumes and was something I'd need to ponder more closely later.

Currently, I was happy to be alive, although I might have a terrible disease. The doctors had done numerous tests involving my intestines and bowels. They kept telling me nothing was wrong. Well, my body wasn't acting normal, so something was wrong! It was irritable bowel syndrome—something they didn't have a name for in the '80s. Coffee seemed to affect me the most, so I quit drinking it. Thanks to Luke I had also stopped smoking. My redheaded temper kicked in after he bummed one too many cigarettes. I wasn't going to pay for his smokes anymore, so I quit. I was tired of being used. Had all this made me selfish or just less tolerant?

By the end of October, Luke was annoying the shit out of me. No pun intended, but if you pay attention there is always a reaction to your words. I had finished ranting about my life, so now there was only silence.

We had absolutely nothing to talk about. Peter had a vast number of shortcomings, but we were capable of intellectual conversation.

By mid-November my parents decided to visit my maternal grandmother's home in Keswick, Ontario, for Christmas. I wanted to go too, but Luke expected to come along with us. He had taken up a permanent spot at the dining room table and was making plans for our future. Well, that future did not include him at our Christmas table. My father asked me whether I had managed to get the time off work. I told him, "Sorry, they told me no." He knew I was lying but never asked why. Surely he had spoken to my boss over drinks at the Legion or Elks Club, or even at the local coffee shop on Saturday or Sunday morning. Yellowknife was small, and everyone knew everyone. My dad spent his days in the mines, but only because he was a mining inspector for the territorial government. He knew people in both industries. He also never shied away from meeting anyone and would have used me as a means for an introduction to my boss, if he didn't already know him.

So, here I was, yet again, in a relationship and wishing it was over. I told myself it was because Christmas was around the corner and well, Luke came from a really dysfunctional family and never had a real Christmas. For that reason I was willing to sacrifice my own happy Christmas with my family. That was my thought process; my emotions were brewing resentment and anger just below the surface.

My conditioning had me playing nice. From infancy we're told to put others ahead of ourselves. Parents, grandparents, Sunday school teachers, school teachers, sometimes even strangers. Why is taking care of our own feelings considered selfish? Do we end up in these situations time and time again because we take care of ourselves last?

By mid-December Luke brought up the idea of returning to school with me in the fall. He didn't suggest Edmonton or Calgary, which were both much closer, but wanted to return to the same building Peter and I had lived in originally. Was this guy slow? Did he not understand anything I'd purged? I was terrified to go back there to visit relatives in case I accidently bumped into Peter. Why would I ever return for two solid years to attend school? It was the last straw. I wasn't about to play house with him; my concern was more whether I could hold out until after Christmas before I dumped him.

By New Year's Eve I couldn't do it any longer; enough was enough. My cousin Lisa had been living with us since the fall. She had left Winnipeg looking for a change herself. Her younger sister, Emily, was my very favorite cousin. She was traveling in Hong Kong or somewhere in the Orient. Lisa had returned to our home on Christmas Eve, engaged. Now all Luke could talk about was getting married. It was just too much. At two in the morning on New Year's Eve, at some underground party with the music blaring, I just ended it. My feelings were important; what was inside me was important! I hated feeling this crazy turmoil inside. What kept recurring was that my feelings were important. Enough of my time had been wasted in meaningless relationships, and not another minute would pass me by. I'm sure missing my parents and sister played a role in my abrupt decision. Resentment was running rampant in my mind. I hated Luke for making me miss out on spending what might be the last Christmas with my Gran.

I turned to leave, and Luke was right behind me. He literally stayed there for days, begging me to take him back, "But tomorrow is my birthday! Are you still taking me out?" Yes, my timing was really, really bad, but why was I now being punished? Was there ever a good time to break up with anyone?

He finally left the house before my parents arrived home. My mother received a call from him on Monday asking whether he could still come over for suppers or meet her and my father for lunch. Was he mentally insane? *They're my parents! Go away!*

It felt like Peter all over again. This time I had nowhere to move to. Was that my lesson? Stop running away from my problems? There was a long history of that behavior. Running to Peter to start with was about getting away from the gossip and useless teachers. This needed to be cut and dried; maybe I even needed to be mean.

I fell off the wagon after one night of drinking and called Luke. *Will I ever learn? Please, God, let me learn.* For the first time in my life my mother gave me a lecture. Maybe my life wouldn't have been so screwed up if she had done that sooner. I had never been held accountable for my actions. As the director of drug and alcohol abuse for the government, she traveled all over the north, counseling people. Of course now she was just coming into her own power at forty. Could I blame her for my lack of direction? She had been only eighteen when I was born, Dad, twenty-one. I am sure they did the best they could with what they had to work with—me. I rarely was forthcoming with any information. There was always the fear of getting in trouble, which must have happened or where did the fear erupt from to begin with?

Even though I couldn't stand Luke, breaking up was still difficult on some level. Actually it was the being alone that was difficult. Why do we attach ourselves to another human being? To make us feel whole? Should we not find that wholeness within ourselves and take that wholeness into the relationship? Two whole people would be so much better than two halves.

After the last word was spoken and I walked away from our relationship permanently, Luke wasn't even half a person. Monday morning as I was crossing the street to my office building he veered his car and tried to run me over. He would have managed if I wasn't so agile on my feet, even in high-heeled boots and on an icy sidewalk I managed to escape injury. Now my anger was at a breaking point, and I mumbled under my breath with tight lips, "Pull it together, Tracy," all the way to my office building, up the two flights of stairs, until I sat down at my desk. I had been in this new permanent accounting position for two weeks. Fifteen minutes later my phone rang, and before it reached my ear I could hear the word, "Bitch!" and then the receiver slammed on the other end.

This continued every ten minutes until the woman across from me asked what was going on. With the open office concept, it was difficult for her not to notice and more difficult for me to discuss. Walking over and bending near her desk, I told her everything that had happened over the course of the morning. She suggested that I talk to her supervisor about the situation, as his father was head of government security. Tell someone about my personal problems? I never had because it was all too embarrassing; there was so much shame attached to my personal life. The phone rang again, and, encouraging me, she walked with me into her supervisor's office.

One of the things Luke and I had fought about was his lack of drive and ambition. He had never worked during the year and a half I had known him. Weeks before, he had started a new job within the government. Otherwise, there would have been no recourse other than speaking to the police, which never occurred to me. The police never got involved with situations like this in the '80s. But, since Luke was a government employee, he was told to stop his abusive behavior or lose his job. Times were changing, and I was changing with them.

Luke changed his tactics. After work I would find him waiting for me on the sidewalk outside my office building. He would tag alongside me no matter where I went, updating me on all his plans to improve his life. "I found my own place and applied to college," he'd tell me. "I'm working and saving money." I didn't dare respond to any of his comments, since it would only encourage him to seek me out more often. I repeated silently to myself, *Be strong and disengaged.* Who knew when he would flip out again or what that would look like next time?

I couldn't be nice after he tried running me down, but because of my upbringing, my conditioning, I was cordial. There was another part of me that was concerned for my life. Apparently I didn't know what he was capable of. I hoped my neutral behavior would keep me safe.

CHAPTER 2

Aloneness

WINTER HAD TURNED A CORNER, and although spring was not even on the horizon, the days were longer. There was still snow everywhere, and everyone was bundled in their parkas, mitts, hats, and Sorel boots. At midwinter, December 21, there might be five and a half hours of daylight; in March it was closer to eight and a half. The days were longer and the temperature had improved slightly. No longer were we dealing with minus forty degrees Celsius but minus twenty-five! Truly, it was a vast improvement.

Enlightenment struck me! When I had committed to change the previous year it only had to do with my location. Nowhere in my mind had the decision been made to change the type of guy I would date. Therefore an exact replica of Peter had appeared. Thankfully, this lesson had taken less time to learn. There was an understanding now of what my rights were as a person. Happiness could be mine through my thoughts and decisions.

In high school looking for a longlasting relationship hadn't been a priority. I was only looking to have fun. Now I needed to make a choice as to what and whom I would accept into my life. Intelligence was a must; I missed having real conversations. This person needed a job that would easily support him and afford him the luxury to invite me to dinner or the movies. Why had I never allowed myself this before? That answer was easy. My mother was a strong and independent woman— something I wanted to be—but she paid all the bills. Somewhere inside I had unconsciously decided that was part of being a strong, independent woman, and the universe had provided me with those types of experiences.

My father made good money; it just all went toward his truck, plane, and toys. There was a similarity between my father and the guys I was attracting—to some degree, anyway. This additional realization stunned me into silence without thought. How do these things get so mixed up in our minds? That question left me pondering.

It wasn't all about boys. I did have girlfriends. I was a social butterfly, except for the awkward stage during junior high. Out of the hundreds of people I knew only two could be called best friends. Kathleen had lived two doors over from me during my last two years of high school. She might be an inch taller than I, but just as thin with long, straight, mousy, brown hair. Her mind was always trying to figure things out. Many of our conversations became a debate. Not because we didn't see eye to eye, but because Kathleen loved to contemplate both sides of every scenario. She was the first person to invite me out to a party after I moved to Yellowknife. The party was fun, although I felt my reputation tanked a bit that night after I got caught necking with some guy. I was sure she would never speak to me again, but that wasn't the case. Our friendship stayed strong even while we lived in different cities during our postsecondary years. I flew to Edmonton several times over those three years to get in some necessary girl time. She had finished her three years with a Bachelor of Art degree and was currently working for the territorial courts. We saw little of each other because of all the traveling involved with her job.

Cynthia moved to Yellowknife the same summer I had. Her curves were voluptuous, and she had the most beautiful long, wavy, mahogany hair. There was always a smile on her face, with moments of uninhibited laughter coming from deep within her soul. It always made me smile. We had connected because we lacked a shared history with the other girls. Whenever the girls around us would start talking about, "Do you remember when ...?" we would migrate to one another, and our friendship eventually evolved. Currently she was living with her parents in Edmonton while attending college. She had stayed with my family and me the previous summer while working to make money for school.

Since I was not seeing Cynthia at all and Kathleen very little, I was lonely for companionship. Most of the women I worked with were much older than I and married with children. It wasn't that I had closed myself off from becoming friends with them; we were just currently in different stages of our lives. There was one girl who was only a couple of years older than me. She had a superhot boyfriend, which surprised me. Her image was completely opposite. I'm not saying she was ugly, but she was completely punked out from head to toe. Stephanie's hair was pink, she had a lot of earring piercings, and major black eyeliner. Her clothes weren't anything I would wear, but they did work on her supertall, lanky body. Truly, I try not to stereotype, as it is completely damaging for everyone involved. But the two of them seemed like such a contradiction to one another. One day we walked together to the Second Cup during our morning coffee break, and our friendship took off from there. Now that Luke was out of my life, my stomach and bowel issues had disappeared. A latte had no effect on me, and Stephanie was a hoot! She had a tremendously generous heart.

Socially, life was moving slowly. Jobwise, it was not something I wanted to do forever, although it was enough for me to put away some money to buy a new car come June. That was my plan. My qualifications surpassed my current position. An education was a really good thing. My mother had been right when she said, "Make sure you have something to fall back on." Now every Friday I read the new job postings in the internal government newsletter. So far nothing had cropped up, but I knew something would.

There was one guy at my previous employer who was interested in me. He was nice-looking and tall. He invited me for lunch and then stood me up, so now he was off my list. He wanted another chance, so I invited him to dinner and then a night out to the Legion with my mother and me. Surprisingly, he accepted.

My father would not be at dinner. He had changed jobs in February. Now he worked for a fly-in, fly-out mining company six hundred kilometers northeast of Yellowknife. His rotation was two weeks home, two weeks away.

After dinner my suitor, my mother, and I met a few of his friends in the parking lot across from the Legion. As we ventured across the street to the front entrance, I literally bumped into John. Now, it seemed like I had known John forever, but actually we had only met the previous summer. He was an old friend of Kathleen and her fiancé, Tom. John and Tom had graduated high school together and then John had wandered through Europe before he settled down and attended university. Although John had been their roommate, every time I visited Kathleen in Edmonton, John had been indisposed. Our paths had never crossed, and until last summer I was starting to wonder whether he existed at all.

Currently his six-foot mass was solidly pressed against me, so I realized he did indeed exist. He was bundled head to toe in his parka with his big Sorel boots, carrying a bag of rented videos. It was surprising I recognized him at all!

"John!" I exclaimed, looking up with my head tilted increasingly backward.

"Tracy?" I could see the surprise in his sparkly blue eyes.

"Hey, what are you up to?"

Showing me the bag of videos, he replied, "Just a quiet night at home watching movies."

"No, no, come with us. Come have a drink." With a smile from me and a bit more persuasion, he followed us in.

The guy from work was not pleased. I didn't care. He and his friends were being incredibly forward in front of my mother and her friends. My mother was not impressed, either. The thought that cropped into my mind was, "Oh my God, another Peter personality!"

How could I not have noticed? No wonder I had faltered about spending time with him. After that realization, the night became a bit of a blur from numerous tequila paralyzers. I did remember dancing with John a lot and laughing at his Newfoundland accent after he had a few drinks. What's-his-name eventually left.

The next morning I woke up not exactly knowing where I was or who was beside me. This had never happened to me before, and it was mortifying. My first thought was, "No more paralyzers. They always get me into trouble." Next came, "Oh my God! What did I do in front of my mother?"

As the embarrassment of not remembering continued in waves of realizations, I dared to open my eyes to see who was next to me. It was Kathleen's house, so either it had to be her fiancé, which was not likely, or John, which was more likely, but how did I feel about that? The last thing I could remember was dancing when my mother left at midnight.

Thankfully Kathleen was not home, although her plane was due to arrive any minute. I would never be able to live this down. Surely Tom had left already for the airport to pick her up. There was a small window of opportunity to get out. I got dressed quietly and called a cab. While I was waiting by the front window, John came over and whispered into my ear, "I've been waiting a long time for this to happen." My body went rigid. I had no idea what to say. Then he invited me to lunch the following day.

During the cab ride home I contemplated his words over and over again. There had been no indication that he felt that way. He was not the type of guy I would ever have approached. Sure, he was tall and good-looking, but he was smart—really smart. Could I hold up my end of a conversation with him? He had a university degree and a good government job. We had conversations and bantered all the time. A part of me thought he was out of my league, while the other part thought, "It's John."

Reality kicked in when I arrived home. It was only eight o'clock on a Sunday morning, but I was already having a really, really bad day—well, sort of. My mother was up doing laundry, so there would be no slipping into bed and ignoring the situation. I could only imagine what she would say. In the past she had rarely held me accountable. She hated confrontation and those discussions usually ended up with me yelling. Both of us had changed; an explanation would be necessary. This is good; accountability is healthy.

Our relationship had grown over the past nine months, in a positive way. We were becoming friends. We would talk a few times a day by phone and meet for lunch. Occasionally we would go out together in the evening. I might not remember last night, but my mother drank tonic water or orange pekoe tea and would remember everything. Her comments were welcome, but there would still be judgment, mostly by me. To face her was to face myself.

I told her what John had said that morning and was surprised that she knew there was an attraction. I hadn't seen it. Apparently, before she had left the night before she had turned to John and asked him to make sure I made it home all right. She finished now with, "Perhaps I should have been more specific about whose home." That comment lightened the mood as I crawled off to bed.

Barely an hour later Kathleen called for all the details. Tom had blabbed. He was so excited about our union, I could hear him celebrating in the background. Having their support if this relationship moved forward really helped.

Monday morning I fretted over what to wear for lunch and how would we get along. Truthfully, I didn't really know John all that well, and I wasn't sure what a relationship with him would look like. I didn't want anything dysfunctional. I wanted a relationship I didn't have to work at, something grown-up. Surprisingly, lunch was great. We had a lot to talk about. Our relationship grew from there. Within a few weeks he came over for dinner to meet my parents—actually, my father. Everything went well except the comment my dad made about John's pierced ear: "Wasn't it in the gay ear?" If that was the worst thing my dad had to comment on, all was good.

For the first time in my life I wasn't being entertained by going to the bar. We were doing "couple" things. We would hang out with Kathleen and Tom or stay home and watch movies. Sometimes it was as simple as takeout Chinese food, a dinner party, or a night of board games or cards. Occasionally it became more elaborate, like a costume party or a full day of croquet matches. John sent flowers to work every week. Attached I would find a lovely poem. Three months later he asked me to marry him.

Life was really good. I was having a blast, but marriage? There were two problems with that. I didn't know whether I wanted to get married right now; I was only twenty-one. The other was that John kept asking me during a night of drinking. On four separate occasions he said, "Let's get hitched at city hall!" Each time I would laugh and tell him to ask me when he was sober.

A year ago my life had been in the toilet. Currently life was great, and a lot of it had to do with John. He was sweet, kind, intelligent, treated me like gold, and had a real job and huge ambitions. But I didn't know how much I really loved him. I felt love for him, but it wasn't like the two other times. Love with Peter was dysfunctional. There were times I could take him or leave him. When I left him my heart was only sad and, of course, furious. Paul, the guy I had fallen head over heels in love with during one of my breaks from Peter—well, to me, that was what real love felt like. He had swept me off my feet. Of course when he crushed my heart, I had never felt such intense pain before, either. Didn't that experience sound more like love?

I was happy, and I did love John, so we talked about moving in together. That step was more comfortable. We would find a place for July first. We started shopping for furniture and all the extra little things necessary to get established. That I could handle.

It was a Wednesday, and John and I planned to go out for an early dinner after work. It was nothing unusual; typically we dined out a couple times a week. Tonight it would be at one of our favorite spots. We talked about our upcoming holiday in Edmonton to pick up my new red Toyota Tercel that I had been saving for, for months. There were two days set aside to meet his parents. I was excited, as John adored his family. We talked about the long drive to Manitoba to visit my grandmother, afterward collecting all the items that I had left behind in a storage facility in Winnipeg the previous year. Then, to my surprise, as dessert was being served, John asked me to marry him. In his hand was a velvet box with a gold band lined with emeralds and diamonds. He told me that it wasn't a real engagement ring: "We'll get something special made later."

I'm really engaged! Life can turn on a dime.

The meeting with his parents went very well; they were wonderful and friendly. We set a date to get married the following summer, and there was lots of wedding talk. His mother teased him about having children with red hair and freckles.

In Winnipeg we stayed with my favorite aunt. Aunt Beverly was really my father's cousin, but we had spent so much of our life together that she became Auntie. She had divorced when her children were little. I admired her strength and independence in raising her girls. She had red hair and freckles and was extremely fashionable, as were her daughters. Her eldest daughter, Lisa, had been living in Yellowknife with my family until her engagement the previous Christmas. Emily, my favorite cousin, was a year younger than I, although she called me "little cousin," since she was at least four inches taller than I. With her complexion as fair as mine, we had spent hours in the shade together as children. John and Emily got along beautifully. This I was happy for, as I was trying to convince her to move north. She had recently returned from Asia and needed a change. Actually, she was lucky to be alive after a horrific car accident the previous month. She was still in recovery and wouldn't be able to travel for at least six more weeks. She agreed to think about it. That was a start, but it didn't stop me from pursuing the issue. In facing my fear, I had moved forward, and wonderful things had happened for me.

The first of the month arrived, and it was time to move into our one-bedroom apartment. We had both been involved in the decision, and even that felt great. John cooked and cleaned! Life was so simple, so easy. He also paid the phone bill—a bonus! This was nothing like my relationships with Peter or Luke where I had poured more than my fair share of money into everything we did. Nor did I want it to be. I had made things change by deciding what I would and wouldn't accept in my life. It felt good.

That "Happy Ever After" thing seemed present. Everything was perfect until John couldn't shut the television off. Sports, sports, sports. It was driving me crazy! He bought a second television to put in our bedroom, *so he wouldn't bother me*, he said. How was this supposed to help? Now I never saw him.

Television had never been an important part of my family's household. I remembered watching Walt Disney on Sunday nights as a child. Occasionally, I watched *The Young and the Restless* in college. It was the noise; it didn't let my brain rest. Movies I enjoyed because I knew they only took up two hours of my time. By November my loneliness was overwhelming. My time was filled with mundane activities like polishing the furniture, polishing my shoes—I had even recently taken to polishing the leaves of my plants!

I had a significant amount of free time. We didn't argue over the television; I just ignored him and it. Drama and friends had always taken up so much of my time, and I didn't have any hobbies. I had figure skated growing up, but that didn't seem like a viable option. I couldn't think of anything I was interested in doing, so I filled my time visiting my mother. Occasionally, I was able to visit my cousin Emily, who had moved in with her sister a month ago. The moment she had moved to Yellowknife, her life had become a whirlwind. One of the women in my office invited Emily to run for Miss Yellowknife. She had been in pageant preparations since, had won the title, and was now preparing for the Miss Canada Pageant.

As I started looking for things to fill my time, that is what exactly happened. I applied and was offered a new job with more money and more responsibilities. Now I was spending more time learning and become acquainted with all the projects with which I was involved. Stephanie had gotten married, but she still had time for me. She had booked us to see a psychic who was in town for the weekend. My mother had taken me, at the age of sixteen, to a tea reader in Winnipeg. It was very interesting.

My life was now in such a different place, I couldn't wait to hear all the wonderful things she had to say about my future.

The psychic fit her role perfectly, wearing a flowing violet gown with a multicolored scarf on her head. The table was covered with silky material and had a crystal ball in the middle and a few decks of cards off to one side. There was an exciting energy surrounding her and all her magical items—or perhaps it was just surrounding me? I sat across from her in a room that was well lit, intently listening to her recalling my past relationships, correctly. Then she discussed my work and how it was only a stepping-stone along the way. Next she spoke of my true love, who was yet to come: "This man is tall and dark. He is a doctor, lawyer, or engineer."

With a questioning look on my face, I leaned forward and questioned her, "You mean the man I'm engaged to right now?"

"No, you're not going to marry the man you're with now."

It was a good thing I was sitting or I would have ended up on the floor. John and I hadn't gotten much done in regards to our wedding plans, but we were engaged to get married. My reply was almost hostile: "What?"

"He is not your hermit. Your hermit is still to come within the next year." She repeated, "He is tall, close to six feet. He will have dark hair, and his profession will be that of a doctor, lawyer, or engineer. You are meant to be together for this lifetime, as you have been for many others."

"But I'm marrying John next summer; the date's set!" She was now very aware of my discomfort in this discovery, but she persisted as though she were on a mission.

Raising her voice and looking me directly in the eyes, she continued, "If you marry John you will not be happy, your marriage will not last three years. He is not the one meant for you, and the window of opportunity to meet your hermit may disappear!"

This was such alarming news. I was in absolute disbelief. I walked away from the reading in a zombie state to find Stephanie. She was in the waiting area, sitting with a grin of pleasure on her face.

I needed to pull myself together. "Hi! So, Steph, how was your reading?" I asked in an upbeat tone. It didn't work. She was already aware that something had gone terribly wrong with my reading. I told her all that the psychic had said. Then she nudged me along: "Oh don't worry. Remember? This was just for fun!" She was right; this reading was just for fun, but what part of it would John find funny?

John was eagerly waiting to hear the news. Our relationship wasn't perfect, but I hadn't considered breaking up, even with all the television nonsense. Lying has never been my forte, so I made light of the reading, hoping not to arouse any hostility or hurt his feelings. Monday morning I received my bouquet of flowers signed, "Love your Hermit."

The entire experience was behind me, although occasionally I would sit and contemplate what the psychic had said. Was John my hermit or was there someone else out there somewhere?

John and I celebrated an early Christmas before he traveled home to be with his parents. I would not be without my parents again this year. John would return by New Year's Eve, with a list of family and friends, I hoped, so we could get started on our guest list. Our wedding was only eight months away. Some of it had been planned, like the date, August 12, 1989, and the location. My parents were moving south to Edmonton in late March, and we planned to get married on their acreage. Invitations hadn't been picked, and dress shopping had not even entered my mind. I was just all hung up on the guest list.

John returned empty-handed. By March the wedding plans had halted completely. I'm embarrassed to say that I was totally surprised when John told me he just couldn't get married, nor did he want to have children. He believed the world had become too corrupt to raise a child. I had been riding a roller coaster of happiness and not checking in to see whether maintenance needed to be done along the way.

John had apparently been plagued for months over what to do about the situation. He had been isolating himself more each day. He no longer watched television but spent time soaking in the tub. I hadn't recognized it as avoidance, because I was thrilled with the peace and quiet! What I had found strange was the amount of time he spent talking on the phone to his mother. She, I felt was the culprit. Her "Oh John, your children will have red hair and freckles" bullshit. She had known all along he didn't want children! It was I who had been left in the dark.

Now, sitting in a ball on the couch with stunned disbelief, I looked up and asked, "How long have you felt this way?"

"Quite a while," he said and then sheepishly added, "Since last fall."

It was March. Last fall was months ago. Had the television been his first avoidance mechanism? Without ranting out loud or internally, I packed the bare essentials. At the last second I grabbed my duvet off our bed. Actions speak louder than words. Without it, I hoped John would be uncomfortable at the least, but truth be told I hoped he would freeze!

My mother was surprised to see me walking in the door. I told her what had happened, but still the tears didn't come. My mind just whirled in confusion. Everyone around me was stunned about the news of our breakup. My mum now made the assumption that it must have something to do with his earring. Was it in the gay ear? I just rolled my eyes.

The next couple of days revealed a lot more about the situation. John called me to go for lunch. He told me he loved me and wanted us to stay together, "Could you live a lifetime with me, without marriage or children?"

For years I had never thought about getting married, nor did I want to have children, due to that one babysitting gig when I was ten, but to have that choice taken away from me for this lifetime ... could I agree to that? It was something I would have to think about. Looking across the table at the sadness in John's face, I wanted to tell him I could, but this was an adult decision. "I don't know. I need a few days to think about it," I replied.

I tried to live those two scenarios in my mind's eye. Did I want to grow old without children? Maybe. Did it matter if we didn't marry if we loved each other? Maybe not? Three days later I told John, yes. Was "yes" my truth? Or was it bred from fear? My parents were leaving in three weeks, and I would be homeless, abandoned. I wasn't ready to look at all the truths involved in my decision.

Our union had John more relaxed then he had been in months. I was more tense. When would the other shoe drop? By May both of us knew our relationship would not last long, but we continued to play the game. John brought up the possibility of moving into a three-bedroom townhouse. We would fill the two spare rooms with Tom and Emily. Kathleen had broken off her engagement to Tom last fall when she departed for law school. He had been living in her parent's rental and felt it was time to move. My cousin Emily needed more space than her sister's home allowed. We would all move in together the first of June.

After we relocated to our new home, we grew even further apart. John would spend time either at work or playing poker with his buddies. I went out. There were too many people in the house! It was too crowded and overwhelming to stay home. Even in college I hated having roommates. Kathleen was back from university working for the summer. Cynthia was done with college and had returned to pay off school loans. The girls filled in my time with dinners and days at the beach or the lake waterskiing. Once a week we played softball. I pulled out my sewing machine, and the rest of my spare time was filled with designing outfits, shirts, skirts, and dresses. Everyone loved my outfits, and most couldn't believe I had made them.

By the month of July, John and I were arguing constantly. He wouldn't even go out for dinner anymore. I started giving marriage and children more consideration. I currently didn't want children, but I wanted the option to choose later down the road. I also realized I wanted the ring on my finger, the big ceremony, the commitment to marriage; that was my "Happy Ever After!" It was then that I realized our relationship had run its course.

It was a beautiful Wednesday evening, and I met Kathleen and Cynthia for dinner and drinks on a suburban patio bar. The place was new and had a different energy than the local downtown pubs. It was time to share my decision with them. They thought I was joking. "You'll never break up with him," they teased me. I couldn't blame them for their thoughts as it had taken me years to end things, finally, with Peter, and months with Luke. But I had thought this through like an adult and had even found a place to stay for the summer. A man in my office was looking for a house sitter—someone to take care of his dog. That would allow me time to find something more permanent. The only thing left was to tell John. They both sat in stunned disbelief. "You're serious," Cynthia said. Making changes in my life had become, easier.

The discussion with John took five minutes. We were both on the same page. Neither of us was happy in the relationship or thrilled about ending it; it was just the right thing to do. The fear of doing nothing and wishing I had done something, then living with that regret day after day had become too much. My other choice was to move through my fear of being alone. With the words said, living on the other side of that fear was refreshing. There was not an ounce of animosity between us, just friendship. The last sixteen months had not been a total waste. I was capable of handling a committed and monogamous relationship without drama. Now with a blank slate ahead of me and so many possibilities, there was only relief and freedom. And the ability to breathe again. It seems to me that in order to move forward, some action has to take place to allow change to occur. I was currently in transition.

CHAPTER 3

Adventure

THE HOUSE IS WONDERFUL! THIS was the first time in over two years that I had space to myself. God, had I missed it. I was even getting over my fear of dogs. The one who came with the house was a lovely, five-year-old white Samoyed. He was so well behaved and happy. But I needed to remember that there was a time crunch: I had to find a permanent residence. I contacted a woman who had placed an advertisement in the local paper for a roommate. We met over coffee and decided that I would move in at the end of the August.

Fresh out of a relationship, I was still looking for love. It surprised me. Although I suppose my relationship with John was over long ago. Knowing what I didn't want in a man was easy and had been my guide thus far. But the question was more about what did I want in a man? He must:

1. be close to six feet tall, so I can wear heels;
2. have a university education;
3. have the ability to carry on an intellectual conversation;
4. be employed, and preferably also self-driven;

5. have his own vehicle;
6. have his own place;
7. be social and enjoy dancing;
8. be tall, dark, and handsome—for a change. John had been fair.

Then Ray, a friend from my office, introduced me to a guy at the bar. They had been enrolled together in the engineering program at the University of Alberta. Ray slipped away, and we continued talking for quite a long time. He was tall, dark, and handsome. He was educated and could carry on a conversation. I started checking off items from my list, unconsciously, as the conversation continued. Yes, yes, yes, yes … realization hit. Huh. I just needed to see him dance. Definite possibilities here. Damn, what was his name? All summer I had worked on remembering people's names. No matter what tool I tried using, moments later I would forget.

There was another guy who was really nice and always made an effort to seek me out. He worked at the airport and invited me to go on a helicopter ride one night. It was pretty cool. Memories of my childhood in Manitoba floated back. Every summer there was a fleet of helicopters that relocated to help fight forest fires. One was always parked in our large backyard. Helicopter guy was nice, but there wasn't any real chemistry. Perhaps he would be useful for a fling, but I was looking for someone who was interested in being in a serious relationship. My heart skipped a beat when a sudden awareness struck me. Was I really looking for a serious relationship?

A few weeks later I walked the three blocks to meet Emily for lunch. Halfway there, in front of the Legion, I nearly bumped into Ray's friend. Without thinking, and looking directly at him, I blurted out with delight in my voice, "Hi Mike" and kept walking, nearly tripping over my own feet a few steps later when I realized what I had done. Was that his name or had I just totally screwed up? Mike? After a lengthy discussion with Emily over lunch, I returned to the office and sought out Ray. "What is that guy's name you went to university with?"

Looking up from his desk, he casually asked me, "The one I introduced you to in the bar?"

Impatience seethed from my very being. Was he trying to be difficult? "Yes, yes, what's his name?"

"Mike," Ray said as his concentration returned to a piece of paper in front of him. Unbelievable! I had remembered his name, but how?

For the next couple of weeks Mike was all I could think about. The small opportunity I had to speak with him in the bar repeated itself in my mind. Then one night, as Kathleen was dragging me home from the bar, I saw Mike leaning against the back wall. There was some guy next to him whom I didn't recognize, which I found odd. Didn't I know everyone in town? My hope of detaining Kathleen for a few more minutes to have a quick conversation with Mike on my way out was abruptly aborted when Helicopter Guy intercepted me. Damn, he was using up all my extra minutes. Kathleen caught up with me once again, grabbing my arm and tugging me toward the exit just as Mike leaned toward me and asked if I'd like to dance. I did the only thing possible—placed my hand on his arm and looked into his eyes and said, "Sorry," as sincerely as I possibly could. "Please let him know I like him," I pleaded with God as I was dragged through the exit.

Our mutual friend from high school, Olivia, was in town for two weeks, and we were all supposed to meet for food at midnight. We found her at fifteen minutes after twelve, three blocks away on the back of a moving motorcycle. Her long brown hair flying in all directions as she laughed, barely acknowledging us as she passed. I turned to Kathleen and totally flipped out. I was so pissed off. Seriously! I could be dancing, with Mike!

She offered to go back to the bar with me so I could talk to him, but the moment had passed. As we continued to walk home, my anger and frustration subsided. Silently I thought, "I need to find something positive about the situation. I can be grateful that at least some form of contact was made, although brief." As I continued, "I hope he didn't think I was brushing him off."

Kathleen kept reassuring me that everything was fine. We would go out the following weekend and find Mike. My mind kept winding back on itself, repeating, *You screwed up, Tracy.*

All week I thought about him. The weekend came, and Kathleen, Cynthia, and I couldn't go out, or, rather, it was a long weekend, and there was no point in going out. Everyone would be away camping, including us.

The following Friday night came, and the three of us found Mike at our third stop. It seemed like an eternity since I had seen him last. It was the only place I had ever seen him, so perhaps we should have arrived there first. The reasoning behind that was easy: I needed time to calm my nerves before our encounter.

As I entered the bar, our eyes connected. There he was, all six feet of him, on the other side of the room. His dark brown hair well kept, with just a few strands making their way across his forehead. His hazel eyes vibrant even behind his round, blue-rimmed glasses. If I had to categorize him it would have been preppy, the extra length of his Levis rolled to sit nicely on his loafers. His body was on the lean side, although there was clear evidence of his arm and shoulder muscles through his T-shirt. On his right wrist he wore a couple of bracelets you would find at a flea market. The girls and I quickly made our way over to him for introductions. Kathleen and Cynthia left almost immediately, as they felt like intruders. There was so much tension in the air. I was overly nervous but desperately tried to play it cool. Nothing could stop me from blathering. The waitress came by with a tray of shooters, and I purchased two, offering one to Mike, hoping that would bring him more into the conversation and slow me down some. It seemed to work, so while he spoke I reviewed my checklist again. Yes, close to six feet tall, he had an engineering degree from a reputable university, he could carry on a conversation, which he had proven during this silent interrogation. He bought me a drink—bonus points, as I drank tequila paralyzers, and they were rather pricey! Now he had bought me two, so he must have some money. Bingo, he has his own apartment and owns his own car! Yahoo, let's see if he can dance. Oh my God, he can. Can I be so lucky?

We danced, we talked, and we stayed until all the lights turned on. Neither of us wanted to break the spell by separating. He asked whether he could walk me home. It was one thirty in the morning but there were still remnants of the setting sun on the horizon—or was the sun already rising? He walked me to the door. "Would you like to come in for some tea? We could order pizza?"

"Sure." He made the tea, and I ordered pizza. We settled on the couch and chatted for hours. At some point we both leaned in for a kiss. That kiss was like nothing else I had ever experienced. It was electrifyingly! I could feel a vibration in the air around us. As our kiss deepened, it led to all sorts of other things. There was something cosmic—even magical—about our union. I stared into his hazel, almond-shaped eyes for hours. There was something so familiar about them.

It was August 12, and the irony of the situation was that I had picked that date for John and me to get married. That date apparently represented a union to me, just not the one I had originally anticipated. Then words from the psychic drifted into my mind, "You will marry someone tall and dark. He will be a lawyer, doctor, or engineer. You have been together in other lifetimes. He is your hermit." Could Mike be "The One?" That would explain that cosmic familiarity about him.

Mike left around nine the next morning. He was committed to playing in a golf tournament and needed to meet his friends by ten. I would have happily canceled my plans to spend the day with him. Instead, Kathleen and I spent the day at a friend's cabin waterskiing, then stayed for dinner. Mike promised to call me around nine o'clock, so there was no hurry to get home and wait by the phone. I would only drive myself crazy, hoping and praying he would call and that it hadn't been a one-night stand. It hadn't felt that way, but all my insecurities were dispersing horrible thoughts through my head.

John was at the lake, along with about ten other friends. We had only seen each other briefly over the last few weeks. Mike's name came up, and I tried to make light of it, not wanting to hurt John's feelings. It was then that the news presented itself about a woman in his office he had already started dating. My heart never skipped a beat; I was happy for him. We both had moved on. There is something to be said about timing.

Mike called exactly at nine and we planned to meet the next evening. It was so different going out with someone I knew so little about. He didn't have any previous connection to me or my friends, and in fact, he had a whole group of friends I was unaware existed. I thought I knew everybody in town. This new information gave me an entirely new perspective, and my world had just gotten a little bigger.

It was Sunday, so we decided to see a movie, *Dead Poets Society*. Afterward we found an open café and sat and talked. He was seventeen months older than me, a Pisces baby. He spoke about his parents and younger brother. He loved sports, but it was more about playing them— soccer, volleyball, basketball. He had played hockey and baseball as a kid, but injuries with his knees prevented him from continuing seriously. The following weekend he had a triathlon, and the first week in September he was going to canoe the Nahanni River. He had been taking canoeing lessons along with three friends all summer to prepare for the Class III rapids involved in their journey. Surprise overtook me that Yellowknife even offered canoe lessons. There was so much more to this town then what I had grown up with and knew. I talked about my parents and my sister, who was only five months older than his brother. Coincidently, his trip to the Nahanni would take place at the same time and for the same duration that I would be attending my cousin Lisa's wedding in Winnipeg. He drove me home and leaned in to kiss me. There was that electrical charge again. It was so alarming that I ended the kiss early and actually jumped out of the car. *Oh my God, what must he think of me?* I'd never experienced a kiss like that before. It was so powerful.

We spoke on the phone or saw each other every day. I also worked part-time in the evenings at the front desk of a local hotel, and a couple of times he popped in to say hello. When we were together we enjoyed each other's company. We talked about our dreams and ambitions. There was easiness between us; he didn't need me around all the time—no clinginess, which I liked. Luke had never left me alone. Once while I was sun-tanning, I casually mentioned my hunger, and voilà: he handed me a sandwich! He was an overpleaser, and that actually annoyed me.

Friday night I met Mike at his apartment. Things were very different. We sat on separate couches in his living room with the music blasting while he stared straight ahead. There was no eye contact between us, and he just ignored me. I started doubting myself and our relationship over the past week. Had I made everything up? It was so odd; what had I gotten myself into? Perhaps he was putting distance between us because he too felt that electrical magnetic pull. Later that night, after we arrived at his friend's party, everything seemed normal again.

Then the following week during lunch I happened to bump into him outside a sandwich shop. He was coming out as I was going in. He said, "Hi," and kept walking, climbed into his car, and drove away. It was so very strange. I had no idea what to make of it. Kathleen mentioned that she found Mike shy. Shy? He had never acted shy around me, but it was something to think about.

He sent me a huge bouquet of flowers for my birthday. They were beautiful. I put them on my desk next to the bouquet John had sent me as well.

The following week we both left on our vacations. Visiting with family and friends while attending my cousin's wedding was really nice. Even spending a week in Winnipeg didn't freak me out too badly. I had found out through my sister that Peter had moved out of town, so there was very little chance I would bump into him. I still harbored a fear that he had some kind of control over me. Probably something to do with the way I left, with no real closure. I managed to return home unscathed and was happy for it.

My parents, who had been stuck in a vehicle with me for over twenty-five hours, were probably just as happy! I had talked their ears off—Mike this, Mike that. We had been dating for a mere two weeks, and I couldn't get him out of my mind.

He was at the airport waiting for me when I arrived home. We had agreed that he wouldn't shave the entire time he was away; he was curious how much beard he could grow. I was terrified that I wouldn't recognize him. What a strange thought. His beard was so long, and he did barely resemble himself. Thankfully he didn't keep it.

We had both missed each other deeply and became inseparable after that. The strange behavior diminished. For Halloween we dressed up as Wilma and Fred Flintstone. I used a stuffed purple dinosaur as Dino. We didn't win any prizes, but we had fun. By mid-November we discussed getting married. I suggested we move in together, but Mike was adamant that I meet his parents first. As much as that drove me crazy, it also made me happy.

It had only been four months, but my current roommates were driving me nuts. Thankfully so were Cynthia's. We found a two-bedroom apartment and planned to move around mid-January.

Christmas was around the corner. Mike wanted a picture of me to show his parents. I fretted about what to wear, how I should stand, or should I sit? The stress of meeting them would be so much worse, but that wouldn't happen until July. Mike had met my parents on a short shopping trip to Edmonton in November. They adored him, as did my sister.

Christmas was fast approaching. Mike hadn't seen his parents in over a year and had flights booked to Lethbridge to see them, as well as his extended family. He had lived in the same town until graduating from university. I could only imagine what that was like. I had lived in half a dozen places before I was six and a few more since that time.

My parents were celebrating Christmas in their new home on the acreage. My father invited his parents and one of his brothers and family. My mother was fit to be tied, as she was home for three weeks recovering from a necessary breast reduction. She wasn't to lift her arms or really move at all. My dad hadn't thought about that; it was more about showing off his new home. I was now starting to recognize the drama that played out in my parent's lives, and I released it and gave thanks that my grandma was available to help with the Christmas dinner. What would we have eaten with only Jane and me in charge?

Mum thought Dad was doing it on purpose. There was just too much baggage to continue their relationship in a healthy way. Grandma was not impressed either, and I heard her mutter derogatory comments about her son more than once. They were unaware that Mum had even had surgery until they walked in the door.

I recognized the drama, but until this point I had conditioned myself to ignore a majority of it by occupying my time with other things— currently that was cooking, cleaning, and playing with my little cousins. Boxing Day, December 26, was spent exploring the Boxing Day sales. My auntie had a list of places where she needed to make purchases, Fabricland being one of them. I was grateful to be able to sneak away early to pick Mike up at the airport. He had a six-hour stopover and would be joining us for supper.

When we arrived home, all the adults were drinking shooters. This was not normal, I explained to Mike. My grandpa, who had been diagnosed with throat cancer the previous year, was sober. He had been a heavy beer drinker his entire life and quit cold turkey after receiving his diagnosis. This I found very impressive. He was impressed with Mike. Their joint interest in mining had them talking for most of the day. The rest of the time Mike spent with my little cousins, showing them how to reach the next level in Super Mario.

We were having such a wonderful time, that, before I knew it, we needed to leave for the airport. Time never slipped away on me! I berated myself all the way to the airport, getting lost, but arriving with fifteen minutes to spare! Apparently that was not enough time, according to the flight attendant, with whom I argued passionately. I did not remember the last time I had been so irate. Mike tried to calm me down. They rescheduled his flight for the following morning.

I was fuming all the way home, still cursing the attendant. I was having a terrible time moving forward, away from my anger. A change in schedule always upset me. I just never adjusted well to the unexpected. Or could the tension of the drama back at the house really be the culprit? Is it what set me off? Was this my way of releasing all the anxiety that had built up inside of me over the last week?

We returned to the house, and no one was surprised when Mike entered with me. Bets had been made that he would indeed miss his flight.

January was dark, cold, and very quiet. Most inhabitants stayed home and hibernated. Outside it was minus forty, in Celsius and Fahrenheit. With the wind chill, colder. That was one little trivia tidbit I remembered from 1977 when Canada converted from the imperial to the metric system: both measurements intersected at -40! February brought more hours of daylight, but still, few people ventured outside with smiles on their faces. March brought our winter festival, Caribou Carnival. It wasn't the end of winter, but everyone felt like celebrating. There were ice castles and dog sled races, and people were smiling and laughing. In April the snow started to melt, and the air was warmer; spring was getting nearer. May brought hopes of summer and twenty hours of daylight. For me it brought an engagement ring.

It wasn't a surprise. Mike sent Kathleen, Cynthia, and me shopping, with a budget. They helped me find the perfect ring. It was sized, and a few days later Mike picked it up while I purchased sandwiches from the delicatessen next door. Over lunch he officially proposed, and I officially accepted. Then we got in his Golf Jetta and drove sixteen hours to Edmonton. Having two vehicles between the two of us in such a small town was redundant. The previous month I had sold my car, and now the plan was to trade Mike's car in for a Jeep Grand Cherokee—something more suitable for the cold weather and rough terrain. Was it the male version of an engagement ring?

Showing my ring to my mother was wonderful, but the weekend would have a quick turnaround time. This time shopping for a vehicle was different. We were trading something in, so there was the disappointment in the price the dealership was offering. Really, that was our fault, as they knew we had a short timeline. For me there were two additional surprises—one, that Mike owed his parents a significant amount of money for his car, and two, that they just happened to own the same color and model vehicle of our new vehicle, but with four doors. Had he held back secrets until I said yes?

It took me the entire drive home to come to terms with this new information. How much debt was I taking on? I had no debt, and in fact I put a little extra away every payday into a savings bond. Purchasing the same vehicle as his parents was a different issue. I supposed they had good taste, and soon enough my mind started wandering. We set a wedding date for the following summer. It would be as close to August eleventh as possible. And the purchasing of bridal magazines began. The rest of the planning would take place over the three weeks of our summer vacation. The week I spent with Mike's parents gave me a better idea about the church service, the number of guests, reception, flowers, food, and cake. The next week was spent with my mother solidifying ideas into decisions and procuring a dress. This time it felt very real.

We returned home to Cynthia's departure. She had decided to move to Edmonton to be closer to her parents, leaving Mike and me the apartment. Before our vacation, we had let go of Mike's lease and had either sold or moved his remaining items in. Although his apartment was cheaper, it was also old and dingy. Both of us decided that the space and light of my apartment suited us better.

Life fell into a comfortable routine. Mike would drive to work at seven, and I would walk at eight. He would collect me for lunch, which wasn't quite what I expected. He would stay glued to his many magazines the entire time. Perhaps it was a habit from spending too much on his own? Many arguments erupted, and no solutions were found. He loved his magazines. At the end of the day Mike would arrive at my work at half past four, spending my last half hour talking with my boss about sports. They got along amazingly well, eventually joining a few fantasy pool leagues together.

That gave Mike a night out and me a night in, alone. Cynthia was in Edmonton, Kathleen had returned to complete law school, and Stephanie had gotten married, pregnant, and delivered a little boy in July. They were now in the midst of packing to move to Edmonton where their families lived. Natasha, a friend from grammar school whose family move to Yellowknife coincided with ours, had returned from university, but we were on the rocks. Not a surprise, as our relationship had always been volatile. Emily, well she was living off her fame as Miss Yellowknife and had started working with the airlines and was flying globally, more so on her time off!

For the first time in a very long time, I felt friendless and very lonely. The quietness that had entered my life on these occasional nights was uncomfortable. I was not used to so much available time. The first place my mind went was, "What can I do to fill this time?" There was a period of my life between the age of ten and fourteen when I was constantly making and replacing friends. Currently, I didn't feel like making new friends. It was a lot of work, and then there was the sharing of my history. I'd rather not go down that road.

Mike and I had a plan. We would work and save money in the north for five years, then we would move south with enough money to buy the house of our dreams. Before that was to manifest, I wanted a better job. In order to get a better job, I needed to complete an accounting designation. I needed to go back to school, not full-time, as all the courses I needed to take were available through correspondence. I may not have done well in high school, and not great in college, but I had taken one course to complete my college diploma by correspondence and found out that when I was focused, and my life was void of drama, I did amazingly well!

There were two accounting designations available. With more confidence now than ever, I decided to take my Certified General Accounting Designation (CGA). I always thought I'd be working in the human resources field, but finance was now my home, and getting the necessary piece of paper to move into management was my next step. By January my life was full of courses and wedding plans. There were a lot of decorations that needed to be made. Anyone dropping by to visit found something, ribbon, beads, or paper in their hands to be transformed into a wedding decoration.

In March I traveled to Edmonton to confirm the church and reception site for August seventeenth. Flowers needed to be ordered, as did the cake; bridesmaid dresses needed to be decided on; and fittings need to be started on my dress. Then there were a million other little things to take care of. Oh gosh, a photographer! And a caterer!

Most everything was accomplished in one very long and busy day. I couldn't wait to go home and crawl into my parents' hot tub. My mother was insistent that we stop and pick up my dress on the way home. I whined and moaned about being too tired but eventually relented to my mother's demands. I would have preferred being alert and happy when I was reunited with my dress. The boutique was located in a strip mall with easy access. As we entered the shop, Mum made mention of the cop car parked out front. "It's not like there are any coffee shops nearby. Why would he be parked here?" She was always stereotyping.

Approaching the clerk at the front desk, I said, "Hi, I put a deposit on a dress last summer and want to pay off the balance and pick it up today."

She looked out the front window and then glanced to the back of the store. "Just one minute. I'll get the owner for you." Mum and I looked at each other. Something very weird was going on. The energy in the shop was completely different than it had been during our last visit.

A tall, thin, blonde woman walked toward us. "Hi, I'm the owner. I understand you've put a deposit on a dress?"

"Yes, my daughter and I were hoping to pick it up today," my mother replied.

"I don't want to alarm you, but I am having a bit of an issue. My husband has filed for divorce, and every time I make a sale the sheriff comes in and removes the money from my till." My mother and I gasped in unison. We were appalled that such a thing was possible. She continued, "A friend gave me a heads-up, and I was able to remove all the dresses in my shop that had a deposit. If you follow me, I can take you to your dress."

My mind was awhirl, but before I had more than a moment to think, Mum answered, "Sure, how do we get there?"

"Drive around to the back of the store, and you can follow me."

Turning to my mother, I asked, "Are we really going to do this?"

"Yes, and act normal. We don't want the sheriff to get suspicious." We both got into the car and continued a discussion about how absurd this entire situation was as we followed the owner. Entering the basement, we saw hundreds of bridal gowns belonging to brides who might never wear them. "You came just in time. We're shutting the boutique's doors today. I don't know what we're going to do with all these dresses."

It was heartbreaking to think about, and my eyes swelled with tears. If I hadn't given in to my mother's adamant intuition, I could have been one of those brides. I didn't know how she would even find my dress in the masses, but at least I knew it was here, somewhere.

The owner emerged twenty minutes later with my dress and offered us a sixty percent discount for our trouble.

"It's been no trouble, thanks," we replied.

How was it that my wedding dress set off my mother's intuition and not mine? God moves in mysterious ways. We were well under budget now, and I could afford the flowers I really wanted.

Invitations were sent out, and tallies were coming back. My dress was being altered, as were the bridesmaids' teal gowns. I was sewing my veil and adding all the bling. Cynthia and I would make the two hundred plus Chocolate Grand Marnier truffles a week before the wedding. Appointments were booked for the bridesmaids' hair. Jane would be my maid of honor with Emily, Stephanie, Cynthia, and Joanne, who was a close friend from elementary school in The Pas. I had asked Kathleen, but she was too overwhelmed with summer school and finishing her law degree. It was a wonderful time and I was happy.

My mother's astrology friend checked the planets, and our wedding day would be clear and warm, "A perfect day to get married," she said.

I'm not sure whether it was my age, now twenty-four, or the fact that I was really growing up, but my perception about everything was changing. Situations and relationships no longer looked the same to me. I had thought I was just living my life, but in reality my life had been quite self-centered. It had never occurred to me that people liked different things, at least not in the way that was becoming apparent now. Before, I think I heard it and either ignored it or remembered it as a statement.

Now I was thinking more about why people were different, what made them like different things, and what made them put up with certain situations while others would not. Why did some people avoid the truth of a situation while others didn't, and why could one person see a truth that another didn't recognize at all?

There was one woman in the office who bragged about how wonderful her son was. He was a drug dealer. Everyone knew it but her. Another thought she could repair her marriage by having a baby. Now her husband was just sleeping around on his pregnant wife. I even saw it in the advertisements on a few store fronts. The signage was meant to encourage you to enter, but to me it came across as needy.

It was all so fascinating. Everywhere I looked, people had different perceptions regarding the same situation. How had I missed this? It was a new awareness, and I found it fascinating.

In June, Mike and I traveled to Edmonton, where both our families were finally to meet one another. We coincided the neutering of our recently acquired cat, Fitzgerald. As usual we were flying free with my Dad's company's plane. We would fly to the mine site and then continue on to Edmonton. My dad was already at home, so instead of visiting with him, we sat in the lounge with Fitzgerald and waited to reboard. There are unexpected moments in our lives that change everything forever, and this was one of those moments. Mike bumped into a colleague from Yellowknife. Kevin mentioned that they were looking for a mining engineer, adding, "Send in your résumé. You'd be perfect for the job."

After a wonderful weekend, except, of course, for Fitzgerald, Mike did. An interview was organized for the following week. He flew to Edmonton, and directly after the hellos, they offered him a job. They continued on for dinner and drinks, but the deal had already been sealed with a handshake. There was a surprise: we would have to move to Edmonton. There had been some company cost-cutting, and everyone was being relocated or would have to get there on their own dime.

This, of course, would interfere with our five-year plan, which we were only in the first year of. But sometimes life throws you a curve ball and Mike's eagerness for this new experience could not be contained. We would move. Surely I had skills and would find work. What kept haunting me was an old Yellowknife saying, "People who can't find work in the south move north to gain success."

We came up with an alternative, and thankfully my parents agreed. We would live with them for six months rent free in order to save money to buy a house. Getting married and moving in with my parents hadn't been next on my list of Things To Do. This new job would have Mike away Monday through Thursday. More alone time … but at least in Edmonton there were my mother and a majority of my friends! And longer summers and shorter winters; the bonuses were starting to add up.

Mike negotiated two weeks off for our wedding and honeymoon.

Then, it was the week of our wedding and, as I looked around, I had more pregnant friends than nonpregnant friends. When did this happen? I made a note to include a larger nonalcoholic punch bowl.

It was my wedding day, and the limo was waiting. My dress was amazing, and I looked like a princess. The dress was white satin. I had always imagined myself in ivory because of my complexion, but I now realized that white was the only choice. My dress fell off the shoulders and had three small roses on the cropped sleeve and a bow on the bum with a substantial train. The bodice was covered in sequins and pearls that matched my veil beautifully. My white satin slippers had a bow that complemented the bows on my gown perfectly. My hair had grown out, and I was wearing it up, loose on the sides. It was my day, and I looked fabulous!

Of course, an hour earlier I had been in tears. Why? I'm not entirely sure. The tears had spontaneously erupted after I had returned to my parent's house from the hairdresser. I raced into the house looking for an available room, but there was nowhere for me to go. All the rooms were full of people! It had to be nerves and then I could hear the bridesmaids arguing among themselves about who set me off! Eventually my mother and Stephanie calmed me down, then handed me a glass of champagne.

We were to be married at half past two. The girls and I arrived at the church a little early, making it impossible to exit the car with such a large crowd meandering around outside. "Around the block," I instructed the chauffeur.

To Mike, the groomsmen yelled, "She's here!" Then they mumbled, "She's leaving." I had not thought about the consequences of my exit. Thankfully it was only five minutes of pondering my departure before he heard the words, "She's back!"

The astrologer was right: the sky was blue, and it was warm. Actually, by midafternoon it was unusually hot. There are only two weeks a year that Edmonton needs air-conditioning, and they are never in August! The candles that were my only centerpiece burned down in less than five minutes, and the homemade truffles turned into hot chocolate blobs in cellophane. Neither tea nor coffee was a beverage of choice, and someone had to make a run for more ingredients to restock the punch bowls. Nothing is perfect; I was starting to understand that. And not one mishap threw me into a tizzy, and that was a blessing.

Although everything seemed a little better after I removed the seven layers of crinoline and the confining corset! After dinner and the first dance, people moved outdoors. The back of the venue opened to a gradual hill that led down into a garden area with an artificial lake. It faced west, and the setting sun gave us the most spectacular photographs. This had not been planned but was a delightful surprise. I had wanted an outdoor wedding, and it had turned into just that. I was a princess for a day, and there was so much love and joy surrounding us, my Happily Ever After had just begun.

We honeymooned in Niagara Falls, which is a cliché, but Mike had never been east of Manitoba. In Toronto we stayed at the Skydome. The previous year there had been a sex scandal during one of the televised baseball games. That became the big joke at our gift opening, "Don't get caught!" We just smiled and shook our heads.

We attended a couple of baseball games, one in a skybox, which was supercool! We went to the Canadian National Exhibition (CNE), which brought back flashes of a trip with my family as a child. Something possessed us to buy dinnerware—a twelve-piece setting that even included little espresso cups and saucers. Later we found out that neither of us liked them, but both of us thought the other one had. We enjoyed dinner at the rotating restaurant at the top of the CN tower. Eleven hundred and fifty-one feet above ground! Love was apparently stronger than my fear of heights. I ate my entire dinner holding my feet up off the floor, as though that were going to save me if I fell. Mike went up higher, to the observation deck, without me.

In Niagara Falls we stayed at one of those cheesy honeymoon suites covered in red velvet with a heart-shaped hot tub, which turned out to be rather romantic. And since there was a theme, we had dinner at the rotating dining room of the Skylon Tower overlooking Niagara Falls.

Walking in the front doors of the Tower building was so familiar to me. I grabbed Mike's hand and dragged him toward the escalators and down into the basement. I was so excited to show him all the cool things I had done there. Memories came flooding back from when I was little—just three, maybe four. I could hear the carnival music and see the Ferris wheel. There were other rides and games, but when we arrived at the bottom of the escalator, the space was empty—no rides or games and not one bar of music. I stood there baffled. The memory was of my parents and me, laughing and having fun. A huge smile spread across my face and a feeling of joy entered my body. It was such a blessing to be given back this memory. With my disappointment replaced, Mike and I turned around and headed up the stairs for a lovely dinner overlooking the falls. New memories would follow.

Snapshots of our wonderful trip included *The Phantom of the Opera* and street caricatures of the two of us together. Then we returned home to start our married life in separate homes. Mike living with my parents, and I in Yellowknife for yet another month. Time dragged by before the packers and movers arrived. I never looked twice on my way out of town; there was nothing I was leaving behind.

CHAPTER 4

Conditioning

MY FATHER WAS HOME EVERY second week. Mike was home every weekend. There was a vast amount of time now to spend with my mother. It had been two and a half years since we had spent this much time together. Jane was not factored into our equation as she was currently living and working in Yellowknife. She hoped to save enough money to start university the following September. Currently, my priority was to find a job. And of course complete my CGA course work. Interviews came easily, but I never seemed to make it to the final one that would have guaranteed me a job. It was very discouraging. What was I doing wrong? I tried to stay focused and positive about my assignments, but my motivation was wearing thin there too. Without work to prompt me out of bed my life just slowed down. My routine turned into watching *Sally Jesse Raphael*, then *Days of Our Lives* followed by *The Young and the Restless*. Somewhere in between breaks I'd get showered so my mother was none the wiser when she arrived home from work. Infrequently I would complete an assignment, loathing every moment. The days blended together. I had been happy ... now it seemed so long ago. Depression was my new friend. I could fake my emotional state during the weekend, although with Mike home I was much happier. We would connect with friends in the city.

Our six months with my parents were almost up, and it was now time to start looking for a home of our own. With only Mike's salary, we were limited as to what we could buy. Eventually we agreed on a three-bedroom townhouse condominium in a smaller community between Mum and Dad's acreage and the city of Edmonton. The airport wasn't too far, and the community had wonderful walking paths, shopping, and restaurants. We signed the papers. Two weeks later I received a job offer. What the hell was that all about!

In hindsight, it didn't leave us financially strapped, and that was a good thing. If you ask for patience, God will give you something to try your patience, for how else will you find it? Although I didn't remember asking.

My job offer had come from a subsidiary of the company my father and Mike worked for, Corp Air. It owned and operated the Bowing 727 that flew the employees back and forth to work. They also had a contract to fly Esso employees to Russia. I was now their new junior accountant. My job started the week we moved. I went from depressed to full-out excited! I was learning new tasks at work and decorating at home—no more lull in my life! My mother had made me sew all my own skating costumes when I was a teenager. Yellowknife had a limited number of clothing boutiques, so it was nothing for me to spend an hour whipping up a skirt to wear for an evening out or a new suit jacket for work. I had also designed earring holders for my girlfriends as Christmas gifts. Now I was sewing valances for the living room, drapes and duvet covers for our bedroom, and toss pillows for everywhere! My creativity had emerged in full force. I was recovering chairs and designing a makeup table and cover.

Once I slipped out of my funk, I recognized that Fitzgerald was in one. On the acreage he had been surrounded by Mum and Dad's three cats and Skeeter, the dog. His new home had him confined on a leash. There were no mice to catch or mallard birds to chase. He'd get excited when the cat cage came out as he knew it meant a trip to the acreage for the day. We thought the lack of excitement had him whining, "A friend will solve the problem." We found a little three-month-old kitten at the SPCA. He was mostly black like Fitzgerald, but with more white on his belly and paws. Someone had found him eating garbage in an alley. When he stuck his paw out of the cage to play with Mike's leg, we fell in love. I had named Fitzgerald, so Mike got to name this new cat. He picked Kramer, from his favorite sitcom, *Seinfeld*. And the kitten fit the name perfectly.

The street part in Kramer was well engrained. We had to place the garbage in the cupboard or stack a few really heavy books on top so he couldn't get into it while we slept. Of course this all occurred next to his food dish, so it left us a bit baffled. Fitzgerald was appalled by his new brother, as his own mannerisms were more like those of a tidy butler. He became so annoyed that he started peeing in the toilet! "I'm not sharing a litter box with you," I imagined him saying. It took weeks for him to warm up, or at least to accept Kramer to some degree. It was so interesting to watch the evolution of their relationship. One day Kramer went running down the hall into the living room. Fitzgerald was lying at the entrance, stuck out his arm, and clotheslined him! He was then placed into a headlock, and Fitzgerald started cleaning him, much to Kramer's dismay. Fitzgerald tolerated him a bit more after that.

Life wanes and waxes. There are ups and downs; that is the natural progression. Balance is a bit more difficult to accomplish. Enjoying the downtime was important, for it would never last long. I wish I had realized that at the time, instead of berating myself to stay busy for those few months I had off.

Being in our own space on the weekends when Mike was home was blissful. During the week was a different matter. One night a week Mum and I would go for dinner. Cynthia and I signed up for tennis lessons that took up another night. The third night the two of us would spend hours gabbing on the phone while watching the same television program. My life had changed. Never in my life had I spent so much time watching television. Nighttime was the worst. Other than the brief period when I house-sat, it had been five years since I'd lived on my own at college. Now I found the nights Mike was away … well, I now feared the dark. Okay, not specifically the dark, but what I couldn't see in the dark. And on some level I was aware that there were things in the dark I couldn't see.

Ever since I was little I've talked myself through situations having to do with the dark. I don't remember being scared of monsters under the bed like so many other children, but I was scared of the closet and what I might find inside. Oh, and basements; they are eerie. It all started when I was about eight. Before that I had never had a problem sleeping, day or night, that I can recall. Once I crashed, I slept through until morning. But that one night when I was eight, something woke me up and directed my attention across the room to the Mickey Mouse bubble gum machine. No matter what I did— blinked, crossed my eyes, turned my head and looked sideways—the form took the shape of a witch with a long nose wearing a pointed hat. There was no way I could get it to change back to Mickey Mouse. Eventually I fell asleep, exhausted.

The dark had always felt too enclosing. Even walking home in the dark from work as a teen exhausted my nerves. Rarely did my parents ever offer transportation, so it was something I learned to "grin and bear." The entire time I would look over my shoulder, scared of being attacked. The basement was just as terrifying. Settling my senses took practice, and I could never relax when ascending the stairs. It always felt like someone was chasing me.

In college I slept because of pure exhaustion. My parents' house on the acreage was worse than any other place I had ever lived. I didn't even like being alone there during the daylight hours! I was sure people had died there, brutally. At the very least, people had been severely injured. Mum and Dad's front door had a little window, and I could always see a face looking in. One night I had a dream about this short little monk. He was carrying a rolled-up carpet, and I just knew there was a body inside. The dream was ever so vivid, and it took me weeks to recover!

So I had trained the cats to come to bed with me. Still, it was difficult to go to sleep. Most nights I would watch TV until I was exhausted and then I easily fell asleep, always setting the television to turn off thirty minutes later. The difficulty was with finding something to watch so late; *Unsolved Mysteries* was the only thing that held my attention, but watching a show about murder where the perpetrator was never found did not help my psyche relax before bed!

I moved the phone closer and placed a baseball bat under my side of the bed. Many nights of frustration later, it occurred to me that if I was going to be murdered in my sleep, perhaps I should just get a good night's rest first! For whatever reason, that train of thought worked. That in itself baffled me. What else was my mind willing to accept as truth? Was our truth made up of lies?

At our one year wedding anniversary, life was in a very nice place. We had balanced time with each other, friends, and family. We were both working and had a nice home with two cats to entertain us. We didn't think about the past, nor were we really thinking about what was next in our future. We lived life week to week, until it hit me: I wanted a baby. Mike was not keen about the idea, which of course led me to think he didn't believe in us. But by Christmas we were on the same page, and the baby was due in September. We were very excited.

Mike's parents had become grandparents for the first time in October. This would be my parent's first grandchild. I was terrified to tell them. My mother's voice kept creeping into my mind from my teenage years: "If you get pregnant, just let me know, I'll push you down the stairs!" It was a huge chunk of cellular memory from my teenage years, and it ran deep. Fear put in check, Mike and I shared the news, and all our parents were happy. Although my Grandma's reply threw me off. "Should you be telling everyone so early, Tracy?" Was she warning me to be cautious, or was it a premonition? My grandma just knew things.

Over the last two years we had spent time at Mike's family cabin and visited my Gran in Ontario, but with a baby soon to arrive we decided to take a different kind of vacation, just the two of us. Las Vegas was nice in March. We would take a side trip by car to the Grand Canyon and

Phoenix to watch spring training with the Chicago Cubs. First I would have to get over the preconceived notion that a pregnant woman should not go to Vegas. Where did these rules come from?

At six weeks, I started spotting and decided to go to the emergency room to make certain nothing bad had happened. I couldn't contain my fear for our child. Miscarriages ran rampant on both sides of our family. Mike was at the mine and my mum was working, but thankfully my dad was around to hold my hand through the whole ordeal, quite literally. He worked on easing my mind and calming me down. The ultrasound showed the baby's beating heart. That image brought such relief. The spotting stopped a few days later, and all was forgotten. The baby was fine.

Vegas was a perfect getaway. We saw a few shows, walked the strip, enjoyed people-watching, and were in bed by ten. Phoenix was hot. Watching spring training was exciting. Mike was astonished by how beautiful "a big hole" could be as we observed the Grand Canyon. I had been lucky enough in grade seven to go on a school trip through the Grand Canyon and Las Vegas on our way to California. Mike hadn't believed me when I tried to explain to him how magnificent the Grand Canyon was. Our visit didn't last long as there was over three feet of snow in spots, and we had not prepared to be so cold.

A week after returning from our trip, I had the most bizarre dream. I'm not sure where I was, but it felt like New York City. I was standing in the middle of hundreds of high-rise apartment buildings, looking upward at hundreds of clotheslines strung between the buildings. Each line was full. There was chaos in the air. Something big was about to happen, but I didn't know what. Then the sky lit up as though there were fireworks, but bigger and vaster. Just as I was settled into contemplating the sky, a huge explosion happened. The shape was more of a mushroom cloud that filled the sky with reds and oranges. It woke me out of my sleep. Dread blanketed the room, and I knew it represented the end of the world.

I telephoned Stephanie the minute I got into work the next morning. It had been so vivid. At 3:30 that afternoon the bleeding started. The dream made total sense. My world was ending. It was a Thursday, and Mike would arrive home at four thirty in the afternoon. I had been at the emergency room, and they had sent me for an ultrasound when Mike met me. By then I knew our baby was gone. The ultrasound confirmed it. My uterus was empty. There was no evidence that our baby ever existed. They called it a blythe ovum. The baby had died and dried up. I was distraught, but a part of me had already come to terms with it during the day. Maybe the dream had healed a part of me before the miscarriage had actually happened. Mike was devastated; I wasn't sure whether he would ever recover.

It's odd how attached we had become to this thing that hadn't even taken a breath. As humans we have so much love to give, and we can focus it on just about anything.

I had an appointment with my obstetrician the following week. It was originally for my three-month checkup. My doctor couldn't get me in any earlier so I bled and cramped for the week leading up to my appointment, and just waited. The doctor thought he was still seeing me for my three-month prenatal appointment and came in congratulating me. No one had informed him of my miscarriage. I felt a bit sorry for the guy but was still so devastated with my own grief that I became angry with him. He scheduled a D&C for the following week. He promised I would be the first surgery of the morning. First it had been a week to see the doctor, now a week to remove my trauma. Every day was a horrible reminder of what happened, and there was no moving forward until after the surgery.

We decided there was no reason for Mike to take an entire week off work for a few hours. My mother was not good around emotional upsets, so fortunately Stephanie found a sitter for her children and sat with me at the hospital. A couple of hours turned into a full day. There was a problem: I was never listed for surgery and would now be the last patient of the day.

Who keeps screwing things up? And now, on top of everything, I wasn't allowed to eat. I needed food so badly. I was miserable, angry, and now starving. But things got even worse. At eleven in the morning a group of interns came through, asking me questions. I was tired of answering questions and just wanted to go home. I was rude and didn't care. Stephanie tried to comfort me, but nothing helped. Her Catholicism kicked in, and she found me a nun. I stared at her in blank disbelief. "What is a nun going to do for me?"

"You can talk to her." That did not appease me.

I hated everything and everyone at that moment, and if I had been consolable, perhaps it would have worked, but I was still so stuck in my mad place. Acceptance came with time. Mike and I were both very sad. Our hopes and dreams felt shattered. Fortunately, we hadn't started to get the nursery ready. My grandmother's words kept haunting my mind: "Should you be telling everyone so early, Tracy?" I had forgotten to knock on wood.

We were advised to wait three months but waited two. The baby was due March 5, a day before Mike's birthday. It was like a gift, a sign. But our excitement was overshadowed by our nerves. What if I couldn't carry a baby? My grandma had miscarried several girls, and Mike's mother had also miscarried girls.

I tried to steer clear of that thinking; this time felt different. I was sick, all day. Special K, green apples, and salt and vinegar chips became my friends. The last two surprised me because I had never liked anything sour before.

Once we arrived at fifteen weeks, we relaxed a bit as the ultrasound showed a healthy baby girl. Soon I was able to feel her move. At six months we started discussing names and preparing the nursery. A girly name was out. We wanted something that could go either way.

Sharing the name was not an option. Everyone seemed to have known someone with such-and-such name whom they hadn't liked. Secrecy seemed vital. My mother was the worst. She hadn't done great with us: Jane got an old lady's name, and my mother gave me two first names, but no middle name.

By mid-February my new doctor suggested I get induced. The baby was getting too big and having her naturally would be a problem if we waited much longer. The date was set, February 22. The nursery was done, we had bought clothes, and we had picked a name.

Prenatal class had prepared Mike much more than me. He knew exactly what was happening, I was out of my mind. We arrived at the hospital, and the nurse placed me on the "the drip" to induce labor. All needles terrify me, but IVs have me seeing red. Three and a half hours later my contractions hadn't started, and our baby's heart rate dropped dramatically. The doctor decided to break my water. Then they screwed a heart monitor into our baby's head, which seemed more distressing to me.

Five hours later, after two hours of pushing and two tanks of laughing gas, our beautiful daughter, Brett Madison, was born, at 6:03 p.m. She weighed seven pounds, four ounces.

My mother, now Nana, was pacing outside the delivery room door with a pizza "for the father." She claimed she thought Mike would be hungry, but we all knew she had brought it as a trading mechanism, baby for pizza. Pictures started immediately. Most of them with Nana embracing Brett, her head held high, looking around to see what was going on. She didn't have much baby fat but instead was long and lean. Dark hair on her head like her dad's and a bit still on her back that I tried not to be concerned about. You could tell she would have dark eyes, and her toes were long and skinny like her father's. Nana was pleased with her name.

Once I was settled, the room got crowded. Cynthia and Stephanie arrived, and Brett was swept from one person to the next.

Is any parent really prepared to take complete care of their baby? It felt wrong leaving the hospital without some sort of assistance. But life moves forward, and here we were, parents. At home I placed her on the change table with all this fantastic sunlight shining in. Big mistake! Of course she would get a rash; she had been cocooned for months. I was losing my mothering confidence quickly. On day five we woke to Brett's piercing cries. Nothing would soothe her. I tried feeding her, but she didn't want me. My milk had been slow to come in, and there was just not enough to keep her satisfied. I was in tears, not sure what to do next when Mike suggested we use the four-ounce can of formula the hospital had sent home. Everyone said breast milk was best, so to feed her formula seemed wicked. She drank the entire bottle in a little more than a minute.

Although it was a Sunday, we had a seven-day-a-week walk-in clinic only a few blocks from the house. At eight in the morning I packed up Brett, and the two of us headed out the door to the clinic. The wait was the length of time it took me to fill in the necessary forms for Brett.

The doctor was an ass: "Breast milk is the best thing for her." He continued in this fashion and yelled at me for even considering formula. "Eventually she'll get hungry enough and eat. "

It took everything in me to hold my tongue as the words repeated themselves in my mind, "Breast milk is not best if she starves to death first!" I walked out of his office distraught and helpless. I walked through the adjoining door to the pharmacy and stood facing a long row of infant formula. What was I to do? The choices were overwhelming. I screamed the following words in my mind: What was best for my daughter? Starving while she waited for my milk to come in? It had been five days—shouldn't it have arrived by now? How much longer could she go without food? And if I was going to buy formula what brand was best? Was nothing easy? *God, what do I do?*

I was exasperated when the nurse from the clinic next door came over to me and said, "You know what's best for your baby. Don't let anyone else influence you." As I turned to her, the tears started to pour out of me. She held out her arms as an invitation—one I couldn't resist—and held me until the tears finally stopped.

I did know what was best. She was starving and needed nourishment. I couldn't provide it, but one of the brands in front of me could. When we arrived home with a case in hand, Brett drank a full eight ounces—unheard of in a newborn. She was starving, and I needed not to take it personally. I had been induced two weeks early, and perhaps that is why my body was not producing milk? The trauma of starving had been too much for her, though; the minute her eyes opened from sleep the screaming started. She would not calm down until she had drunk more than half a bottle of formula; she would even cry through the first couple of ounces. This process repeated itself for ten months. Even when she started eating solid food, the edge had to come off with a bottle first. I had no idea how to release that early trauma from her body.

I don't know how it happened, but this little person, Brett, became the center of my world. My focus had changed. Mike was no longer front and center; it was this small child. I loved and adored her and found it very difficult when my six months of maternity leave was over. How things change. I couldn't leave her with any of the caregivers I interviewed. Stephanie would have been my first choice, but I didn't want our friendship to suffer. At last I took my concerns to her. It was the best decision I could ever have made. Stephanie was great, and Brett thrived there. She craved interaction, and Stephanie's children provided that. When Mike and I took Brett for dinner with us, the noisiest place in the restaurant made her the happiest.

My husband became more of an accessory. I loved him, but I was so wrapped up with Brett that something shifted between us. I had never imagined that so much could change. I had planned on always being a working mother, but now I could easily have quit my job. Within a month of returning, I renegotiated my job down to three days a week. "With you home on Fridays, and me home two other days of the week, that means only two days of daycare a week," I told Mike in my effort to convince him that the financial changes would affect us little.

Mike agreed easily, as did my boss. Without the experience to negotiate, I didn't do nearly as well with my contract. In the end I worked more for less, but we all have lessons to learn. One day I would learn my worth. In the end I got what I wanted, which was more time with Brett. Hadn't I been taught that you have to give up something to gain something else; you can't have it all?

The rollercoaster ride had leveled out again, and life was perfect. On Mike's Friday off, I would work, and he would learn to be a hands-on dad. That was very important, because if anything were to happen to me ...

he'd need to step in. He also took the chore of grocery shopping off my list. Occasionally they would come and meet me for lunch. Other times Mike would fill in his day videotaping Brett: "A day in the life of Brett." In the evenings I could then watch what the two of them had been up to during the day.

One morning when Brett was eight months old, I woke up with the most uneasy feeling in my body. Something bad was going to happen. I checked on Brett, and she was fine. There was this unnerving feeling that I was not supposed to leave the house. That knowledge made me more upset as it got closer to the time for me to leave for work. If it hadn't been our accounting month-end, I wouldn't have given a second thought to staying home. We were now both dressed, but it was impossible to head out the door. After ten minutes of pacing, I finally decided this was ridiculous. "Let's go, Brett." Buckling her into her car seat, I got in and started driving away. Two blocks from home, at a speed of 30 km/hr. (19 miles/hr.), the vehicle slipped on an icy patch and slid into a lamppost.

We were fine, although the damage to the car was severe. We returned home, and I called my boss and informed him we had been in an accident and were staying home for the day. He needed me and would pay the cab fare. The bad feeling had passed; it was now fine to leave the house. We bundled ourselves up for the second time and headed out the door.

I may have been busy with month-end, but it didn't stop my mind from wandering to all the strange things that had been happening since I'd become pregnant with Brett. I knew who was on the other end of the phone before picking it up. Once I knew Natasha was calling, and we hadn't talked in over three years. I answered a question correctly from a radio program before they even asked the question. I'd think of a movie I wanted to watch and find it in the programming that evening. In high school when the teacher said to turn to a page in our text book, I always turned to the exact page. Strange things had always been happening, but presently the number of occurrences had increased—so much so that it had my attention, and Mike's too. If that "funny feeling" showed up, we would change our plans until it went away. Mike was really good about it, never questioning or arguing. Perhaps it had nothing to do with my insight, and he was just happy to change plans and stay home.

Brett's first Easter was exciting for me. My grandma was coming to visit her first great-grandchild! It was during a walk with my grandmother that my mother announced she was leaving my dad. I was thrilled that she was finally leaving. This would be the fourth time, and I hoped it would stick. My astonishment came from her mentioning it in front of my grandmother, her mother-in-law!

There are some relationships that happen that you aren't even aware of, and this was the case with my grandma and Mum. "It's about time, Sandra," was my grandma's response. My jaw dropped.

As a mother, this was a bit shocking for me. Do you get to a point where you can see your children for what they truly are? This adult world was very interesting.

Mum didn't enjoy living on the acreage or the thirty-five minute drive she had to and from work every day. She found herself an apartment one bus ride—fifteen minutes—from work. Dad would never consider compromising location, as the acreage was adjacent to an airstrip, and his plane could be parked in the front yard. It was time, and they both knew it. Dad was dating the following week.

Although I was happy they were apart, the dynamics of having to deal with two parent households are challenging. What were the rules? Could they bump into each other and be civil? Was I able to discuss one with the other? It was so new, and the fact that Dad was dating made it more complicated. By fall he wanted me to meet "her." The whole situation was a mess, which only led me to believe it was she who was pushing for the dinner. She picked a night during the week, a work night, and one when Mike would be absent. So how was this a family dinner?

I was grumpy before setting foot in my father's house. "She" was in my father's kitchen and had the audacity to offer me wine. "Thanks, but I know where to find it," I tried to say with a positive tone. As I turned, she tried to cut in front of me to collect the bottle from the fridge. *What is this, high school?*

Not only was I not sitting at my usual spot at the table, but she had me as far away from my father as possible, and with my back facing the living room, where Brett was playing on the floor. Between my end and my father's end of the table sat her daughter, son, sister, and mother. Family dinner for whom? Not *my* family!

She mentioned that her daughter had just completed her Accounting Designation. "You quit taking courses, didn't you, Tracy?" *Bitch* entered my mind automatically as I concentrated on cutting my meat. Then out of nowhere she leaned into my father and said, "Oh Richard, but you love me anyway." Giggling like it was some private joke. Is this woman for real? Majorly insecure; if I hadn't hated her so much, I'd almost have felt sorry for her.

I finished dinner and left before dessert was served, trying to be as cordial as possible, "Sorry, I have to go. It's getting late, and I need to get my daughter home to bed." Brett and I left. My anger was so extreme that when morning came I was still in state of upheaval and called in sick. I needed to talk to my mother. Could I talk to her about my father? At this point I really didn't care; my emotional overload was too extreme. Thankfully she was in her office. I told her everything that had happened. Unexpectedly, she got off the phone and called my dad; he called minutes later.

"Your mother said you're home today. You're not feeling well?"

"No, Dad, actually I'm not." I paused momentarily. The words *tell him the truth* floated through my mind. Did I really want to go there with my dad? I continued, "I'm quite upset about last night."

"Do you want me to come over and talk about it?"

A stuttered "Sure" escaped my lips. The last thing I wanted to do was have a conversation about my feelings with my father. We had managed to avoid sentiment for twenty-eight years. There were no "I love yous" in my house, not even an "I'll miss you, or I missed you." This was going to be very uncomfortable, and I was terrified.

He arrived at the door with a box of doughnuts. Opening the door to let him in, I looked up and told him, "Dad, I don't eat doughnuts. I don't like them, never have." Twenty-eight years old, and we knew so little about each other.

He used her name: "Christine believes you're upset because it was difficult for you to see another woman in your mother's kitchen."

The laughter came bubbling out before I could stop it. What was this Psychology 101? What a standard answer, but then she had been married three times and my guess was she had not learned much during that time. "Dad, I'm thrilled Mum left. I wish it had happened years ago. Neither of you was happy."

My father then fell into one of my kitchen chairs, speechless, staring blankly back at me. There was such pain and confusion in his face. Not all children want their parents to stay together; the misconception always confused me. Perhaps I'm just an oddity; actually, I know I'm an oddity. I sat down across from him.

Once my father caught his breath, he asked, "Why are you upset, then?"

I told him at length how "she" had made me feel like I didn't belong in my own home, that her comments felt like they were directly meant to belittle me, and that she had tried to make me feel like he now had a whole new family that made me less important. "And Dad, why did she pick an evening when Mike was out of town? It's because she never would have behaved that way if he had been around. Mike wouldn't have put up with it. She orchestrated the entire evening to make me feel like an outsider."

He confessed that her own mother had said many of the same things to her the previous night after I left.

"She has some major insecurities, Dad, but I'm not getting dragged into her drama."

"Ya, I told her this morning she's in big trouble if she's managed to piss off the nice one of my daughters."

That made me laugh. "Oh my God, I can't imagine what will happen when she meets Jane!" My sister would eat her alive. Jane didn't put up with anyone's nonsense.

Never in my life did I think my father and I could have a serious conversation, one that didn't end in a shouting match. We had communicated, and our relationship had changed because of it. "She" didn't last long, but then there was always another one …. Perhaps I should thank her. My entire being had totally resisted the dinner, but such a good thing had come of it. I needed to learn to tap into when that feeling was more about danger or when it was more about healthy upheaval.

Or had I? I had attended the dinner against everything I had felt.

The Wonder Years

CHAPTER 5

Exhaustion

MIKE HAD WORKED FOR THE Echo Bay Mines, Lupin Property for a little more than three years and had received several promotions. The previous New Year's Eve the wives had been flown up to the mine site to celebrate with their husbands. I looked very pregnant, and the pilots and crew had given me a hard time for weeks before the flight, none of them wanting to deliver a baby on the plane or at the site. During my visit the mine manager had made a point of telling me what a wonderful employee Mike was: "He's doing an amazing job and is definitely going places." The praise had been wonderful to hear and was perhaps meant to prepare me for the future.

Barely a month into working part-time, Mike flew out to Vancouver Island for a job interview. Even though his boss's statement had come the previous year, I hadn't thought about moving. Yes, we would need a bigger house if we had a second child, but nothing too far away from my parents. Although, now I was considering the benefits of the island weather, no more snow.

Mike came home, adamant about not taking the job. The life and safety of the project was not something he was interested in getting involved with. I was deeply disappointed with his decision and quite frustrated that I didn't seem to have a say in changing his mind. Not that I wanted him to work in an unsafe environment, but didn't a wife have a say in all matters? Once he decided no, there was no changing his mind, which was so frustrating for my ego! Now there was a part of my brain that couldn't stop thinking about the possibility of moving, somewhere else. How exciting would that be!

Mike's mine manager has been transferred to their Washington State operation in the United States and was requesting Mike's expertise within the engineering department: "If you could just spend a week here to organize the department for me, that would be really helpful."

Mike spent two weeks in early November organizing a mine planning program and returned home with a job offer. Had I made this move happen? I most surely wanted to move, but out of Canada? That had never crossed my mind. Everyone and everything would be so different. Of course this perception came only from what I had seen on television.

Mike knew his worth and negotiated a good deal. This job would allow him to be home every night: no more missing milestones in our child's development. Our packing date was December 26, and move-in date was scheduled for January 2, 1995. We had done the look-see and purchased a beautiful three-bedroom, ranch-style home on a half acre lot located one block off the lake and ten minutes north of the town of Republic. I had spent very little time in the mountains or the valley of any mountains; but the views from our new home were breathtaking. We were nestled in between Wauconda and Sherman Pass and only thirty miles south of the British Columbia border and the town of Grand Forks, BC, which was much closer than the nearest American town of Colville.

My winters had just become significantly shorter, making my summers that much longer and that much hotter. I would miss the sunrise and sunset, but again I guess there are always trade-offs.

The house was perfect. It was less than a year old, spacious, with huge windows that had spectacular views. Fitzgerald and Kramer were thrilled to be off-leash! They roamed the tall grass in our valley and adjusted nicely. The local newspaper even made mention of one of them chasing a deer!

My vision of a working mother had transformed when Brett was born. I no longer wanted to work and here I was, jobless. Had I made that happen too? Not being allowed to work, because now I lacked a green card, was harder to swallow. With the opportunity and choice taken away from me, I felt a little caged. Yes, I had ultimately been a part of this decision, but my new title did not sit well with me. Housewife and stay-at-home mum; I just didn't like the stigma attached to either of those titles. My mind was in complete resistance.

Interaction with my mother, Cynthia, and Stephanie had filled a good part of my life. Now I had too much time on my hands and a ten month old who was walking and getting into everything, because of course it was a ranch house, and everything was accessible! What were we thinking!

The image in my head of a town made up of fifteen hundred people in the United States or Canada was redneck. I couldn't imagine I would ever find anyone with similar values with whom I could befriend. Town would be full of smokers and drinkers and people who let their children run wild. That is what all the small towns I grew up in where like—weren't they?

I soon learned, with much relief, that that was not the case. All these mining wives were imports just like me, some even from Canada. The local newspaper advertised a playschool that accepted children age zero through five years. A phone call to the teacher confirmed that indeed Brett was more than welcome to attend class on Tuesday and Thursday mornings for a cost of thirty dollars a month.

My nerves were a wreck, and I was dealing with the worst case of irritable bowel syndrome (IBS) since breaking up with Luke. I didn't know how to talk to other moms, and I had never been comfortable around other people's children. The only moms I had spent time with were mine and Stephanie. There was a stroller group that lasted six weeks while I was on maternity leave, but not even a coffee or playdate had come of that.

Stephanie's children had not prepared me for playschool. There were so many children—nearly twenty—and it was so loud. Parents were preoccupied. I was seriously overwhelmed but grateful at least to have Brett to hang on to for comfort, which lasted about a minute! She wanted to be in the middle of it all and couldn't get enough of the other children. Her walking at ten months did get the attention of a few parents, and conversations started. Everyone was so friendly, and Brett was in heaven. She loved to be stimulated—overstimulated, actually. In the car she needed a huge variety of toys to keep her occupied. This was perfect for her. I would learn to adjust for her sake.

The child next closest in age was eleven months older. Not that any of that mattered to her, and my bit of heaven was the adult conversations. Being alone at home for the last week and a half with little adult time had been very difficult. Two days had been filled with unpacking, but now the house was completely organized. With everything on one level, Brett had a lot of space to move around. I was exhausted. A team of parents couldn't keep up with her, which was the comment after our first day of playschool.

Again, I anticipated with great excitement weekends when Mike was home all day. We would go shopping in Colville or Spokane. As we didn't have a sitter, there wasn't any alone time to take in a movie or go out for dinner, so Brett was always included in our plans. I learned to reorganize my Tuesdays and Thursdays to get some downtime. Brett and I would stop after school at the local grocery store and pick up the essentials. All the clerks were getting to know her by name. Everyone was so nice. I would purchase a couple of chicken fingers for the ride home because I knew once she ate, nap time wasn't far behind. I didn't dare wake her up at home to feed her, since she wouldn't go back to sleep. Those two hours of quiet were precious to me. It didn't take long to let the laundry, house cleaning, or supper prep go in favor of reading. It felt like years since I had really read anything. Before the move a coworker had lent me *The Mists of Avalon* by Marion Zimmer Bradley. There were moments when I felt like Viviane or Morgaine! I felt some magical power within me just waiting to be tapped into. This fictional story felt like a part of my past, and the concepts were entirely plausible.

The weekdays that Brett didn't attend preschool were exhausting! I was having a terrible time trying to find balance between playing with Brett, which was almost impossible because she changed activities too rapidly for me to keep up, cleaning the house, and of course quiet time for my own sanity. In the end nothing seemed to get accomplished. Actually, that's not true—lots got accomplished; it just kept coming back around to have to be done all over again! Laundry was always going, tidying up was a constant, especially if you are a Virgo and have anal tendencies. Mike was more anal than I, so I never felt like I had accomplished enough to satisfy him! I felt like a broken record, always telling Brett, "Later Mummy will do that." At eleven months she was now talking. Not full sentences, but she could string two or three words together.

With Mike home every night, I was able to get a better routine going. We would trade night to night, dishes and bath time, which was causing me less stress. Not because of the work itself, but now I was able to release my resentment with Mike sitting in the living room reading his newspaper or watching one of the many American sports that he had suddenly taken to.

The resentment was making its way into my heart. I could feel myself pulling away from him. Did he even notice how much I did? Or was it just expected? How could he not feel guilt about how exhausted I was? Didn't he see it in my face or hear it in my voice?

One night before it had all been sorted out, I just lost it and handed Brett off to him: "She needs a bath. Her jammies are laid out in the bathroom." Was all I ever needed to do to give him a little direction? To move out of my anger and take action? He willingly took her. I checked on them, and they were having such fun, playing. I was a bit jealous. I never had time to play so freely; it was always about what the next chore was and then eventually being able to flop into bed.

By the end of February, things started to pick up in my social life—my daytime social life, that is. There was quite a connection between the playschool mothers. So many activities were organized outside of school time. We had recipe swaps, quilting parties, and of course celebrated our children's birthdays together. The children were always with us. These events were highly anticipated and very rewarding, but what I really wanted was a best friend, someone like Stephanie, Cynthia, or Kathleen.

I found her at one of the recipe swaps. She had two children, and the youngest was a year older than Brett. The children got along nicely. We would head north into Canada for a morning of swimming or take the pass to the east for some weekly grocery shopping in Colville. It was nice company, for a while.

We all have our own little idiosyncrasies. Kathleen loves to debate and will actually pick the minority's point of view just to argue a point. That was the lawyer in her, long before that inkling had entered her mind. Stephanie is wild and crazy, and nothing stops her from accomplishing her goals. She encourages you to accomplish your dreams! Kathleen and Stephanie showed me what strength looked like. Cynthia taught me that sometimes cautious was necessary before jumping in. She was also the first person who allowed me to be there to support her, whether it was dealing with an old situation or something new. I gained the ability to think outside the box. She brought out the caregiver in me. Without them I wouldn't be who I am. But the main reason our relationships have lasted so long is that our values are very much the same.

My new friend's values were very different from mine. Occasionally I'd reflect on my upbringing and would become angry that my mother did not instill enough rules or discuss values. Once you have your own child, these things become much more important. Then the realization dawned on me that my parents must have done pretty well if here I was making comparisons. I could see that she was what her environment had created, so then wasn't I?

Discipline was an important part of my current survival system. By the time Brett was one year old she was held responsible for her actions. She was a smart little girl, and I was aware of that. Of course the discipline needed to be age appropriate, and I had read a dozen books regarding that topic. If I didn't discipline her now, for my own sanity, what would it be like when she became a teenager? Would she ever listen to me at fifteen if I couldn't get her to listen to me now? I didn't agree with all the child-rearing books, but there were bits and pieces in each book that I assimilated. Truth be told, Brett wasn't like other children. Her energy level was way beyond normal, and learning to listen to me and eventually teachers was imperative for her survival in this world. If my hard work now would help her in the end—well, I believe that is what parenting is all about. It wasn't about being liked; my job was to be a parent.

Time-outs were necessary; learning right from wrong was necessary to build a strong foundation. Saying sorry for injuring anyone was a must, and a child must learn from consequences. It can be hard on some, but I felt all of these things were building blocks for everything else.

My girlfriend never held her children responsible for their actions, or perhaps I should say, never followed through with anything she said. And they knew how to play her. She was too soft of heart, perhaps lazy. As a friend, do you mention that you can see the children manipulating her? Or will that jeopardize your relationship? And if you decide to tell her, how do you go about it?

The opportunity passed me by, and now I was standing knee deep in a dilemma. We were all at a quilting gathering. The kids were having a good time like they always did until Brett came to me crying and holding her eye. Through her tears and with information from the other children, we were able to learn what had happened. Brett had been poked in the eye by my girlfriend's son. "I didn't want her looking at the picture on the wall," was his reply.

Accidents happen, but this seemed to have been done with intention. But had it been malicious? That is what would make the difference. He was three and in my mind old enough to be held accountable for his actions. The injury was so bad that Brett's eye was bloodshot for five days.

He didn't lose any toys or privileges and was granted attendance to preschool the next day. I was outraged. She told me he was sorry. I didn't hear him say he was sorry, and Brett didn't hear him say he was sorry, so I mentioned that perhaps he should apologize to Brett directly. She brought him over to apologize. He looked his mother directly in the eye and said, "Sorry." Brett wasn't even standing next to me; she was across the room. This was not an apology, and it left me frustrated with her lack of comprehension.

Knee deep. She didn't get it, and that was fine. We all have our own lessons to learn; heaven knows I did. But boundaries had been crossed, and I would not take the chance of this happening again. This would be the last time. There were just some people who were unhealthy for us and our family.

Friends come and go. Some last forever, while others are just around long enough for us to learn something new. That's what I chalked it up to. Letting go of the friendship was sad, but after reevaluating our relationship, I realized we just weren't on the same page. There were other women in our group I felt more connected to and with whom I had healthier relationships. Of course those thoughts get you through your decision, but they don't necessarily ease the emotional pain.

Being at home full-time was now enjoyable, and even being labeled a housewife didn't bother me much anymore. The first couple hours of the morning had become my favorite time of the day. Brett and I would sit on the couch to watch *Little Bear* and then *Rupert*, and we'd cuddle while I enjoyed my morning café mocha.

A lull of contentment must have entered my life, for why else would I have wanted another baby? *And please, be a boy.* I referred to the information from a book I read—something about male sperm swimming faster so you needed to get pregnant immediately after your egg released. We were pregnant in the blink of an eye. Then reality set in: "Am I nuts? How will I manage two?"

Six weeks into my pregnancy I miscarried, again. This time I wasn't devastated, just deeply disappointed. My heart hadn't been wrenched out of my chest. I was, well, resigned. Brett was a healthy child—one who seemed like more of a monster currently, but she was an angel when she slept. The D&C was routine, other than a fainting spell when they tried to insert the IV for the fourth time. I came home sad. Mike became withdrawn.

I do not believe in coincidences. Both pregnancies that ended in a miscarriage were because we had tried to conceive a boy. Both my grandma and mother-in-law had had difficulty carrying girls. Perhaps I had difficulty with boys?

Brett turned two on February 22, 1996, and the new baby was expected August 30. Thankfully we had air-conditioning! Man, it was hot in this valley.

Thank God we had baby gates! Brett hit her "terrible twos" long before two. Closing in on two and a half, she was still a cyclone, but now it included an aggressive nature. If she didn't like something or was angry, she would become physical—not so much beating on the other children, but she would just push them down or out of her way if they were too slow or in her way. None of the children had been hurt, mercifully, but there had been a couple of really close calls. I was pregnant and getting tired of constantly punishing her and exhausted from all the apologies she had to make. Was this karma?

Time-outs were prevalent inside, as well as outside the house. Brett was always dressed up like a princess, and I was starting to feel like the villain in her current fairy tale!

Mike and I had a decision to make. Where did we want our new baby to be born—in the United States or Canada? We decided on Canada for a variety of reasons. One was that I needed to drive over the Sherman Pass to see my doctor if we delivered in the United States. In the summer it wasn't a problem. As I had become pregnant in November, I could be dealing with treacherous road conditions. The road to Canada was less dangerous, and the hospital was much closer. We had never considered it as an option until some of the other women decided to go north to deliver. We were told that it was also less expensive. The idea of all of us flying on the same passport was also appealing. Brett and I had obtained green cards, and it was just a matter of filling in paperwork at the border to do the same for our new child. In three years we could all apply for citizenship together.

Mike was a nervous wreck. With five weeks to go, he was already calling me at six o'clock in the morning to update me on his whereabouts. No one we knew had cell phones, and in the valley, I'm sure they wouldn't have worked. My biggest stress was about going into labor after midnight. The border crossing closed between midnight and eight in the morning. If I went into labor during the night we would have to call the Royal Canadian Mounted Police (RCMP) and have them open the gate to let us through.

A month before my due date I woke up to the phone ringing. It was Mike telling me which mine site he was working at for the day. Halfway through our conversation I was brought to full alertness. Brett came running into our bedroom, bubbling with excitement. "What? What is it, Brett?" I wasn't entirely awake yet and couldn't comprehend what she was saying.

"I poured my own juice, Mama. Look, I poured my own juice!"

And sure enough, she had poured her own glass of grape juice, and, with the lid on incorrectly, there was overflow dribbling down the cup, landing on my cream-colored carpet.

"I have to go!" I said, scrambling to hang up the receiver. As quickly as a woman who is eight months pregnant can, I jumped out of bed. The trail led me down the hallway, through the dining room, family room, and into the kitchen—little grape spots everywhere. She was so excited, and I didn't want to burst her bubble, so I took the glass and congratulated her on her achievement. Then I explained that we really needed to keep the juice in the kitchen. "Look what a mess grape juice makes, honey." It was 6:10, and I was pulling out the steam cleaner.

An hour later the two of us sat down and had some breakfast while we watched *Little Bear*. At 8:30 while I was in the shower, she put her favorite videotape backward into the VCR, where it became lodged. We had discussed this multiple times, so she was placed in a five-minute time-out. This entire process was then again repeated at 10:30 while I was changing loads of laundry. My patience was wearing thin. While I was trying, yet again, to remove the movie, I heard running water.

"What is that?" I asked myself out loud, turning around to pinpoint the noise.

As I came around the corner, I saw Brett standing on my wooden dining room chair, peeing. It was running down her leg onto my chair, over the edge, where it was dripping onto my cream-colored carpet!

Time-out was over, and a spanking was issued. She had been potty-trained for more than six months, so this was not an accident! I now recognize that she did indeed stay in time-out and hadn't left her post, but by that time my morning had not put me in the best of moods. While she spent time in her room with the baby gate in place, I hauled out the steam cleaner for the second time that morning. Once finished, I checked in on her to discover that she'd pulled all the books off her bookshelves, emptied her drawers, and was fast asleep among all her belongings. Bliss at last!

With peace in the house, momentarily, I continued doing loads of laundry. Between loads I made a refreshing blueberry Italian soda. I took a long sip and placed it on the table and went to get the next load of laundry to fold. When I returned, I placed the laundry basket on the table, pushing it back to make room for my folded articles, and yes, you guessed it, knocked the contents of my drink all over my beautiful carpet.

Within seconds I grabbed a cloth and kneeled on the carpet and cried. This was not a typical day, but one at a time, my days had become more challenging. Overwhelmed with so many issues, I could no longer see straight. Suddenly my thoughts chased one another. Could the day get any worse? This wasn't the life I wanted. How the hell did I get here? My husband was thrilled to be living here, watching nothing but sports. I had started to dislike him. It was only a couple of nights earlier that I couldn't even stand watching him eat supper. His chewing was loud and annoying. I had a demon child and was expecting ... what? Even my friends wondered what was wrong with Brett. She had been diagnosed at sixteen months with asthma, which kept me awake 24/7 for weeks on end several times a year. When I consulted the doctor, he had told me to place her on Ritalin.

"No! There must be another solution," I remembered saying as I relived the entire conversation in my mind.

"Would you like a prescription for Prozac?" he offered.

"No! How is that going to solve anything?" I had left completely annoyed and bewildered at his inadequacies as a medical professional.

I didn't feel depressed; I felt insane. As I sat huddled on the floor cleaning, there was another voice in my head, and it was saying, "There's a way out." I stopped suddenly and listened intently. "There is a place you can go to, and your worries will no longer exist."

That excited me. Could it be true? My tears stopped as I tilted my head and continued listening. In my mind's eye I could see a door opening, just waiting for me to walk through. "Let yourself go insane," it whispered. "Then you can live in whatever world you want to."

Could I really do that? A millisecond later I yelled, *"No!"* The door slammed shut, and I was left wondering what had just happened. It was a split-second decision that could have gone either way. I recognized that I had made a conscious choice to stay in my present world. Was it really that easy to go insane? I shook my head and allowed the thought to fall away from me. I would figure this out, and it would get better. Isn't that what I had done for years? Decided on change and then moved forward to implement it? I pulled out the steam cleaner for the third time and started cleaning up the mess I had created.

Once I had time to sit and think about it, I realized that more stuff was coming through than it had in a long time. My psychic abilities had really kicked up a notch while I was pregnant with Brett and had only increased since.

It hadn't been long ago that I woke up from a dream of which I have no memory, but tears were streaming down my face. I was slightly aware that I was repeating the word good-bye. The words "I love you and will miss you," simply escaped from my mouth. It took a few moments before I realized the good-bye was to my Gran; she must have passed during the night. She had come to say farewell to me. My mother called an hour later and confirmed what I already knew.

Had Gran come to visit because she knew it wasn't possible for me to attend her funeral? No one in the family with whom I spoke had a similar story.

There were littler things I was also aware of. The occasional high-pitched ringing in my ears were downloads from the Universe – what was being downloaded was a mystery to me. And some nights I couldn't fall asleep because my mind had to review the events of the day, much like looking at a movie reel. I now realized that since childhood I placed part of my pillow or my forearm over my third eye chakra, my forehead, and it stopped the visions and made sleep imminent.

After almost going insane, I reevaluated my situation. I made more time for Brett and tried not to cringe when eating dinner with my husband. I placed my concentration on the baby's room.

Then she was coming! Eight days early! Mike and I dropped off Brett with friends, but by the following morning when we woke in the hospital, my contractions had stopped. The doctor suggested I go home and come back when things started up again. "No," came my urgent reply. "I'm not taking the chance!" My doctor looked at me with questioning eyes. I continued, "I don't want to get stuck on the other side of the border after midnight when it closes. Please let me have this baby today. Also, tomorrow's my birthday, I don't want to have this baby on my birthday!"

Who wants to go through labor on their birthday? And could I not have something that was just mine? Stephanie had her oldest on her birthday, and now she spent every birthday catering to someone else; she was totally forgotten.

My doctor agreed to induce me, but seconds later my water broke. No doubt the baby had heard me and decided, if that's the way you want it, Mum, fine. Here we go! The delivery was fast, and the labor was vicious. The baby did not fare well. The shoulders got stuck on the way out. The doctor waited for a contraction to dislodge the rest of our baby. I waited, becoming quite frantic that nothing was happening. It was the longest minute of my life. Finally he placed his foot against the bed and yanked, delivering eight pounds, six ounces of blue baby. They whisked her away, since there was no breath. It seemed like an eternity until we finally heard a cry. It was then that we found out we did indeed have a girl. Taylor Alexandra Elizabeth was born two and half years and one day after her big sister, at eight pounds, six ounces.

This delivery was nothing like Brett's. I could have crocheted a blanket while delivering Brett. It was so easygoing until I took in the two tanks of laughing gas. With Taylor I was totally out of control! I was standing. I was lying on the floor. I was on the toilet, then off the toilet, and I was being hung over a bar. I was being moved this way and that way. I wanted to be massaged; I didn't want to be massaged. Poor Mike! And he was on crutches from a baseball injury to his ankle that had occurred the previous week.

Once her cry came I immediately went into shock. My body wouldn't stop shaking. They wanted to place her in my arms, but I was terrified of dropping her or giving her shaken baby's syndrome! They started stitching me up. An hour later, when they were done, the shaking finally subsided. We were rolled into a private room, and that is where I fell in love. She was absolutely gorgeous. They say you don't know the color of a baby's eyes, but hers were going to be blue, and she had a full head of red hair. She was so chubby compared to Brett.

Before I fell asleep, I tucked her into bed with me. I couldn't let her sleep in that cold, plastic bed; it just seemed wrong. I never did that with Brett; I was terrified of rolling onto her, and of course there had always been rules in my head! This little girl was so small and alone in her bed three feet away from me. It was only one night, and she had had a rough day. I was breaking the rules, but later when the nurse came by, there was a smile on her face. We had finally bonded.

The following morning, on my thirtieth birthday, Brett, Mike, and my father arrived at the hospital. My dad had driven past the hospital the afternoon before on his way to our house around the same time Taylor was born. If he'd stopped, he would have met his new granddaughter within minutes of her arrival. He had looked for our car, but we had just traded in our old one, and he didn't know the color of the new one. My dad has this keen awareness of births and deaths; it is quite eerie.

I greatly appreciated Dad over the next couple of days. Mike's foot was now looking much worse, and getting around was nearly impossible. I sat all day as my dad was terrified that they had released me too early, and I would hemorrhage. Memories of my birth must have resurfaced in his mind.

Brett was thrilled to have her Papa visiting too but was more interested in her baby sister. Her eyes were so big and inquisitive, taking in Taylor's tiny fingernails and toenails. She was never very far away, usually on the edge of her sister's blanket on the floor, pretending to read her a book, watching the diaper changes with lots of comments like "Pooie!" or "Ah, she's peeing, Mama!" Occasionally I would find them sleeping, curled together on the floor. There is nothing more precious than a sleeping child—okay, there is, when there are two. My parents had pictures of me sleeping, and I never understood it until I had my own.

My dad left, and Mike's parents arrived. They left, and my mother arrived. She flew in, and I planned on driving back to Edmonton with her for a two-week visit. Mike would then meet us in Lethbridge for his grandmother's eightieth birthday during the Canadian Thanksgiving weekend in October.

Mum was heading home and wanted to cross the border when it opened at eight. It was 8:05. I was still sitting on the couch sipping my coffee when she entered the living room, yelling. She never yells, so this was very unnerving. "Get your ass off the couch and start packing the car!" I know she was just trying to snap me out of it, but all she got was a blank stare as I slowly hauled my ass off the couch. Her expression changed to one of serious concern.

This behavior wasn't like me. It was all so confusing. My personality was to get things done. I was ready before everyone else, and no one ever needed to tell me to get moving! Currently I just didn't want to move.

There was no energy stored, and there was such a long day ahead of us. The last month had been hard—no, really, the past year had just taken everything out of me: a trying two-and-a-half-year-old and now a new baby. Breastfeeding hadn't worked this time, either. There was lots of milk, but my nipples were cracked and badly bleeding. Then there was my husband. His eating habits almost made me barf. His mannerisms drove me crazy. Sex had become one more thing on my to-do list. Who wants to have sex when all day long people are pulling at you and needing you for something? I just wanted to be left alone, I was exhausted. Things would change for the better, I kept repeating, but they hadn't. My life sucked.

So with my mother now using encouraging words, distress lurking deep in her eyes, I gathered up our belongings and packed them in the back of our Ford Explorer and climbed into the driver's seat. It was close to nine by the time we crossed the border.

Halfway there, we stopped for the night and arrived in Edmonton the following day. Mum and Dad had settled things financially, so she had bought herself a house in the same neighborhood where she'd been living for the past two years. My dad kept the house on the acreage but had to sell both his planes, which still upset him a year later. A few days into my visit I was starting to feel much happier, more alive. Perhaps it was time to leave Mike. I wasn't happy with him anymore, and single parenting might be a better choice. Jobs were abundant, and there was a daycare around the corner from my mother's house. I was sure she would let me stay with her until I got on my feet. The more I thought about it, the more I thought about it. What was wrong with my husband, anyway? He helped out with the girls when I asked him to. The part that annoyed me was that I always had to ask him; he never took the initiative on his own. He enjoyed playing with them, inside and out. They lit up when they saw him. Then it dawned on me that I couldn't take his children away from him. I needed to find another solution.

When we returned home after Mike's grandmother's birthday celebration, things changed. The main thing was my attitude. A break from the mundane had been good for me. Seeing my girlfriends had been good for me! I realized that a combination of being overwhelmed, perhaps postpartum, and a few close friends moving away from Republic had pushed me over the edge. I now found joy in watching Brett interact with her sister, sitting next to her on the couch or floor, always with a book or a toy to entertain her. When Taylor was a little bigger she would push her around in the doll stroller, or the two of them would sit on the little pony and ride around together. I was learning to relax, and life was getting easier.

Then I started to enjoy my husband more. With the birth of our second child, he had decided to get a vasectomy, and with that freedom, our sex life improved. Not tremendously, but slightly. My children had come first in all things and Mike had come last, which had contributed to our relationship dwindling. I never mentioned to him about my thoughts of leaving; it would have hurt his feelings. There was work to be done— that is where I would concentrate my efforts.

And it happened. Instead of working from six in the morning until five every day, Mike started coming home closer to 3:30 in the afternoon. This changed our relations tremendously. It allowed us to have an afternoon coffee together while the children were still napping. Before this there had been no "us" time. When the kids went to bed at eight in the evening, we both were too tired and just wanted our own space. We'd hired a sitter a few times, but there just weren't many choices available for a night out. We needed to rebuild and rebond.

Then we connected with a lovely couple whose children were the same age as ours. Having similar values and interests were great, but the best part was the conversations. The struggles we dealt with daily were comparable in nature, discussing them brought out humor and reduced the stress. Laughter is healing.

Ask for change, and it will come knocking at your door. Make sure you're ready for it.

By January we were enjoying each other's company and our children more than we ever had. I was stronger and more capable of handling all the day-to-day events that occurred in our lives.

It was the first week in February when Mike came home earlier than usual. We sat to have our lattes when he announced, "I got a job offer today."

"Really, what job?"

"It's in San Francisco."

"There's mining in San Francisco?"

"No, but there's a head office of a really large mining company from Australia, and they want me to come for an interview next week. They would like it if you could join me on kind of a house-hunting trip. Kevin gave them my name." Kevin had told Mike about the job at Lupin as well.

At this point I took a real interest and looked him in the eyes and told him, "We're going to live in Walnut Creek."

"What?"

"We are going to live in Walnut Creek. Rosie O'Donnell just introduced an audience guest, and she was from Walnut Creek. It's in the East Bay." With more psychic connections than ever, I was really paying attention to the signs around me.

There was a question mark in his eyes and a shrug in his shoulders as he replied, "Okay."

Mike's parents came to watch the girls. The interview was informal and pretty much a "When can you start?" thing. We spent the rest of our time in Walnut Creek and various other areas that had been suggested as nice communities to live in, with an easy commute.

I felt like a small-town hick venturing out in this fabulous city. My clothes were wrong, my hair was wrong—ugh. So while Mike was at meetings, I decided to find someone good to cut my hair. Surely they were all staring at me because I looked so out of place. Those insecure feelings from when I was in junior high were emerging. During that period in my life, my hair had gone completely frizzy, there was nothing that could be done with it. I wanted it straight like all the other girls, but eventually I got a perm. There was such excitement about this new experience, but I was terrified about fitting into the California lifestyle. Without realizing it, I was once again taking what I had seen on television and the movies and assimilating it into my life as a truth.

Over the next couple of weeks there wasn't much time to worry about anything. There was too much to do. Brett had been baptised just before we moved from Edmonton, and although it wasn't planned, we were going to be moving directly after Taylor was baptised. I felt terrible, like I was using the church. Family was coming to celebrate Taylor's baptism and Brett's third birthday, and to send us off on a new adventure. Thankfully our pastor didn't cancel the baptism, although she did have every right to. My grandmother was coming from Manitoba. It would be our first visit since my grandpa had died in January. I wanted it to be a happy weekend, and it was.

Only days after everyone left, the four of us, and the two cats, were all in our vehicle heading south. We rolled into Walnut Creek on Mike's thirty-second birthday with the cats a little frazzled, Brett feeling cooped up, and Taylor covered in chicken pox. We found our temporary accommodation—a two-bedroom apartment condo, settled the cats in, let the kids run around a bit, and ordered pizza to celebrate. We had left three feet of snow and were now surrounded by green grass and blooming gardens.

With all the activity before we left, I was amazed when my grandmother commented that she believed Brett's juice was causing her hyperactivity. A month earlier, a woman at church had looked at Brett and told me, "You should get the book *Raising Your Spirited Child* by Mary Sheedy Kurcinka. It did amazing things for me, and I really think it would help you."

I had read the book and used a lot of the techniques. The best part was that apparently there were other parents having the same problems we had. I took comfort in that, but with my grandmother's observation, a new discussion took place.

Pure juice with no sugar additives was the only thing she had ever drunk. But all juice, even in its natural form, contains sugar. That sugar was giving her a kick and then when she came down off her sugar high, she wanted more. My grandmother had observed the cycle. I of course had been living the cycle and saw nothing. Rather than beat myself up, I realized that now at least there was something else to work with.

The real problem was keeping sugar out of her system. I would find her scaling the counters and scavenging through the cupboards looking for anything—the sugar bowl, chocolate chips, something to give herself a "fix." The whole thing was unnerving.

In Canada we have five main banks, and each of them can be found in every province or territory, so moving and having to transfer money is not a problem. The banking system in the United States is very different. Each state has its own banks. We had a money draft and needed to open an account to deposit it. Wells Fargo seemed to be the best choice and more widely found. A new branch was opening in Walnut Creek. The only morning Mike had available happened to be St. Patrick's Day. The bank was busy because it was new, and because of the holiday it was dressed for the occasion with balloons, cookies, and lots of customer service representatives. At ten in the morning the clerks were trying to give Brett cookies.

Most adults, honestly, do not understand when you tell them, "My daughter cannot have cookies. She has a sugar problem." Brett had been off sugar for approximately two weeks, and I couldn't believe the intelligent, sweet, wonderful child she had turned into. Behind my back the clerk gave her a cookie and then a second one. I tried to pry them out of her mouth with no success. By 10:30 Brett was out of control. It was taking everything in me not to beat her. Mike was trying to open an account. I was chasing one child and sending evil glances to the clerk who apparently knew more about rearing my child than I did! I captured Brett and brought her back in line when again, her hand slipped out of mine and she leaned over and bit the shoe of the man standing behind us. Her saliva left a perfect imprint of her teeth on his toe. I was horrified! As much as I wanted to offer to replace his shoes, I was afraid that they might cost thousands of dollars, and we could not afford that! As I was giving my most sincere apologies, I looked around for Brett, finding her with a horrified look on her face, in the basket under her sister's stroller. She was so embarrassed. Mike finished up, and we were able to leave.

Within a few weeks I was able to narrow down the behavior not only to sugar, but specifically to apples and apple juice. This awareness came from a snack of apples at the park. Afterward Brett just started pushing down children who were in her way. Eventually we had to leave the park as a punishment. The numbers of apologies that had to be offered were taking a toll on me. *Sugar and apples, sugar and apples, I must remember.* Then I flashed back to a bottle of apple juice at six months. She had broken out in a head-to-toe rash, and I never gave it to her again. Then at fourteen months a friend watched Brett for a couple of hours. I had forgotten to mention the apple allergy, and she had fed Brett apple sauce, and there hadn't been a reaction. I'd thought the doctors must have been right about the six-month episode being something else. How could I have forgotten? What kind of mother was I? Why hadn't I realized this sooner?

So much to remember, so much to do.

CHAPTER 6

Premonitions or Confirmations?

MIKE LOVED HIS JOB. HIS attire needed to change from jeans and T-shirts to suits and Italian loafers. He'd grab his paper on the way out the door to work at six o'clock in the morning and read it on the BART rail system all the way into the city. True, the train made his day longer by a couple hours, but he seemed to love it. It was his transition time; it was when he could read his magazines and relax without annoying me.

I kept busy looking for a house to rent within our price range. Our home in Republic was for sale but hadn't received any bites. Two weeks later I found the perfect place. It was already vacant, so we could move in immediately. My major concern was that the back of the house had three sliding doors that opened into the yard with little or no effort by Brett. I was worried that the girls would escape without my knowledge. I called my grandma to discuss the problem.

"You already knew about that," she replied after hearing the story

"Knew about what?" I asked her.

"Don't you remember? You dreamed about it while I was visiting. You saw your new house, and you were concerned because the back of the house had multiple sliding doors."

My God, I did remember the dream! How could I have forgotten? I'd even mentioned it to my grandma. The sliding doors would not be a problem, as they were a sign. I signed the lease without any further questions.

As it turned out, it wasn't the sliding doors that were the problem, but the front door. We needed to install a security chain, at the very top of the door, to keep Brett from wandering out with little or no clothes on. If the terrible twos were bad, then nearly four was formidable!

Off sugar and apples, Brett was still a handful. Once or twice for her own safety I actually kept her strapped into her car seat, in the car, in the garage. All the doors of the car and garage were open for ventilation, which was necessary, but now the whole block could hear her screams. She wouldn't stay in her room for time-out, and I was at my wit's end disciplining her. I had signed her up for a Gymboree class, and that was helping both of us. Taylor wasn't any work. She would sit in my lap or play in one spot all day. Even when she started to crawl—and later walk—she always stayed close. Through the gym I meet a mom who was part of a "Mother's Club." I was unfamiliar with this term but was thrilled when she told me that it was an organization that hosted playdates, dinner parties, and campouts for parents and children.

Joining that Mother's Club saved my life and sanity. Twice a week I would meet a few moms at Starbucks, which furthered my addiction to vanilla lattes; this was the walking group. We would strap our children into the strollers and walk for a couple of hours, breaking for coffee or Italian sodas at the halfway point. Once or twice a week I would meet with another group of parents and children all of the same age at a local park. Every week the location changed, as there were dozens of parks to choose from! Mike was able to join in on the dinner parties and camping trips. My free time was filling in, and life felt really good. Again.

In September Brett started attending a cooperative playschool. The staff was fantastic and offered a lot of useful information. Mike and I had found a teenage babysitter directly across the street. She adored the girls, and we adored her. All these changes allowed us the opportunity to get away, if only for a few hours. Our first mistake was doing this during the evening, after the girls were in bed. We weren't using our babysitter to her full potential, and frankly we were too tired to do evening dates. We realized that lunch and a matinee were much cheaper than dinner and a movie, and this we could stay awake for. Also, the sitter then took over the job of playing with them all day! Why wasn't this the norm? We hadn't attended a movie in years. Now we saw *Contact, The Game, Titanic, Good Will Hunting,* and *The Truman Show.* If we didn't plan a date, the girls went to bed early, and I would cook something amazing out of one of my many cookbooks. I loved to cook, and it had been so long since I had made much other than kid food. There had been years where Mike hadn't eaten the same thing twice. Experimenting was fun, and I was glad to have time for it now. We would pair supper with a great bottle of California wine and enjoy each other on the outside patio. Our relationship was coming along nicely.

We'd been in Walnut Creek for a year. Oprah was starting to annoy me. Don't get me wrong—I love Oprah; how can you not? She has helped millions of people, except me. Every time I'd think of a new way to make changes in our lives and follow through on it, weeks, sometimes days, later, she would present it on her show. Why couldn't these shows be aired before I figured it out? Why must I always learn everything on my own?

I had been yelling a lot. I noticed that now the children and Mike were following my lead, so I lowered my voice, and really, moments later, so did they. It was a fantastic discovery! Then Oprah aired a show discussing that exact topic. Ideas had shown up to help me resolve some of the issues in my marriage; then Oprah did a show on it. I had this most wonderful idea for writing a book—exercises for the stay-at-home housewife. It was all about turning mundane tasks into exercises, and then she interviewed an author of a book filled with the same ideas!

Were these premonitions or confirmation that I was on the right track? I was having a hard time getting past mad, mad at God and Oprah for making me figure so many things out for myself! Couldn't a little bit of help be offered up beforehand?

There were, of course, other irritations, but all and all, we had settled in nicely. I had come to realize that there were always things that needed to be dealt with, but solutions were always available. Our current issue was the high cost of living in the San Francisco/Bay Area. Everyone in my mother's group was dealing with the same thing, especially the new imports like us. It had been cheaper to live elsewhere. Budgeting had always been an issue for me. It wasn't that I couldn't do it; I had a spreadsheet that showed money coming in and money going out. It was just getting harder and harder to balance the two rows. To save money, I menu-planned and watched for the "free" days at the local museums or zoos. We ate out at restaurants that offered a discount if we arrived before six p.m. Not having that additional disposable income kept us humble. Should we give up everything? That would make us miserable. We were working on finding that happy balance.

It took big things to get my spirits down, or at least took a while to build up to that. When I was up, I was up. When I was down, I was down. Mike was miserable because his newspaper had not been arriving before he left for work for five days in a row. I could not comprehend it. "So what?" was not the reply he was looking for. No paper equated to a miserable morning commute rolling into a miserable day.

"I need you to call the paper and find out why it isn't being delivered early anymore." God, he could be so anal sometimes!

Being the dutiful wife that I had trained myself to become, by keeping the kids clean, the laundry clean, the house clean, and supper on the table at 6:30 every night—oh, and handling all the bills—I called. Lo and behold, they had lost their carrier and were still in the process of finding a new one to cover the route. Until then the paper would be arriving later than usual. I called Mike and told him the news.

He asked, "Why don't you deliver the paper?"

"What?"

"You should call and find out what they pay for delivering the paper."

"I'm thirty years old—thirty-one in a matter of days—and you want me to deliver the newspaper?"

After I hung up the phone in disgust, I pondered this new opportunity. It would solve our financial crunch, and I could finally use my green card. I pondered the fact that things happen for a reason. I called back. The pay per hour was reasonable, and I would be done before Mike left for work. The biggest hurdle was that the paper was delivered seven days a week, so there would be no sleeping in. Mike agreed to do the Sunday delivery. Problem solved. We had been asking for more money, and I was being handed a job. We had to say yes.

The day I started was the morning the front page read, "Princess Diana Dead." I think most people in the world remember where they were when they heard the news. I was beside myself. It couldn't be true, could it? At every door where I delivered the paper, I wanted to knock and tell them what had happened. Comprehension had left me. She was a great person and had done so much to bring attention to so many causes. This made me realize that I too could change at least my world in some way. I could become nicer, friendlier, be more giving. I was having problems with a woman in my mother's group, and now I had the means to change it.

My paper route was rather enjoyable. And it had expanded over a four-month period from thirty papers a day to one hundred and twenty. We would start at five in the morning with Mike folding the papers while I got ready to deliver them using the girls' Burley carrier attached to my bike. By Halloween surprise hit me when I put on my witch's costume and, while I was pulling up my fishnet stockings, my thigh felt – weird. Had it been so long since I'd touched my thigh? Certainly it couldn't be that much smaller, but it felt smaller. My attention had been elsewhere. It also occurred to me that my underwear had become baggy and apparently not because it was stretched out but because I was losing weight. I hadn't even noticed

I had taken my measurements before becoming pregnant and again a few months afterward but had given up because things just weren't changing as rapidly as I had anticipated. As I reviewed where I was now and where I had been after Taylor's birth, the difference was two and a half inches less on each thigh and close to four inches off my waist! No wonder I wanted to date my husband! No wonder I was feeling happier and healthier; I was!

My feet no longer hurt in the morning when I got out of bed, nor did my knees. Why is it we don't notice when we feel good—only when we feel lousy? My neck hadn't been stiff in months. This was a revelation. During my pregnancy with Taylor, my left hip had become so painful I could barely move. After delivery I started visiting a chiropractor my girlfriend had suggested. Since I had started this new job, my visits had become further apart. Interesting. I felt nearly twenty again!

My job became a cross-training exercise regimen. There were fifty pounds of papers on the back of my bike, toning my thighs as I pedaled. At each house I jogged up the walkway before throwing the paper the last little bit where it landed perfectly on the front step. I was working my arms too. There were other newspapers that were thrown poorly, in bushes or far away from the front door, and I would pick those up and deliver them as well. I never thought about it; now it was routine. This extra consideration brought me huge tips. Many people in the area were retired or older and couldn't crawl under bushes or other places to retrieve their papers mostly because of walkers or canes. I was making over five hundred dollars a month plus tips for thirty hours of work. Okay, I wasn't a bank executive, but a housewife filling in an hour of time every morning, but it was exciting. Mike was happy about receiving his papers on time for work, and I was happy about less body fat!

As Mike walked out the front door, I would cruise into the driveway. That gave me an hour between six and seven to read my book before the girls started their day. Those couple of hours every morning really made a difference in my life, mentally and emotionally. If I had sat down and planned what would make me happy, I never would have come to the solution I stumbled across. Thank you, thank you, thank you.

I've always been a social person. I really wasn't happy unless I was either out with someone or on the phone talking to someone. In fact, Mike and I argued about this many times. He would get upset that I spent so much time on the phone when he was around. If I wasn't on the phone, he wouldn't talk but would read his newspaper or one of his many magazines. My response would be that if he was busy reading and didn't want to talk, why should I get off the phone?

My first week of delivering newspapers was alarming. I couldn't form a thought in my head. There was no one around to talk to, I wasn't reading a book or dealing with the children, and I didn't have a paper and pen to jot a list of chores for the day. There was never any downtime during my day; it was full of reminding myself what I needed to do next, putting in a load of laundry, pulling something out of the freezer for supper, checking on the kids, changing a diaper, making a snack, dropping clothes off at the dry cleaner, adding to the grocery list, returning a phone call, or checking on the kids again. At that very moment, with only a list of house numbers to follow, I felt a little like Homer Simpson. There he was looking at a tree, and all that showed in the bubble above his head was the picture of a tree!

My God, what had happened to me? I knew that I used to have independent thoughts. The problem was I never, ever just sat alone, quietly. There was always something that needed to be done or someone around, and if not, I'd call someone. It took me a week before I was able to let thoughts drift in and out of my mind. What an awakening.

The parents in my mother's group started asking how I was losing weight. I really didn't want to divulge that I was delivering newspapers. I was embarrassed and worried about being judged. Obviously, some of my old insecurities were affecting me. *Get over it, Tracy.* It was time to be exactly who I was and to be truthful. This conversation took place in my head, and the struggle was resolved in less than twenty seconds. When I told them, they were all impressed, and more stories were revealed. It was agreed that the best way to lose weight was to turn exercise into a job!

Months flew by, and my days started to take on a nice rhythm; a real routine had developed. There were friends with whom to chat and make plans outside of our playgroups. Brett and Taylor were happy and kept busy with activities, preschool, and playdates. Life was interesting and entertaining. My day mainly evolved around the kids, and thankfully they were great sleepers. By eight o'clock Mike and I had our evenings to ourselves. Ninety-eight percent of the time we chose to stay in, now enjoying each other's company. We loved living in Walnut Creek—our house, the weather, and the lifestyle. We had gotten our relationship back on track. Things would eventually change, but at this moment we really wished that wasn't the case. We were happy.

There were the daily ups and downs. Like the day before Brett's fourth birthday, we were driving home from playschool, and she asked me, "How do babies come out of their mummy's tummy?"

I had anticipated that at some point in my life this question would arise, but not now. Thankfully she couldn't see my face as I took some deep breaths and tried to figure out what an almost four-year-old needed to know about giving birth. It had to be the truth. I didn't want her to be confused later on. "Babies come out a mother's vagina." As I held my breath trying to decide what to say next, Brett replied, "That must really hurt, Mama!"

My answer was, "Yes, honey, it does. It really does." I hoped she would remember that statement until she was well past her teen years and preferably married and ready for a baby in her late twenties.

Then there was the morning when, after changing the laundry over, I came out to the open living area and found that, rather than playing or watching a movie, Taylor was sitting in the middle of the dining room table. I couldn't blame Brett as she was at school. My fourteen-month-old had crawled up there herself. I actually looked around for the cats but knew they were not responsible. Comprehension as to how she got up there still eludes me. Pretending it wasn't a big deal, I swooped in, picked her up, and asked, "Want to play with Mummy?"

In February 1998 Mike's company announced that the head office in downtown San Francisco was closing. Hundreds of expats were either given retirement packages or were being sent to various operations overseas. There were two choices available for Mike—Yellowknife or Brazil. He knew he didn't have to ask me which one I would rather go to. He would take a look at the Brazilian operation. There was no chance in hell of moving me back to Yellowknife!

"What is BHP doing in Brazil?"

"Mining iron ore."

"Well, you haven't worked with that mineral yet." He had worked with gold and silver.

My mind was abuzz: Brazil, Brazil. I knew nothing about Brazil other than that there was an amazing carnival once a year and a huge river called the Amazon. Grade ten social studies was a long time ago, and Google was still in the future.

They wanted us to go and visit the villa and operation immediately. The company organized for Mike's parents to fly from Calgary, Canada to watch the girls for a week while we flew to Brazil. This all took place in early March. We were told this wasn't a honeymoon. "Please take this trip seriously."

I don't think either of us needed to be reminded of that. This would be a huge commitment that could last up to three years. We would be given a house, and most utilities would be paid for. They would cover half the cost of a vehicle of our choosing, and pay for all education. This would include Portuguese language lessons for all of us. The package would also include one trip home a year. Home was to be our place of hire—San Francisco—not anywhere in Canada.

CHAPTER 7

Compromise

BRAZIL IS A VERY LARGE country. It is the fifth largest in the world, with Canada in second place, behind Russia, and United States in third. It borders ten South American countries. We'd be living in the southeast corner, over 400 km or six hours by car northeast of Rio de Janeiro. Our flight took us from San Francisco to Miami to Rio de Janeiro, then on to Belo Horizonte. After that we drove for one and a half hours to the Villa of Samarco where we would be living. The mine site was another fifteen minutes farther down the road.

Walnut Creek was well into spring. Brazil was moving into fall, and it was beautiful. I guess it could be called jungle; to me it just looked wild and rugged. The highways were wide, and the area on either side was cleared quite far back off the road, so it was hard to confirm. Most of what we could see was rocky terrain and cattle-grazing fields. The cattle—in fact, all the animals—looked undernourished.

We would be living on one side of a mountain that overlooked a valley and across to another mountain range. We toured the mine site. I had to walk across catwalks three stories high. Heights have not been my friend in a very long time! The next day we were taken to look at what would be our three-bedroom, twelve-hundred-square-foot house. Let's just say there was a lot of ventilation and no hot running water. I know! Where was he taking me?

Next we explored the local markets and shops. Everything was decades behind. So many memories of our childhood arose. The man Mike was to replace had accepted a transfer to Yellowknife. They planned on mining diamonds. The Northwest Territories had diamonds? They mined for diamonds in South Africa, not the Arctic. It just sounded wrong.

If we took the assignment, we needed to understand the change our lifestyle would undergo. Some good, for sure, but some changes would be very difficult. We would be making quite a bit of money, and our living expenses would be minimal, so our savings would increase immensely. But, I would have to boil water for the entire time we lived there for washing dishes, bathing, and laundry. How far behind was this country? Although living in a foreign country would be quite the experience, and learning another language, priceless. The girls would grow up in a tropical climate. There was lots of history and culture to learn ... and my list weebled and wobbled.

The local supermarket didn't carry any packaged food. It was well equipped with fresh food, which of course would be healthier. Everything would have to be prepared from scratch. The fruit flies surrounding the produce area and the smell of meat hanging in the open would be a problem. Seeing the live chickens with their legs tied together at the market for daily purchase would be more difficult to get used to. *Big breath.* What were my choices? Yellowknife? Absolutely not! Australia and the United States were already full of expats being sent to Yellowknife, so no availability there. Brazil. There were worse places in the world to live, like Yellowknife. Brazil's economic market had leveled out, and the Brazilian real was currently worth the same as the U.S. dollar. Mike and I made our decision on the long flight home. We would take the assignment, we would take a chance and see how things went.

We moved at the end of June, a few months shy of the San Francisco office closure. We wanted Brett to finish her school year. I knew it was only playschool, but if we kept moving every sixteen to eighteen months, she would never get an end-of-year party. Also, we needed to prepare ourselves mentally for the move. We started studying Portuguese as soon as we returned in March and felt relatively fluent when we arrived in Brazil. With the extra time, we managed to see a bit more of California before we left. There might not be another chance. We camped in the Red Woods, drove down to Monterey Bay to see the aquarium, and hiked through Yosemite Park. Mike had a cousin in LA, and we really wanted to visit him and Mickey Mouse, but our schedule had a time constraint.

My dad came for a visit and so did my mother, not together.

So many decisions needed to be made. The plants I had brought with me, some from my college days, would have to stay behind. The company was "encouraging" us to leave our pets behind. I was having a hard enough time with my plants; there was no way in hell I was leaving our cats!

We were packed. There was an air shipment, a boat shipment, and the rest of our items would be kept in storage. I'd found a good home for all my plants. Now we were ready to set off on another adventure with two kids, two cats, and twelve pieces of luggage.

With Miami as our jumping-off point, we decided to add a four-day layover in Disney World. We'd visit with Mickey Mouse and consider it our last fling with the civilized world. It was getting a little tricky, though; the State of California allowed us ten days to get the cats immunized, send the report to a state authority, have them stamp it and return it to us, leave the country, and arrive in Brazil. This we found out after we booked our four days in Disney World. We counted backward and hoped the document would be returned to us within a couple days. The U.S. postal system always comes through; they are so efficient. Everything was done on time, and we would get to meet Mickey and the gang.

The cats weren't the only ones who needed to get vaccinated. The rest of us did as well—for rabies, typhoid, yellow fever, hepatitis A and B—and our tetanus needed to be updated. The girls and I would travel to Mike's office to see the company nurse for these vaccinations. Every time we arrived at the train station, the girls would start to cry. I tried to organize it while our family came to visit. "Let's all go downtown and visit Daddy!"

Then the day came, and it was time to leave. We flew first class from San Francisco to Orlando, with a plane change in Houston. During the summer there was a pet embargo. This we were informed of at the last minute and made the necessary purchases of carriers that would fit under the airplane seats. Our cats were large, the cages were not, and they barely fit. They would be able to fly under the plane in a larger carrier from Miami. I think the smaller cages were for gerbils, but it was the only thing we could find.

When we went to reload in Houston, the ticketing agent told us that she was going to have to call someone of authority to take a look at our pets before she could allow us back on the plane. She claimed that our cats clearly did not have enough room. What upset me the most was how they could allow us on the plane in San Francisco, then change their mind at the next stop?

She asked, "Do you have anyone you can leave them with?"

Mike was seriously annoyed. "No! We're moving to Brazil and loaded in San Francisco this morning!" Our flight was almost completely boarded, and we were still waiting for an attendant. She told us we would have to wait until the next flight. Mike was done with waiting and told the flight attendant, "We're getting on this flight. I guess you just got yourself a couple cats. Their names are Fitzgerald and Kramer."

The kids started crying. Panic took hold of my body. Fear crossed the attendant's face, and she said, "Fine, just get on board."

Would he really have left them behind? Did he know she'd relent? With all the crying and yelling, I guess I would have too.

At the age of twelve I had gone on a school trip to Disneyland, and during spring break in college vacationed in Disney World. Neither our children nor my husband of thirty-three had been to a Disney Park. I wish I could say it was like having three children, but really there were four! We saw every Disney character possible. We went on every ride accessible.

Loved the fireworks and ate lots of snow cones. It was an exhausting four days of bliss. Taylor loved Pooh Bear but was overpowered by his life-size stature. Brett loved Pocahontas, but I think all the attention she received alarmed her. Pocahontas was not typically the most sought-after princess on the property. I got my butt squeezed by Meeko. Mike got to have a ride-along in a NASCAR. We have a picture of him beaming! The cats were pampered and cared for next door at the kennel, receiving a certificate stating that they had stayed at Disney World.

The holiday came to an end, and we arrived at the airport to learn there was a box embargo. What the hell was a box embargo? You can't ship anything in a box. Six out of twelve of our pieces were boxes. Mike's company had told us to bring dishes and bedding, as it would be months before our items arrived in Brazil. I was panic-stricken. People around us were getting things like televisions wrapped in saran wrap a foot deep. How would we wrap bedding and dishes?

"What? It doesn't matter as we are flying first class? Oh, thank you!" Relief swept through me. Tears entered my eyes.

We arrived in Belo Horizonte completely exhausted. Even the cats had shut down. Irritation was present on their faces. I hoped that whoever was picking us up had a very large vehicle to jam in all our things. That was one worry I didn't need tonight, but I was a compulsive worrier. My IBS was back, and I had given up food days ago to relieve the cramping caused by all the anxiety I was experiencing. The van showed up, and somehow everything fit. One and a half hours more, and we would be home and able to fall into bed. Ahh, sleep.

The house was packed with at least half a dozen people waiting to welcome us. They were mostly from the mine. We were shown all the improvements they had made on the house and explained all the food products in the cupboard and fridge. The girls were oohed and aahed over. They lovingly touched their silky hair. I will admit that taking a chance on moving to what I now call Brasil seemed like a good idea at that moment. The house looked amazing. The furniture had been replaced. There were vases of flowers everywhere! The cupboards had been fully stocked, along with the fridge and freezer. I was informed that only the best products had been purchased, so I would know what to buy.

The biggest improvement was hot water. Tears of joy came, relief swept my soul: no boiling tubs of water for dishes, laundry, or bathing. Then my mind went to the previous representative. He had gone three years without knowing that hot water even existed, that it had just been a matter of turning a knob on the water tank located in the attic. The company had even installed a satellite dish so the children could watch television in English! I had no idea you could change the language on programming! Lovely, it was all lovely. There were plates, cups, cutlery, and pots in the cupboard. The beds were made. I was so grateful, but very, very exhausted.

We rolled into bed shortly after one o'clock in the morning and barely felt like we had slept at all when we were awoken by knocking at the door. The clock said seven. Mike and I rolled out of bed to find a woman standing at the door. She was a few inches taller than I, with long, black, thick, wavy hair. Her skin was the color of my freckles. She was surrounded by a group of four or five women. She was saying something ... what was she saying? *Okay, brain start hearing Portuguese, something about work.* She wanted to work for us. She wants to work for us! Oh right, someone last night had said that there was a maid who came with the house, and she would be coming by today. "Retorno amanha, por favor." Return tomorrow, please.

"Do you think she understood us?" We managed to crawl back into bed until ten. We got up and looked through the food to see what we could make for breakfast. Eggs looked the same. There was juice, milk, and bread. With breakfast done, I jumped into the shower. Not much water, but enough to get the job done. I was barely dressed when we heard more knocking at the door. This woman looked more African-American, perhaps five eight and very well dressed. I couldn't understand her, and then there was a moment of comprehension: oh, she's speaking English!

"Hi!" Her name was Maria do Carmo, and she would be teaching our children Portuguese. Yeah! She also explained that the maid, who had come earlier, had worked for the BHP expats for the last twelve years. I was also told about a young girl who was looking for work and would love to be a nanny to my children.

"Sure, I'll meet the young girl." A nanny and a maid? But what would I do all day? I was overwhelmed about making any decisions. Were these things necessary? A maid, sure—I didn't want to deal with all the strange critters with too many legs. And who wants to clean one's house when one could pay someone else fifty reais a week? I did not need a nanny, because then I would need to train the nanny. I wasn't looking forward to it but was surprised when I realized she spoke some English and was useful to navigate me to the various shops in the nearby town of Mariana. Currently every day was an adjustment.

Much more so for Mike. It had only been a few weeks, and he was already bored with his new position. I was bored because I wasn't used to having so much help or free time.

The school system was interesting. Grades four through eight attended school from eight in the morning until noon. Preschool through grade three attended from one until five in the afternoon, so this was when Brett attended. The high school students attended from six till ten at night. That was how my teenage nanny was able to work and attend school. It was necessary for them to be able to work to help out the family financially. Also, there wasn't enough room in the schools to teach everyone at once, so this system alleviated the problem.

Conceição, my maid, was a lovely woman, and she adored Brett and Taylor. She was married and had two children of her own—a boy of fifteen and a daughter who was eight. She lived in a little shanty town five minutes by car. She walked. She told me work started at eight and finished at five. That she arrived so early allowed me to jump on my bicycle and ride a route I had mapped out that was twelve kilometers. I'd say it was for pleasure, but I never do anything halfway. It was all about burning calories and staying toned! When I arrived home, the nanny was supposed to be there but rarely was. I would shower, and she would eventually show up. If there was time before Brett needed to be at school, we might drive into Mariana and pick up a few essentials. Once Brett was settled at school, quality time was available with Taylor. By the time I returned from dropping Brett off, the nanny had put Taylor to bed, no matter how many times I told her not to. It wasn't that she didn't have a nap, but I needed it to be closer to three, or she would fall asleep in her dinner plate!

The nanny would then have nothing to do until three o'clock when she left for school. Occasionally I would ask her to clean the toys or tidy up the children's room. She never did; that was the work of the maid. With my entire afternoon now free, I would fill it with Portuguese lessons with Maria do Carmo or pull out my scrapbooking albums. Reading a book was even possible. If I was at home, Conceição and I would chat so I could practice my Portuguese.

Brett was learning the language rapidly. Being at school five days a week had made a huge difference in her vocabulary. When she came home from school, she would sit in front of the television and decompress by watching English cartoons for an hour. I wouldn't allow her any more than that. It was less than a month later when she came home from a friend's house angry because someone had called her a bad name.

"How do you know it was a bad name?" I asked.

"I know, Mama!"

"Tell Conceição what she said. Maybe you're wrong." Conceição gasped, placing her hands over her mouth and shaking her head. Apparently Brett did understand what was being said. Amazing.

The name-calling was not a common occurrence. Brett was fitting into Brasilian life easily. She had friends on our street with whom she played. Taylor spent her time manipulating Conceição around her tiny, little not-quite-two-year-old fingers! She barely moved on a good day, enjoying sitting in the sandbox, or sitting in a swing if someone would push her. She could play in one spot, content, for hours. Now I found her sitting on the sofa with her blanket snuggled around her, having Conceição surfing the channels for her, and food showing up at her request!

"Conceição, you can't keep doing everything for her," I pleaded.

"Oh, she's only a child. She will have enough years where she will need to do stuff for herself," was always her reply.

Part of what she said made sense, but I wasn't going to have a spoiled rotten child when I eventually returned to a no-maid zone.

Part of Taylor's allure was her white-blonde hair. She may have been born with red hair, but by six months, it had changed color. Everyone adored her hair; they all wanted to touch it and stare at her. "Lindo"—beautiful—they kept repeating!

In the south of Brasil, blond hair and blue eyes were more common. In our area they were not. Everyone had dark hair, and very few had straight hair. Brett received attention as well, her hair being straight and light-brown. She didn't stand out nearly as much because her skin tanned to nearly the same color as the locals. What demanded attention was Brett's personality!

A month of having two additional people constantly in my house was a bit much. Conceição needed little training with twelve years of expat experience. What discussions we had were about what the girls could and couldn't do or have. The nanny never abided by those rules. She was fifteen. The idea of training her to follow our rules was exhausting, and having her around was a bit redundant. That, along with her lack of responsibility, was wearing on me. Ninety percent of the time she arrived late and offered the most bizarre excuses. Then Brett mentioned that she had spent time at the nanny's boyfriend's house and had been left outside while they "kissed" indoors.

We discussed it, and she offered a different explanation. How much would I put up with before letting her go? Why did this culture insist I have a nanny? I had a maid who was perfectly capable and keen on helping me out when I needed someone to watch the children. Was my compliance more about being judged in my community?

The last straw came when I returned from a bike ride, and the nanny was asleep on the couch. It was ten in the morning, and she had turned a movie on to occupy the children. She had also pulled out junk food to keep them happy. I had asked her to take them to the park. She would use my poor Portuguese as an excuse again. "I did not understand you," seemed to be her constant reply.

Brett, who was transfixed by the movie, was still on the couch. She didn't even notice me until I stood in front of the television. I asked, "Where's your sister?" A snore came from the nanny, and a shrug came from Brett.

Mike's company had hired people to repair my kitchen and its heavily ventilated roof. I found Taylor unsupervised in our backyard among the construction workers, snacking on a lump of wet cement.

I sent the nanny home and talked to Conceição, who clarified a lot of inconsistencies I had been told over the past month. My biggest personal concern was losing my exercise regimen. That bike ride toward the mountain range filled me in such a spiritual way. I had only experienced it a few times before in my life and most had been spontaneous. When I was in college at eighteen and living in Winnipeg, one morning in June while waiting for my bus, I found myself in a place of absolute contentment. I could feel the heat of the sun on my body and smell all the flowers in bloom. My mind had emptied out. It was a serene moment. Now I felt that every time I rode toward the mountains and didn't want to lose it.

Conceição assured me that she would love to watch the girls. Perfect! Mike and I spoke that night and let the nanny go the next day. She actually had the audacity to look surprised. She was being paid more than my maid and only accomplished one eighth of the work. *Tracy, remember she is only fifteen ...*

Yes, she is only fifteen, but that wasn't what was bothering me about the circumstances. Every time I thought about the situation, it upset me. There hadn't been an even exchange. That was it! There hadn't been an even energy exchanged. I felt like I was paying her more than she deserved. It had caused an imbalance in our relationship. If I looked at other relationships that made me angry the same thing could be said; I was putting in more than I was getting back. Mike sitting around and watching television or reading his magazines while I was busy with housework and the children was the perfect example. Of course since we now had a maid to clean, cook, and do some of the laundry, it hadn't been a problem. Actually, it hadn't been a problem since Republic.

I was in awe of Conceição. She washed everything every week—the walls, the windows. She scrubbed the floors inside and out. She helped out with the kids. But five days a week was too much for me. I talked to her about working a three-day week, though I would gladly pay her for all five. That would raise her daily rate to a little over sixteen dollars a day—not an issue for me. I had realized that our exchange needed to be equal. With that said, she also needed to be comfortable with our exchange, and a compromise was found.

Our agreement stirred up animosity among all the maids and their employers in the vila. Maria do Carmo was approached to discuss this situation with me. "Tracy, we need to talk. You are paying your maid too much. Everyone is upset," she said in English with her drawn-out Brasilian accent.

I was stunned that people were talking about it, but had no intention of changing my mind. "You will need to tell them I am sorry, but I feel I am paying Conceição what she is worth."

"We know you are not used to seeing so much poverty, but you cannot help everyone."

That statement surprised me even more. Was I doing it out of pity? "I don't have a nanny. Conceição not only does all the cleaning and some cooking, but she also watches the girls. She has been working with English families for over twelve years and has an understanding that another maid does not. She is worth the extra money to me." It was all true. Nothing was because of pity. It was about an even exchange—energetically and financially.

The mother of my ex-nanny approached me in the grocery store a few days after I let her go. Something about it being a lot of money, how could I fire her daughter? I recognized that they had come to depend on the money. I tried to explain to her that I felt her daughter was not responsible enough to do the job. I worried for my children's safety. Pronouncing the word *responsible* in Portuguese is difficult. I was still having a problem with my r's, and the word for "irresponsible"—*irresponsável*—was even more difficult to get across. I tried as nicely as I could to explain the situation, but she didn't want to hear about it and kept repeating that she didn't understand me, "Não entendo." I had been told my Portuguese was good, and everyone else in the *supermercado* seemed to understand, pretending not to pay attention, one ear toward us. I told her she could come by my Portuguese classes and talk to Maria do Carmo. She never showed up. Maybe she thought she could bully me into changing my mind. Maybe she just hadn't understood me.

There had been difficulties before. Charades had become a natural part of my life. It was one game I had always avoided growing up. Now there was no choice. The *supermercado*, bakery—*padaria*, butcher shop—*talho*, and general store—*loja*, all had items not referenced in my English/Portuguese dictionary. For instance, nail polish remover, powder, or bobby pins, which I needed for a Halloween costume. There is no translation for Kleenex unless you remember to call it facial tissue. It is the same with hamburger, which really is ground beef, and ketchup being tomato sauce. Trying to remember the conversion in English and then translate it into Portuguese sometimes was impossible. It took ten minutes talking to the butcher with him pointing at hamburgers before I finally clued in to the fact that what I needed was ground beef. The other option was to just mash up the hamburger. Tylenol is headache medicine or pain killer? Good luck. And the packaging looks entirely different. That was my other problem. I recall things by what they look like. When packaging changes, it totally messes me up! Tylenol came in a small plastic encasing of two pills. Why would I look for that? It usually comes in an enormous bottle in North America! Mushrooms are found in glass jars, so eventually I was able to recognize them, although you could never get them fresh. Milk isn't in the fridge, but a tetra pack. After the incident at the *talho*, the butcher shop, I became compliant.

Christmas was around the corner, and I didn't know whether the butcher shop would be open during the holidays, so I planned on ordering everything necessary for the next two weeks. I had a cheat-sheet my American tutor had given me regarding the different cuts of meat. Everything was so different here. Again, I work with recognition. No cut of red meat was butchered with a bone, so I couldn't ask for a T-bone steak or a rib roast. All their red meat looks the same. Rather than listening to what I was ordering, the butcher thought my cheat-sheet was my grocery list and started cutting up twenty kilograms of beef for me. I did not realize he was doing this. Ten minutes later there were half a dozen women waiting behind me to order. I assumed he was cutting my items off the cow hanging from the ceiling and doing their orders at the same time to save time. Maybe they had called ahead? A few more minutes passed before one of the ladies in line spoke up. All I got was, "Esta todo dela?" Is this all hers?

"Nao minha!" Not mine! Try to explain "cheat-sheet" in Portuguese!

So, I learned to order the same thing every day, whether it was the butcher shop or the bakery. It seemed to me people got scared when they saw me coming their way. Conforming was necessary. I hated to see the fear on the shopkeepers' faces when they saw me. So I tried to fit in.

What I did need was a friend to talk to. Phoning North America was terribly expensive, and, although we had a computer, few people had e-mail addresses. Then there was our dial-up network, which was never reliable. Conceição was even fretting, "Você preciso um amigo." You need a friend.

Our family had been invited out a few times, and it was always nice. We were introduced to *churrasco*, Brazilian barbeque, which was fantastic. Reciprocating made me nervous. Where would we take them? What would we serve them for dinner? It was all too overwhelming for me to think about. What if they hated North American food?

Most people were friendly, wanting to spend time with us to practice their English, which of course would give us the opportunity to speak Portuguese. I had always been the perfect host, and now I was scared of failing. So I didn't organize anything at all.

My reluctance was stopping me from moving forward. There had been so many other times where miscommunication had caused problems. So, we filled our time with sightseeing. There were so many new things to see. The weekends were spent exploring the small cities and towns around us. We stumbled upon Ouro Preto, which means Black Gold, forty minutes away. The gold-rush town was founded in the 1600s, and much of its wealth had been lost to the royalty in Portugal. The architecture is very well preserved, the churches, amazing. It had become our favorite town. There was a nice little coffee house where the girls would get hot chocolate with lots of whipped cream, and Mike and I could order lattes or espressos. Part of its attraction was that it felt a little normal. There was one spot we loved to go for lunch or dinner because we were guaranteed to hear people speaking English. There was also an amazing Italian restaurant hidden in the basement level of a house. The walls were made of stone, and the staircase was unique. The food was fabulous, although not like North American Italian food at all. We spent time in Rio exploring all the sights and sounds and farther up north on the east coast near Victoria there was a little beach community called Guarapari. Everyone was so lovely.

The restaurants were always different and the food astounding. I loved their fast food–style restaurants. The "fast" only came from it being a buffet. The food itself was very healthy—okay, only some of it. The best part was that each plate was weighed for payment. The children could cost less than a real!

Their open-air pharmacies, *farmácia*, weren't like anything I had experienced. They had huge scales open for the public to use. I hadn't brought my scale, so I gave it a try. It was in kilograms, and it had been a while since I'd done that conversion, but I was sure it was too high. Oh my God, I had gained thirteen pounds!

The local food was so good I had Conceição replicating it. I hadn't realized she was using over a liter of cooking oil per week, but I knew where it had settled. She was taken off cooking duties; I was on a diet.

As the weight disappeared, I started to make more friends in the Villa. What the connection was, I don't know. The lady next door was nice, and our children were similar in age. She would practice her English, and I would practise my Portuguese. Mike and I also became good friends with our Portuguese teacher Maria do Carmo and her husband Harry. He was from England and understood eighty percent of what we said. Although there are always cultural differences. During the day I was being invited for coffee or joined in birthday celebrations with the women in the vila. What I could understand had increased tremendously. Maria would always lean over and ask, "Do you understand?" "Voce entendo?"

"Oh, I understand!" Some of the conversations were quite racy!

They say the holidays are the worst when you are not near family. It's true. This was the first year since getting married that we weren't with one or the other set of parents. Traditional North American dinner was also difficult in a plus forty-degree climate. No one wanted to eat turkey. Realization came a little late as to why everyone was at the beach.

CHAPTER 8

Trust

IN THE EVENING AFTER THE children were in bed, we continued our tradition of sitting outside and discussing the day and now our future. As the months progressed, Mike's lack of challenge at work had him depressed. Now every night was a repeat of the last, how he lacked job fulfillment; nothing was challenging enough; and he was sure this experience was ruining his career! I sat there and listened, not knowing what to tell him. Life wasn't easy for me, either, but we had a little over two years left on our contract, and now wasn't the time to become disillusioned. Or I would never make it.

Maybe a weekend away would help cheer him up! He'd always dreamed about attending a Grand Prix race, and there was one in São Paulo the following month. Planning and organizing for the trip did perk up his spirits. Maria agreed to watch the girls for the three days we would be gone. She and her husband didn't have children, so they were thrilled. Conceição would check on the cats. Everything was covered.

On Friday, April 9, 1999, we flew to São Paulo, which is rated as the third-largest city on the planet with a population of over twenty-one

million people. Belo Horizonte, which is the city we most often vi
to do our shopping, has three million. No one we know has heard of Belo
Horizonte and it was the largest city I had ever visited. The entire San
Francisco Bay area had six million, but it is so widely spread out, the feel
of it is very different. Flying into São Paulo, I had no problem believing
the statistics; we flew over high rises for more than thirty minutes before
landing.

There were certain precautions we had been instructed to take when
hailing a taxi cab. The scare in Rio with the girls in October was enough
to heighten our concerns for our safety. The four of us had walked three
blocks toward the beach from our hotel to have dinner. After dinner a
torrential rain storm started—the kind where the rain bouncing off the
sidewalk gets you more wet than the stuff falling from the sky. We could
have waited but decided to take the taxi parked out front. We gave the
driver a business card from the hotel, but as it happened the street was a
one way, facing away from our hotel. We knew he would have to go around
the block to get us back, but he was going more than one or two blocks
away, then five. We kept repeating the name of the hotel, and he'd nod
and continue driving. He finally realized our panic and looked closely at
the card. With that, he apologized and turned the car around. Our hotel
had just recently changed its name; another hotel had the same one, and
he was taking us there. "Desculpas." Sorry. We were visibly shaken.

Was he telling the truth? Or did he figure we were too much trouble
to roll? You just don't know because of the language barrier and our
inexperience with the culture. This time we made sure there was no
misunderstanding before we left for our destination. Not that it mattered;
he could still have taken us anywhere. We drove for a very long time. Our
only savior was trust and that we knew approximately how much our fare
would cost.

Thankfully, the drive was uneventful. We were happy to settle in
and had a few hours to explore the financial district shopping area. The
temperature was significantly cooler than home. Most people were
wearing leather jackets and gloves. It was fall and felt like it. The streets

around our hotel had been closed off to everything except foot traffic for years. There were vendors lining the streets and high-end shops and restaurants in residence on the main floors of every building. Shops like nothing else I'd seen in Brasil up to now—so very modern. The quality of products was of North American standards; it was like real shopping! We didn't go nuts, but we did buy a few items. Then we toured the adjacent park and garden surrounding an old beautiful church. Churches had become my new fascination.

I had wandered through one in Ouro Preto. There was such an energetic connection for me. At one of the altars I fell to my knees, then crossed myself and kissed my finger. I knelt there with my head bowed before my mind opened up and wondered what I was doing. I had attended Sunday school off and on until the age of thirteen in the United Church of Canada. Then only briefly became a member when it was time to get married and have my children baptised. Kneeling was never involved, nor was the signing of the cross. Some past life memory was coming to the surface. I stayed kneeling for a while; it felt comforting in some way. I then got up and experienced the church in a different state of mind than before. Just as I was leaving, I felt that I was being pushed out of the way, and in my mind's eye I saw woman being dragged up a flight of stairs by a priest; he had her by the hair. Stunned into disbelief, I became motionless for what seemed like a very long time. Perhaps it hadn't been just any church that had prompted this memory, but this church? Had I lived in Brasil in another lifetime? Was that the reason the language seemed easier than French ever did? Now I toured whatever church I could to see whether something else would surface, to find more answers to the ones left unanswered. Nothing revealed itself other than a deep sense of peace.

We returned to the hotel at four o'clock. Mike needed to rest, as he had eaten some vendor food and was dealing with the side effects of undercooked chicken. It wasn't pretty. By seven he was faring a bit better and was willing to escort me to dinner in the hotel restaurant.

We are not exactly sure why, perhaps precautions, perhaps premonition, but Mike left his wallet and only took fifty reais and a credit card, and I left my purse behind in the hotel room. We hadn't checked whether there was a dress code, so we dressed up rather than down. As we slid into a booth, the waiter handed us the wine list and explained that there wasn't a chef tonight; it would only be buffet. We both enjoy Brasilian buffet, which is everywhere, but we wanted "service" tonight. We thanked the waiter, "Obrigado," and decided to check with the concierge for a more formal restaurant. The line was twenty couples deep, so we decided to enjoy one of the many wonderful restaurants we had passed earlier in the day. It was after seven and pitch-black, except for a few streetlights or store windows. The night was much warmer than it had been earlier and even in my cardigan I was comfortable. As we walked away from the hotel, we noticed that the shops had closed, and the vendors were packing up their goods. The day was done.

We continued walking, but everything was closed, including the restaurants. We were starting to feel a bit uneasy and decided to return to the hotel. Both of us urged the other to head back, but at the last minute continued on for one more try. I'm not sure what possessed us to keep walking past the hotel entrance. When we reached the farthest corner from the entrance to the hotel, we faced a huge open area with an amazing fountain in the center. It was hard to get a really good look, as a few of the streetlights were burned out. Seconds later we were surrounded by three men, very young men, with guns. They came out of nowhere, but thankfully we had time to back ourselves against a brick wall.

They never touched me and never asked for my wedding ring. They patted Mike down and took his fifty reais and the credit card from his pocket. What shocked me more than being held up was the idiotic way my husband was behaving! It gave me flashbacks to Peter's outrageous behaviour. Mike yelled about the gun being "only" a starter pistol— who cared? It was pointed at his temple! One of the robbers must have understood a little English, as he showed us that the gun did indeed have bullets.

I finally yelled at him, "Just give them the money! Who cares!" They took the cash and card and started to flee.

Mike was still yelling at them, "You'll never use the card; you might as well give it back." Surprisingly, the guy holding the card threw it back.

My husband was making noise that would eventually have caught someone's attention or would it have gotten him killed? We were robbed by men, boys really, wearing flip-flops and leather jackets who seemed to understand English perfectly. Was this just a night job? Couldn't they use their ability to understand English, maybe speak it in a better-paying job? As far as I could see we were the only idiots out and about, so thievery couldn't be too prosperous. Não entendo, I didn't understand.

Visibly shaken, we rounded two more corners and then entered the hotel lobby. We decided not to report the crime. They would never find the culprits, and it would have kept us busy for the rest of the night. Passing the concierge's deck, we headed back upstairs to the restaurant.

We were escorted to the previous seats we occupied then handed the wine list and menus. We both looked up at the waiter, and Mike asked in Portuguese, "I thought only buffet tonight?"

He replied, "Nao, serviço completo." No, full service. Had we just misunderstood the placement of the comma?

Was the whole experience we'd just lived through destiny? Everything happens for a reason, but neither of us understood. Was it just about them needing the money more than we did? Was it a wake-up call for my husband regarding all the whining he had been doing lately? If I had known something bad was going to happen the morning I got in the car accident, where was my bad feeling tonight? Sure, those feelings had shown up moments before we were robbed, but not when we walked out the front door of the hotel. There were so many questions and absolutely no answers. Yet.

The rest of the weekend was uneventful. We got up early and attended the qualifying race. Sunday was the finals. Monday morning we flew home.

The girls were thrilled to see us, which always puts a smile on a parent's face. Maria do Carmo had spoiled them with delicious homemade Brasilian treats like little doughnuts, *pao de queijo* (cheese buns), rock candy, fried pork rinds, and so much more. There was a bit of wariness when Maria asked, "How was your weekend?"

To our dismay, Conceição and Maria had spoken to each other about their concerns regarding our trip. Neither had mentioned anything before we left. "We just didn't want to worry you," Maria said in English with her Portuguese accent.

They reminded me of my grandma, intuition always in play without a second thought. That connection to earth and spirit was so much more prevalent in Brasil than I had experienced elsewhere. Not in a religious sense, although most of the population was Catholic, but in a real connection to the soul. It is the innate part of each of us; some refer to it as a gut feeling, others call themselves psychic; for me it is my intuition. I hadn't been paying attention to it, but things just seemed to be working out for us. One day Mike and I had gone off on an excursion and rolled into a gas station in the middle of nowhere on fumes. The gauge in our car never worked; we just thought it was time to fill up. The angels seemed to be keeping us safe. The gas attendant had shook his head and laughed.

I had seen the very poor children begging for food. I had seen the wealthy walking around with their cell phones. But, on all levels, there was a spiritual connection that the majority of our North American culture was missing. Brasilians had it built into their vocabulary, and it was part of their belief system. Our society was missing that open communication. Perhaps it had to do with the fact that they worked to live and we lived to work. Maybe it was because our country was so much younger, and we hadn't evolved to the point of enjoying life, yet. Would we ever evolve? Many insights arose during quiet moments in the early morning while I sat quietly on my hammock staring at the mountain range opposite. North America wasn't much for quiet moments, but I was sure starting to enjoy mine.

My day started in such quiet and then the girls would wake up. At some point during the day people would hear me yelling at my girls for not listening to this or that. It felt like I went from one extreme to the other. I wanted to find the middle, where I would just flow.

I wonder if I was attracting drama on some level or another, because once routine set in, something always happened. One Saturday morning I felt like I just couldn't hold it together anymore. But I should first tell you about what happened two weeks prior. There had been a horrifying experience with Taylor.

I had just arrived home after picking the girls up from school. Mike was minutes behind us. Brett and Taylor were playing outside on the patio until it was time for dinner. With Mike getting home, Brett had come into the house to show her dad something she had accomplished at school. A few minutes later I came into the living room from the kitchen and asked, "Brett, where's your sister?"

"She's outside, Mama," Brett replied.

The sun had receded behind the mountains within minutes of our arriving home, and seeing anything at this point was near impossible.

"Taylor," I called on my way outside, scanning the front yard. Feeling a pull to the back, I headed in that direction, my mind arguing with me: "They never play in the back." I went anyway and glanced up the hill and then came back to the front and moved to the road. The entire time I called her name, "Taylor, Taylor, where are you? Taylor!" Ending in a screech.

No response. I went down the street, asking each neighbor as I went whether they had seen her. No one had. I don't know how many minutes had gone by—perhaps five; maybe ten. I was in full panic. I returned to the house and told Mike while I called Maria do Carmo. She contacted my neighbors to explain the situation. By then many of them were already on the street calling her themselves. My mind kept wandering to the fact that my beautiful, blonde child might fetch a pretty penny on the black market. Was there a black market? Or was that just in the movies too?

More neighbors poured out. Maria said she would call the police if need be, but we would wait a little while longer. A few houses from ours Mike came across a huge hole in the ground. It was hidden among a clumping of trees. The girls had never ventured in that direction before, but we couldn't take a chance. A group of us had gathered all thinking the same thing. The hole was full of water, mostly rain run-off, perhaps sewage. Mike used a stick to see whether she had fallen in. There was no way to tell; he needed to jump in. The hole was about the length of a large couch and a good ten feet deep. It took him a while to check, coming up for air in between. Mike reassured me that she hadn't fallen in. It was decided that everyone needed to split up. I'd stay, but Mike would go by car with a neighbor to look for her. Why was he in the shower rinsing off? He was torn between getting in someone's car smelly and wet and looking for his missing daughter. *Wasn't this all about time? Just go!*

While I was standing in the front yard judging my husband's insanity, I felt this knot in my stomach. Instinctively I spun around, and there she was, just standing and staring at all the commotion.

I could have killed her, as much as I wanted to just hold her forever. "Where were you?"

"With Kramer in the backyard," she responded.

"Why didn't you answer?"

"I was trying to pick fruit." The first place I had gone to was the backyard, even though the kids never played there. The yard was all uphill, with trees along the right side. It was impossible to see the orange tree at the very top in the daylight, and I never gave the area more than a quick scan. But that had been my problem; I should never have thought. I should have gone with my instincts.

I had never held her so tightly! She had no idea why we were all crying with relief. She was with Kramer, had been her reply over and over, like it was the most normal thing in the world. Kramer knew where she was, so what was the big deal?

That, along with Mike's repetitive conversations about how boring his job was and my own frustration of not being able to make it all better, had caught up with me. So that particular Saturday morning, as I was taking a shower, overwhelmed with what was happening in my world, the tears came. The stress was too much. As I stood there crying,

I heard my dead Gran's Scottish-accented voice singing the Canadian Army ballad, "Be all that you can be …" repetitively. I stopped crying and craned my head to listen. No longer singing, she stated, "Stop worrying. You just be all that you can be, that will be enough. You will get through this."

Then Gran's voice disappeared. I never questioned that it wasn't her. I spent quite a long time in the shower thinking about the message. Was I enough to get through this? I hoped … yes I was; she believed in me. I would believe in myself. All these moments were just another part of life.

After getting out of the shower and pulling myself together, I entered the living room where Mike was sitting. "Gran just visited me in the shower."

Mike replied, "Yeah, what did she have to say?"

Really? No reply about being crazy or you're hearing voices? Whether he believed me or not, I related the entire experience. I supposed that over the last ten years he had become accustomed to my family and all the messages my grandma, mother, sister, and I received in various ways. For me, this one was different; I hadn't really heard voices before, well except that one time. I had mostly gut instincts. I had never wanted to hear the voices, like my mother and sister, or see spirits like they did. That was all too scary.

When Gran was around to converse with, I didn't feel lonely. I know it sounds crazy, and many of you may be thinking, "I'm done with this book." Perhaps think of this next part as a ghost story. Allow the ideas to enter your conscious mind; I hope they will expand from there.

Chatting with Gran was a bit like a game. I would ask her questions and listen for answers. In my mind's eye, I could see her in a blue dress wearing pearls. She looked much younger then when she died at the age of eighty-two; she looked more like fifty. Occasionally she would be with my cousin Judy, who had passed together with her son in a car accident on New Year's Eve Day, 1997. My granddad was never around or my Auntie Joyce or paternal grandfather. I remembered my mother mentioning that some spirits need time to deal with additional stuff after they pass, and for some it can take years.

There had been discussions with my mother and sister about the paranormal over the past few years, so talking to my mother about what I was hearing and seeing was not difficult, now. There had been a time when I didn't even consider it. I still hadn't told her that I in my younger years, I believed that I had killed three of our family members.

Fine, I didn't literally kill them, but I had used thought to "kill" them. At least I think that's how it worked. It seems I can cause things to happen, or perhaps it is more a prediction that things are going to happen. At the age of twelve it was difficult to decipher.

The first time I had just finished gymnastics training. I was walking out of practice with a really nice girl who was in seventh grade with me. I can't say I knew her, but for some reason I felt comfortable enough to talk to her. We were talking about family. I remember she had lost her mother to cancer. Our conversation eventually steered to my great-grandmother. I told her that when I was about eight, just after we moved out of an extended stay at my grandmother's house, my great-grandmother came to visit. My great-grandma emigrated to Canada from Sweden with great-grandpa (who died when I was young) and six children, and later three more were born in Canada. I have been told that my father was her favorite grandchild; I apparently was not her favorite anything.

It seemed like an average day. I was literally running around town, climbing rocks, playing with bugs, and picking berries wherever I found them. I stopped at my grandmother's house for a cookie—two or three, actually; she had the best-stocked cookie jar in town. The door was never locked (no one locked their doors), and I walked in to replenish my energy. My great-grandma suddenly started yelling at me about entering the house without knocking or dirty feet. Something. Who could understand when half her sentences were in Swedish? I was totally taken aback by her remarks. I tried to explain that I was just grabbing a couple of cookies and then leaving. I don't remember whether I got the cookies, but I do know that I was still angry about the situation four years later. I ended the conversation with my schoolmate by saying, "I wish she would just die. Bite my tongue, watch someone else die instead." I don't know what possessed me to say it. I replayed that sentence in my head for years.

Half a block from my house, the air changed—not the weather; it just felt weird, thick, heavy. Then I saw my aunt and uncle's car parked in our driveway, which was really odd. My mother and my aunt did not get along, so we rarely saw them. It was also five in the afternoon on a school day, so my parents shouldn't have been home yet. I was extremely worried before I walked through the door. Something was up; something had happened. Everyone was standing around the television. Mum was pacing back and forth between the living room and the kitchen, cooking something but needing to see what was on television. It was all so weird.

My mother finally noticed me. Leaning toward me with her hands clasped together in front of her, which she only did when she was on edge, she told me that my Uncle Terry had been killed in a work-related accident. Electrocuted. Someone had forgotten to disconnect the power, and he had died instantly. What I found most revolting was that everyone was watching the news. Somewhere in my head I was upset that they were turning his death into a television show. At the time I didn't recognize that my dad and his brother needed to find out more information about the accident, that they wanted to connect as much as possible with the baby brother they had lost. I just thought it was all so morbid.

I had loved my Uncle Terry very much. He was fun and, other than my grandmother, was the only other directly related relative with red hair. We had a connection. I cried and cried, perhaps to mourn his death, but I was also terrified. Had this been somehow my fault? Did I cause this with my words?

At his funeral I watched everyone cry, including his mother, sisters, and wife, who held their young son. I couldn't tell anyone what I'd done. How could I? I felt so guilty and wanted to escape. It was at his funeral that I had my first taste of alcohol. I can understand how people turn to alcohol or drugs, but they're not the answer. I really was just avoiding my emotions, which was the beginning of a very bad habit.

It was almost a year later that I found the nerve to mention to a friend, in complete confidence, what had happened. You know, in hushed tones and all. I told her the whole story, ending it with, "I wish it would have been my great-grandmother." Although she was a little weirded out, we let it go and moved on to other subjects. She never got to find out what happened next, for the fear kept me silent, yet again.

I arrived home from school, and the phone was ringing. I don't know where my little sister Jane was, but she wasn't home to answer it. My grandmother was on the other end of the line, and that in itself was odd for four o'clock in the afternoon. But as I love my grandma very much, I was happy to hear her voice. It wasn't a pleasure call, however. She was calling to let us know that her great-nephew, my cousin, was in a coma on life support and wasn't likely to make it through the night. He had been at a party where alcohol was involved, and a terrible car accident followed. She would call again once there was more news.

I was stunned. I had just broken my vow of silence by telling a friend the whole story, and now another death was imminent. Had I done it again? But what had I done?

Then I remembered a time when I was young—perhaps six or seven— and I always knew what was going to happen or had answers for things I didn't even understand. My auntie, who was only four years older than I, would turn and yell at me, "You can't possibly know that!" She would get so angry at me that after a while I turned off that ability. People didn't like it when you knew stuff they didn't.

Did I know stuff, or was I a witch like she said?

It was about two years after this second incident that I related the story to my two closest friends. We would often sleep over at each other's houses, and of course there were always a few ghost stories involved. I decided to tell my ghost story.

I need to share this information. Maybe they had insight on what had really happened. My only hesitation was I didn't want anyone else to die. My fear was, who would I kill next? Was everything that happened a weird coincidence or had I been killing my family members? I told my friends about the two previous events and how I had not wished anyone dead, not even my great-grandmother. I had learned my lesson.

You probably have an idea of what happened next. It couldn't have scared me more. My mother received a call from my paternal grandmother the day after I exposed my voodoo magic to my girlfriends. Her mother, my great-grandmother, had finally died. My father flew out to Vancouver Island to attend the funeral, while the rest of us stayed home. I shared the information immediately with my friends, and they didn't think it was a coincidence.

After this, whenever someone picked on me at school, my friends would jokingly say, "I wouldn't do that, she might kill you!" In their minds I don't think it was entirely a joke.

At fifteen I proclaimed that whatever it was, however it happened, I wouldn't be a part of it anymore. Whatever it was, I closed down the last part of it that day, for the fear was too great. I now know that is one reason why my intuition never completely cropped up, or at least not nearly as strongly in the years to come. If it did, I tended to ignore it, knowing it could only cause death and heartache. And of course fear in others.

It wasn't until closer to my midtwenties that my mother, sister, and I started talking openly about this whole other world. We all knew something was going on with my grandmother and a few of her sisters. Even on my mother's side, a few of us cousins discussed strange things that happened.

We had used metal clothes hangers to see how large a person's aura was. We owned pendulums and used them to clear our chakras. They are energy centers in the body that run along the front and back; there are seven of them. My mother had read our tarot cards. Introduced me at sixteen to them in Winnipeg, where I had my cards and tea leaves read. Both my mother and sister saw and spoke to the dead. That was not a gift I wanted. That was too much like black magic, like voodoo.

There were certain superstitions I believed in. Before smoking was banned in restaurants and bars, I used to shake salt into the ashtray to ward off evil spirits. I'd never walk under a ladder or across the path of a black cat. I always knocked on wood, and heaven forbid if I were to break a mirror. Now I wasn't sure what to make of this conversation with my Gran and was hoping my mother could shed some light.

Recently she had seen a psychic who saw Gran in a blue dress with pearls and guessed her age to be around fifty. The psychic mentioned that occasionally there were two other people with her, a young woman and her baby. Hearing this information now was wonderful and terrifying! But at least I wasn't crazy. The negative in all this was that my mother felt hurt because she hadn't received any messages; she was told she was doing just fine, so there was nothing to say.

CHAPTER 9

Abandonment

BEFORE WE MOVED I HAD purchased over fifty books; one was a book on meditation. The information given did not seem to be helping me. Being a visual person and only receiving a vague explanation, it was impossible for me to figure out whether I was doing it right. It didn't feel right, so I assumed it wasn't right. What I didn't realize was that most of my day was spent in a kind of meditative state. My mornings on the hammock, biking, and listening to the birds were all about connecting to the quietness within my person, within my soul. I was enjoying the slower pace and in return there was more meaning in my life. I had never really been very superficial, but now most of what I did was to please myself.

For so many years my life had been full of havoc. Honestly, there had never been a time in my life where there wasn't some type of chaos. An abundant amount of moving as a young child, dealing with the name-calling and insecurities about being ugly, confusion around my parent's dysfunctional relationship, and then taking on that dysfunction in my own female-male relationships. Even though there was more stability with Mike, our lives had become a whirlwind. Marriage, moving, a baby, more moving, new friends, another baby, another move, another language, more new friends!

Even when there was a brief lull, in the overall picture there were always friends around to communicate with. That moment of silence was always filled by picking up the phone for endless conversations and gossip. Mike and I had numerous fights about my phone time. He couldn't understand my need for conversations, and I couldn't understand his need for so little. His friendships were few; mine were many. I now understood better. Silence was golden.

Now I found comfort in solitude. Peace and tranquility had found me, not the other way around. Everything happens for a reason; is that why we moved here? So I could find this internal peace?

Please understand that my entire day was not blissful, but there were more moments of peace than ever before. Even with help, Brett and Taylor were a challenge. Mike and his negative talk had me dreaming about faraway places. Since my Gran had started visiting, I jumped at the slightest movement in my peripheral vision. Fear was overpowering me. Would more people come and visit me? I hoped not! There were so many new metaphysical experiences.

As for the rest of the moments, I had learned how to live in this foreign country, to lead as normal a life as possible. My mind-set was in place, we were here for a three-year contract, and I would cope—for my state of mind and for my family's sake.

In June, 1999, we returned to North America for a vacation, our one trip out of a year. I had great hope that this would improve Mike's mood. It did initially, but it also made him want to work in a developed country that much more. By October he was depressed again. Or I should say that his depression had deepened. The only thing that cheered him up was the thought that he might be able to shorten our contract and leave. He spent the available parts of his days looking for a job in the United States, Australia, or Canada. He wanted to feel useful again. He had not found the serenity that had snuck up and captured me. When he looked out, he saw misery, and I believe he thought we were miserable too. He just kept repeating how this assignment was ruining his career. Everything was about his career.

Thank God Brasil had really good red wine! I don't mean homegrown; they had an amazing international store that sold wine from all around the world. A good, rich, red wine in general had gotten my attention, and that is what got me through a lot of Mike's "woe is me" evenings.

We had survived sixteen months, and better than I had originally anticipated. We had hot water, satellite, Internet, and a great maid. We were not lacking. The children had great friends and so did I. Perhaps if Mike had more *amigos* he would have done better in this foreign country. Even without friends I would have made the best of things. This is what you do in life. "You made your bed, now you have to lie in it." I had completed five large scrapbooking albums and read more than sixty-five books.

Mike came home smiling in November; he'd found a job. We argued. He was taking us to Yellowknife. Well, he might be going, but he wasn't taking me: "My life will be over if I have to go back there! I'm not going!! My resistance was so intense.

With his voice now raised, he said, "It's the only place that's hiring right now! There isn't anything in the States, and Australia isn't much better." I just glared at him.

"Fine! If I can make do here, I guess I can make do there! But I don't want to go! It's going to be awful!"

Personally, I wanted to go back to the United States. Sure, it was full of expats, but weren't we expats? We were hired out of the United States, and they stated in our contract that that was our place of origin. The problem was that Mike knew he would be dumped into a mindless job there too. My anger was almost uncontrollable. Wasn't Australia an option? The more I thought about moving there, the more daunting it became. There would be a minimum six-month adjustment period where I would have to learn all the contents of their packaged foods, familiarize myself with the area to find the best schools and location to live, make new friends so the children had playdates, and learn another culture and their language. Then there were utility hookups, which I would have to research to find the best companies to use. I realized it was just too much for me at the moment. What I needed was a low-maintenance move. Why did Yellowknife have to be that choice?

The serenity of my hammock called me. I sat already missing my *lindo de manhã*, beautiful morning. I convinced myself that there were benefits to this move, as there always were:

- It would be a relatively easy move.
- I already had friendships established.
- I knew the language.
- I knew the area.
- We would be closer to family.
- There would always be another move.

The negatives:

- It was Yellowknife.
- There were people there I didn't ever want to see again.
- Mike would be working at a camp Monday through Thursday.
- It was frickin' cold!
- I couldn't ride my bike all year long.
- I didn't want my children to grow up in the dysfunction of Yellowknife.

Depression set in, and it was severe. I didn't want to go. Preparing my mind seemed impossible. We would be closer to family and could reconnect with old friends. That was all good … right?

Overnight Mike became elated, and I became miserable. He didn't even notice, or he just didn't care.

He requested that the Brasilian position not be restaffed. This decision meant that Conceição would have to find a new job. She had worked for an English representative for over fourteen years. Regular Brasilian maids were treated in a ghastly fashion. Items in the refrigerator were counted and monitored. If anything went missing, the cost of the item came out of the maid's pay. Within a month of our arrival our phone blew up. There was a great number of electrical storms, and we were unaware that the electricity was not grounded. I had gone to the *loja* to buy a new phone. The owner asked, "Com chave, nao chave?" I repeated the words several times before finding them in my memory bank: "Chave, chave … key?" Why would I need a key for my phone?

Looking quite reserved and without looking me directly in the eye, he told me it was so the maids couldn't use it.

"Nao, nao chave."

Did you know that university is free in Brasil? Did you know that most people can't attend because they don't have the bus fare? It's heartbreaking. In most circumstances the maid stays with the house, so finding a new job in the area where your child will attend school is almost impossible. Finding affordable housing is the other problem. Most maids get paid only two hundred reais a month. The entire family is expected to help with the expenses. That includes the extended family. I didn't know if anyone would move into our house, and if not, where would Conceição go?

She was married and had two children—a son and a daughter. She was very proud of her home and had received many benefits from working for American families. Her home was less than what we would consider a "roughing it" cabin. Most of the cooking took place outside where there was running water. All the clothing dried outside, except of course during the rainy season, when nothing dried. She couldn't afford a washer or dryer. Our towels and bedding were always wet, but I could at least throw them in my dryer. Her pots and pans were worse than anything I had in my camping boxes. Their beds were made up of a piece of plywood held up by a couple of cinder blocks covered in a very thin blanket. With the humidity, the winter months could be very cold.

She always seemed happy. Her mother had passed while we lived there, and she had an emergency hysterectomy. Stuff was going on in her life that she had to manage. Her dream was to work as a maid in Florida.

The degree of poverty did surprise me. The shanty towns were made of no more than wooden sticks and aluminum waffle board, occasionally, like my maid's, of cinder blocks. People walked miles and miles with a sickle in one hand and a pile of sticks on their backs to be used as firewood. Then I would go to town and see computers, Interac machines, and fancy photo-processing machinery. I have a picture of a road where there is a bicycle, a motorcycle, a car, and a horse tied to a post—all valid modes of transportation sitting next to one another.

It really is the perfect picture to express what Brasil is all about.

Poverty could be seen out my front window. Children of all ages would come early in the morning and pick through our garbage cans looking for food. Time and time again I contemplated putting food in the garbage for them. Or should I call them in and give them food? Although I wanted to call them to my door and offer them food, that would not have helped them or me. The number to come the next day would be greater, and it was like feeding wildlife; they would become dependent on you. Is that harsh? Yes, but I wouldn't be there for long, and that wasn't the answer to the problem. But I did not know what the answer was. Older children would come and sell us stuff—useless stuff, really. We would buy it. Some would offer to wash our car or do work in the garden. I was happy to help if I could.

The problem was too big and too difficult for me to find the right answer, and the people around me kept repeating, "You can't help everyone!" Even my maid would shoo the starving children away, calling them dead children, or something like that, since they weren't expected to survive long. Perhaps I couldn't help everyone, but I could help my maid and her family and anyone else that came along and asked.

I would miss Brasil.

It was Tuesday, December 28, 1999, that I sat in Yellowknife, Canada, contemplating how in the hell I had ended up back in this godforsaken place. The view out the window was white. The ground was covered in three feet of white, and the sky was snowing more white. It should have been picturesque. It wasn't. What could God's plan possibly be? Was this some perverse joke? He couldn't possibly think I would be happy here. Maybe it was Mike's turn for happy. Maybe we were supposed to take turns?

If I was truly honest with myself, the true reason I didn't want to return had little to do with the weather. The return had me looking at myself as a person, the person who had lived in Yellowknife. The good, the bad, and the ugly were floating through my brain, and I didn't like what I saw. There seemed to be a lot of bad and a lot of ugly. I hadn't been a very nice teenager during the Yellowknife portion of my life. I had wronged so many people—my sister Jane, friends, acquaintances, strangers, my parents. Why had I been such a bitch? What made me that way? There were so many things I wished I had done differently or hadn't done at all. The weight of the shame and guilt sat heavy on my shoulders. I felt like curling into a ball, staying in bed, and sleeping it away. I didn't want to face the world or the people I'd hurt or been disrespectful to. I didn't want to face the shame I felt in my heart, and I didn't know how to get past it.

God help me. Please.

Spiritual Acceptance

CHAPTER 10

Moving Forward

ALL IN ALL, THE MOVE was fine. We took extra time during the Christmas holidays to see Mike's parents and reconnected with my sister and mother. Dad had another girlfriend, so we only saw him briefly.

Although we had been living abroad for over five years, in truth, it seemed a lot longer than that. Brett, now almost six, and Taylor, only three and a bit, played in the snow for the first time in three years. Brett had a blast, jumping around and throwing snow everywhere. If we had been at the beach it would have looked much the same. She was almost always happy! For Taylor it was different. Jane had said at birth that Taylor had a dark cloud hanging over her head. Now she sat in one spot trying not to touch the snow, a look of concern on her face regarding all the white stuff surrounding her. Thankfully she wasn't screaming.

Our temporary housing consisted of a two-bedroom apartment condo in downtown Yellowknife. The downtown core was still made up of seven blocks of bars, restaurants, coffee shops, Canadian Tire, and multiple high-rise office buildings. The company would cover the bill for six weeks until we found a permanent home. It pains me to say permanent. Even the cats were not enjoying their confinement or the confusion about their hair loss. They had been shedding the previous week, now their fur was trying to grow in as fast as possible to accommodate the cold weather! Going from the Brasilian summer and temperatures of plus forty Celsius to the dark, cold, winter temperatures of minus forty was shocking for all of us, just less visible for the humans.

The one thing I hadn't missed was the extra time necessary to get the girls all bundled up to leave the house. Brett would be first and would then complain about being too hot before I was even close to being finished with Taylor's boots, snow pants, scarf, hat, mitts, and coat. The car seats both needed adjusting to make room for all the extra layers of clothes. Winter, yuck.

Although I would have enjoyed being miserable at my mother's house a few more days, we decided it was prudent to arrive before December 31, 1999, with all the commotion about Y2K problems regarding flying, banking, and such. Nothing happened other than that we spent three extra days in Yellowknife.

There had been quite a bit I was able to do from Brasil via the Internet. It was amazingly helpful. Brett was preregistered to take French immersion kindergarten in the morning. She struggled for the first few days, replying in Portuguese. I hoped she wouldn't lose her Portuguese. It was impossible to get Taylor into a preschool anywhere, but I did get her on the list for the following September. We filled in the rest of our time with figure skating lessons. My old teacher was there and offered me a job to coach part-time. Maybe that would improve my spirits. A job, something for me! I truly was excited about it and couldn't wait to teach a couple of days a week. It also gave me a couple of bucks to play with. The girls were enrolled in gymnastics and dance as well. Brett had taken ballet class in Brasil, but there had been no activities for Taylor. Having activities available for the girls was the best part of this disaster.

Okay, it was only disastrous for me. The girls were doing fine. Mike couldn't stop talking, but now I was drinking wine in hopes of ignoring his enthusiasm. Had he always been so self-absorbed? Did he not see how

I was tortured? Was it just that he was so wrapped up in his job that he saw and heard nothing else? We never heard from him during the week; he was too busy. I was sad, and now lonely.

I suppose his enthusiasm put more of a damper on my mood, because there was nothing I had that type of enthusiasm for. I loved my children, but currently I didn't feel that love for them; I was numb inside. I started attending meditation classes once a week and my mantra was, "I feel love." I made myself hug the children every morning and evening, hoping to feel something. Hoping the girls didn't notice the state of my mental health. I signed up for yoga class one other evening. I loved it, but there was always a little bit of guilt for leaving the girls with a sitter at bedtime, twice a week. I kept reminding myself how important it was for my mental health to be doing something for me. Perhaps it was fallout for having the luxury of a maid for so long. Perhaps I didn't have the skills to balance everything now. But I couldn't have quit either activity; it was as though my body craved it. It was like being at a bookstore, and, although you don't really need another book, you can't put that book back on the shelf.

There weren't a lot of quiet moments any longer, but when there were, I started to question, "Why am I here? What is my purpose?" For surely God had a plan for me. Not having answers to those questions was so frustrating.

Movement was starting to happen in my mind—a little, anyways. In yoga I reconnected with a classmate. There were rumors, terrible rumors, about her running off with someone and leaving her husband and child behind. A year later she came back to her husband and from what I could see seemed quite happy. If she could forgive herself or at least come to terms with what she had done and move forward, as did he, surely it was possible for me to do so to? My anxieties were around the shame and guilt of my teen years. Her situation had me pondering forgiveness. Just how did people move on? How was I going to move on?

I concentrated on finding us a permanent home. Mike might have dragged me here, but I sure as hell was not buying a house. The thought made me nauseous. Our home in Republic had finally sold in November.

We didn't make a dime, but at least it was no longer an expense. We had saved a lot of money in Brasil, but the thought of spending it hadn't even crossed my mind. I was looking for something to rent.

The mine life was long, and allowed us the opportunity to stay until retirement. Which had never been an option before and I didn't see it as an option now and never found it funny when Mike mentioned it. *Please tell me he's joking!* I had found a new useful skill, using my pendulum, or actually my pearl necklace. It apparently wasn't only used to balance my chakras, a skill my mother had taught me the previous summer. When trained properly it (the pendulum) would answer yes or no to any question I asked. I remembered seeing my mother at a baby shower doing the same thing using a needle or a button on a thread to find out the sex of the baby when I was a young girl.

Holding the chain in my right hand between my thumb and index finger, with my elbow aimed outward at heart level, I would then ask it a question: "Will we live in Yellowknife for more than five years?" As I concentrated on the question, I watched the pearl start moving, bobbing a bit until it started to swing left and right. A no, and a sigh of relief expelled from me. Had it swung toward me and away from me, it would have been a yes.

Multiple questions later, and then some scrying using my pendulum over a map to find a specific location, showed me we would move to southern Alberta, close to Calgary, although not Calgary itself. I would eventually get out of here. That answer relaxed me a little more.

With that information in the back of my mind, the thought of buying a house only for its equity value was more appealing. Currently the houses on the market were crap, so my mind went back to renting. Ask and you will receive. Our realtor just happened to have a three-bedroom condo for rent. "We'll take it!" I'm okay when things fall into my lap.

The condo was cramped, but it matched my mood. And it gave me the excuse to avoid company. We had been invited to a couple of company functions. I passed. It was currently too much energy to paste a smile on my face and try to be interested in conversation. I only called my old friends out of obligation. I couldn't very well send Christmas cards with a Yellowknife return address, could I? It could be awkward. That tradition was too well-ingrained for me to avoid. Those old relationships turned out to be a blessing, and we picked up where we had left off. Finally, a happy feeling.

From the outside it looked like I was doing what needed to be done, I believed that, anyway. But inside I wanted to feel more, I wanted to be more. What the hell was my purpose here on Earth? Good mother, fine. But eventually the kids would leave home and what would I have then? A rocky relationship with my husband?

We were drifting apart. The heat in Brasil really had increased our libido. I thought it had only been stories. At minus forty there was no heat here. Being discouraged and dealing with internal fears and anxieties had not put me in the mood. I tried to resume date night, but with our conversations being so one-sided, they just annoyed me.

One morning in late February I woke to feel my energy returning. By now the days were longer, and today the sky looked to be blue. The sun wasn't completely up yet. It was going to be a great day to take pictures! I had discovered a different world through the camera lens since living in Walnut Creek. I dropped Brett at school and Taylor at daycare, which I was now doing once a week, and decided to explore Yellowknife with a different perspective.

It worked! Yellowknife was fascinating when I wasn't dwelling on the past. For those few hours it was all about the color of the frozen lake with the reflection of the rising sun. In the background there were brightly painted houseboats frozen amidst the lake. The roads there sporadically covered in flocks of white, fluffy ptarmigans, blending in with the snow as nature intended. The love inside of me in those moments was so strong.

As the days moved forward, winter continued to subside, and the days filled with more sunlight, my own dark cloud started to evaporate. Yellowknife had changed. It was a little city. There were cool, trendy restaurants, coffee shops, and pubs. The movie theater had been renovated, and I didn't even recognize it from the days when I use to work there. The bowling alley was actually somewhere people went to bowl and not just drink. They had built a new facility for the swimming pool. Perhaps I should say they built a facility, as the old one had been in an apartment building. There was so much more for everyone to do, especially children. Karate, swimming, cross-country skiing, horseback riding, skating, drama, dance, indoor soccer, and the list continued.

For the first time in years I pulled out my cross-country skis! There was a new track with amazing trails only minutes away. Weekends were busy with other activities, but during the week the girls and I would head out to the trails after school. It was so invigorating! Winter had changed in the north. The minus forty days had disappeared. Winter was warmer in general, reaching minus twenty degrees Celsius in the dead of winter. Surely there was something going on in the atmosphere with the greenhouse gases. There was talk about it, and I had no problem believing. This town had become an outdoor oasis. No one was cooped up hibernating; they were skiing, snowmobiling, tobogganing, walking, or part of a running club. The locals—not so much the transient population—had cabins that were winterized. Before it had never been an option; it had been too cold.

My mantra was working; I was feeling. It did come at a cost. There were many encounters with my past. To change things in my life, change needed to happen, and action seemed to be a part of that change, whether it was good or bad.

I always got nervous leaving the house. What would I encounter? What action would trigger another old memory, old event, or old emotion? It had started the first day I took Brett to school. It never occurred to me that I would know any of the parents; it had been so long since I'd been around people I knew. There was a mom from my old office and a dad from high school. We didn't have a difficult relationship, but they did invoke other memories.

Going from A to B was much worse, as that part of the world was much bigger. Anyone could be out there. I had so much fear about going to the grocery store or downtown, to the gym. Every memory would take me to another memory that filled me with regret and shame. It would then take hours, sometimes days, before I would stop torturing myself. I found it impossible to get to forgiveness, as it had been a foreign action in the house I grew up in. We had just learned to ignore things, which was apparently why I was now stuck in this emotional mess. With that course of action no longer serving me, I continued with my mantra, which had started all of this. Or was it my mantra that was saving me?

Making up all sorts of scenarios before I left the house didn't help. It just wound me up. The only time I felt calm was during meditation, and I turned to it often. I didn't want to bump into the guy who had raped me or either of his conspirators. I couldn't ask my girlfriends about them, as I had only shared the story of my rape with one friend and my other friends would ask, "Why are you interested in what's going on in their lives?" There was also fear around encountering Luke. He had tried to run me down and a vague thought of him choking me was starting to surface. What would he do to my children? Even the thought of bumping into the mean girls from high school set me off. There was fear of all those people, where they were, and when I would encounter them.

When your mantra is love, healing happens. Moving through fear is necessary, and to do that, a shift has to take place. I hadn't become so fearful that I wasn't leaving the house; I tried to live as normally as possible, mostly for my children. I didn't want them to take on any of my dysfunctions.

Brett had her kindergarten checkup, and there was a chance she needed glasses. The shop Mike and I used had moved into the mall, so off the girls and I went. The mall. It used to be a hotel and a bar—how things change. Brett was being fitted with her new glasses by a classmates of Jane's, so I felt comfortable wandering around the shop with Taylor trying on glasses and making funny faces. While my glasses were off, and I was checking out a quirky frame, behind me came the words, "Tracy? Tracy is that you?"

Even with my back turned, the voice was clearly recognizable. In a monotone, I answered, "Yes, Luke, it's me." My mind went directly to Taylor. She was a few feet away behind a display.

"I thought it was you. When did you get back?" As I turned around, I could see him bubbling with excitement.

"A couple of months ago." What the hell was he doing in an optical shop? He didn't wear glasses!

"Maybe we could go for coffee sometime and talk. I've done a lot with my life. I have a company where I own midsize trucks, kind of a niche. I'm doing really well." He's trying to impress me? Did he use the word *niche* so I would know he had attended postsecondary school?

"Ahh, maybe." I was being motioned that Brett was done. "I have to be somewhere, bye." I grabbed the girls and fled the store. Did he not know that I was terrified of him?

After talking to my sister, I found out that he was dating her classmate and had been for five years or so. That information calmed my nerves. Maybe he wasn't psychotic anymore.

Then, walking into the bank, I literally bumped into someone whom I thought had been a friend but turned out not to be.

"How are you?" he asked, leaning in for a big hug.

A little stunned, I replied, "Ah, great. How are you doing?" He rambled on about life, what he was doing, his wife and such. I can't say I heard a word. I just kept wondering when he had gotten so short. I had always thought he was significantly taller than me. His hair had thinned. What was he saying?

"Oh, yah, great seeing you too," I automatically replied as he exited the bank.

Had he forgotten how he'd hurt me? It was the summer after graduation, a bunch of us had gone camping, and I was having an afternoon nap. He crawled into my tent hoping to get lucky. We did not have that kind of relationship, and that is what I told him directly. He asked if he could hang out for a bit so the group of boys around the fire would think he had succeeded.

"Seriously? Will that make you feel better?" I asked him. What the hell was wrong with some people! "If you think that is going to make you more of a man, sure, hang out," I threatened in a disgusted tone. He sat sheepishly in the corner of my tent, accepting the praise when he finally emerged. I shook my head in disbelief. Nothing at that point could have made my reputation worse. There were similar lies about me all summer since my rape. Now I just thought of him with disdain. I could live with the truth, but how did he live with the lie? It seemed he had completely forgotten about the incident. *Bygones need to be bygones, Tracy.*

Then the universe gave me a gift. There were people I wanted to avoid, but of course there were people I'd love to see! After leaving the rink one day after teaching skating lessons, I crossed the road to my SUV. Just as I was about to open the door, I whirled around and yelled, "Bob?"

The man across the street turned around, and sure enough it was he, a guy I had graduated with. How did I know he was there? I had spun and called long before I saw him. It was like answering the phone and knowing who was on the other line.

We had a quick, five-minute catch-up, and then we both were on our way. Such a lovely surprise.

The intuitive encounters continued, and thankfully it was another good one. I woke up one morning with the need to look perfect. I took extra time with my hair and clothes. I didn't know what was up but knew I would see someone. I didn't know where, as I had a long list of errands to accomplish.

Paying the utility bill was first on my list. The moment I walked into City Hall I started to smile. Standing at the counter was John. He hadn't changed much since we were engaged. He was still tall and lanky, although he had cut his long hair.

"Hi, John." He spun around with a shocked look on his face. We embraced in a warm and friendly hug.

"It's so good to see you."

"You too. When did you get back to town? Weren't you living in Brazil?"

"We were. We moved back in January." We continued to talk for ten minutes, catching up. He was living with the same girl he had just met when I moved nine years ago. He loved his job and was still traveling a lot. He asked about my cousin Emily and mentioned that he had expected to see us at her wedding. I told him that we had really wanted to come but could only manage my grandpa's memorial service or the wedding. He thought perhaps his attendance had kept us away. Interesting: he had felt guilt for no reason. How many things was I feeling guilt about that had nothing to do with the other?

All these new perspective were healing. Slowly, but maybe I couldn't handle anything quicker currently. I was releasing my fear by facing all of them. That gave me strength.

It was time to start participating in the activities of the BHP wives. Betsy was married to Kevin, who had worked with Mike in Yellowknife in the '80s. He had also recommended Mike for his job in Lupin and BHP San Francisco. After San Francisco they had moved to Australia and had been back in Yellowknife for nearly two years. They had a son a year older than Brett and a daughter a year older than Taylor. I called Betsy and asked to be included in the next BHP wives' social function.

The majority of the BHP wives were expats. Because of that they spent a lot of time with each other, at the gym, coffee dates, tea parties, lunches, and holiday celebrations. I attended Betsy's birthday luncheon and met a dozen ladies. Then I attended a Partylite and Pampered Chef party. They were all lovely and very friendly.

My old girlfriends were great. We talked about old times and what everyone was currently up to. But our life experiences were different. They had stayed in Yellowknife and didn't plan on ever leaving. That was not my life. I wanted to leave, see new things, experience new things. On that level it was difficult to connect. Perhaps I had changed too much or the years apart had made it more apparent. My life was no longer about going to the bar and getting drunk. And to be fair, theirs weren't either; we just didn't fit together the same anymore. I preferred dinner parties with expensive red wine and intellectual conversation. My paralyzer days were long gone, and I was thankful for that. Their lives had never been shaken up; they saw all the same people day after day. But to their credit, they seemed really happy. Was I?

Knowing a few of the women made my first company function easier. Mike's boss was hosting a going-away party at his home. The group was mostly upper management. Without realizing it, I sat across from the mine manager's (top boss) wife. They are Australian, as were most of the upper management employees. Innocently enough, she asked me, "And where are you from, Tracy?"

"I'm from here."

"Oh. What part of Canada?"

"No, I'm from here. Yellowknife." The look on her face was priceless! She almost fell off her chair. She would have been told that we had arrived from Brasil. No one was from Yellowknife. I suppose I wasn't, either, but I did consider it home – as painful as that was to say out loud. After that I felt like I was treated differently. Not in a bad way, just different; perhaps I had become exotic. Bizarre—that was how I felt when I lived in Brasil.

Being surrounded by BHP wives gave me a certain amount of security. They weren't aware of my "past" unless I shared it with them. It was like having downtime.

All the changes that were happening made me feel calmer and more connected to God and spirit. There was still fear, but it didn't have the power over me that it had had a few months earlier. I was using the mantra, "I feel and give love." Daily my intuition was leading me to physical places where I would encounter people from my past, and I was able to release the fear and anxiety connected with them. My mind was making up fewer scenarios of destruction. Life wasn't pleasant yet, but it was less stressful.

In allowing yoga and meditation classes into my life, I had released a bit of guilt about giving to myself. My mind had moved on to "What is my purpose?" I needed something to call my own—not classes, or the gym, but a real purpose. It nagged at me. Then I'd move into fear: would my purpose take time away from my children? Mediation would bring me to center again, and I would listen to my intuition. In my heart, I knew it would guide me.

Perhaps I didn't know who I was? Was I getting hung up on who I thought other people thought I was? Was it all about judgment? I didn't like to judge others, but I sure was judging myself. I wasn't a teenage girl full of indiscretions. Nor just a wife and mother. I wasn't a backwater American or a trendy Californian. There had been so many labels until Brasil. I hadn't known what Brasil was; it confused me. It was now important to get rid of all that stuff and find out who Tracy was. Not Tracy-Lynn or Lynn, but Tracy; I was Tracy.

My meditations had changed. I was now talking to spirit. Who spirit was, I wasn't sure. Talking to my Gran periodically made this new experience easier. There had been so much fear initially. I believed it was a couple of my guides that I spoke to the most. If something felt wrong, off, I would say, "I will only talk if you are within God's love and light." Some voices went away, others stayed. The biggest difficulty was deciphering between ego and my guides. I found that my guides spoke more fluidly, never stumbling over words or concepts.

My guides were telling me it was time to buy a house. At this point I never questioned it. I told Mike. He listened. So many things had been happening, he was not finding it difficult to trust and listen.

One Friday morning he dropped Brett at school on his way into the downtown office. The words out of my mouth as he was on his way out the door were, "Slow down in the school zones." He called me fifteen minutes later from his cell phone. He had just gotten a ticket for speeding in a school zone.

So now we were on the hunt for a house, and it was tedious and depressing. There were a lot more on the market than when we first arrived, but now we categorized them as fifteen disappointments. They had been either ugly or ugly and expensive. Our realtor had one more coming on the market on Wednesday, and we would get first viewing. Mike was at work, and Brett was at school, so Taylor and I drove past it a couple of times before the meeting. It was cute, on a corner lot, looked like a split level. We parked and went in. With only one foot in the door, I said, "We'll take it! Oh, with the condition that Mike sees it first, before we close."

Some things happen that fast. You know it when you know it. It was like that for Mike and me when we met. The house in Republic was the same way. I was positive Mike would love it, so here I was, making an offer, signing the papers and adding a condition of acceptance: husband must approve purchase. He barely got his foot in the door and felt the same way.

It was beige on the outside, but there wasn't much color in the north unless you lived on the water. It was a four-level split with three bedrooms up and one down. It had a front room, a dining area, and an eat-in counter in the kitchen. It had a great space for an office and a huge family room in the basement. It had everything I had been looking for in the last fifteen houses. It had a great deck and a large, flat backyard. I say flat because most houses are built on rock and therefore, so are their yards. Well, that and marsh. This yard was all grass—huge and grassy—great for a swing set and a trampoline! It had a great, double, attached garage, and the entire house had in-floor heating. In-floor heating—what an amazing concept. And a fireplace for those really cold winter days and nights. Comfort in the northern wilderness: wasn't anything possible then?

We would move in mid-August after summer vacation. There was a family reunion, my mother's side, in Ontario. The last reunion had been in 1993 while I had been pregnant with Brett. This gathering of the family was not a happy occasion. It would serve as a memorial service for Gran and my cousin and her son. There had been a funeral for Gran, but her ashes had never been buried; same for my cousin and her ten-month-old son.

We had so many air miles, but they were all from an American airline, which meant we couldn't fly from one Canadian city to another. We would have to fly into the United States. We picked Chicago as the place to land and would drive north into Ontario.

Ninety percent of our vacations as a married couple had revolved around family visits. And so was this vacation, but after exploring different parts of the world, we had the travel bug. Chicago wouldn't just be a quick turning point; we planned on visiting for a few days. We attended a ball game at Wrigley Field, took an architectural river cruise, enjoyed the Museum of Science and Industry and the Children's Museum, and shopping at FAO Schwarz Toys! We enjoyed the trendy shops and restaurants and drove along North Lake Shore and marveled at how huge Lake Michigan is.

Things had gotten exciting before the vacation, a different kind of exciting. We had spent a night at Jane's in Calgary before catching our plane to Chicago. That night I woke around two and looked over at Mike, who had me blinking. It wasn't him; it was so many different faces. It was like face shifting, if there is such a thing. One face after another would cycle through, man to woman, to young, then old. Every second there would be a new face imposed on his. It was mesmerizing. When I woke up in the morning, Gran's voice was clearly planted in my head.

I haven't heard much from Gran since we left Brasil. I had questioned her a few times about my guides, but that was it. I suppose even spirits have places to go and people to see. Now it was like we were traveling together. She made comments about the experiences of our trip, "Look over there, come this way, or do this."

Her attachment is difficult to explain. We were connected, one inside the other. I could feel her presence all the time.

I had a girlfriend from high school living in southern Ontario, and we planned on spending one night with her. After her family and mine went to bed, we stayed up talking. At one point this face shifting started on her, but then it settled on one face. That freaked me out; her voice was coming out of someone else's face! It launched me off the couch.

She was startled with my abrupt movement and asked, "What's going on?"

How do I explain this? Gran's voice floated into my head, "Honesty is the best policy." That received an eye roll. "All right, I've been seeing different faces impose themselves on your face, which was cool. I saw the same thing on Mike's face a few nights ago, but then it settled on one. An older lady, with short, gray hair and bright eyes. She is still there and is smiling in a very loving manner." Big breath, while I sat back down and waited for her reaction.

Her response was surprising. "It's my grandmother. She recently passed. I've been sure I could feel her around, and now you've confirmed it. Thank you."

I was stunned. I had never really helped anyone with these strange gifts. Was it possible to help without seeming like one of those weird women dressed in long gowns and scarves?

The drive took us longer than anticipated and had us arriving at the cemetery moments before the service began. We would bury Gran. My cousin's family wasn't ready to bury their sister, wife, and daughter yet. Did it really take more than five years to heal? Of course it could. Rhetorical question.

Gran had me transfixed on the setting sun. Every time I tried to look elsewhere, Gran would urge my eyes back. Even as I bent over to throw dirt into her grave, my eyes were locked on the horizon. It was as though she were using my eyes to see, which confused me. Could she not see the sunset herself? Was it color that was an issue? Great, one more thing to ponder.

Her hold let go once the service was over. I was then able to hug, chat, and introduce the girls to aunts, uncles, and cousins. We left and went to the reunion site, but Gran urged me to take her home, now. I talked to another cousin who understood the crazy metaphysical stuff, as I wasn't the only one in the family sensitive to the Other side. She would come with me to take Gran home, as her parents were now living in Gran's house, and she had a key.

The detachment happened the second I walked in the front door. She took off at the speed of light! I could barely keep track of her in my mind's eye. She was moving from room to room. The house had changed, and she wasn't completely happy.

Her journey with me was complete. How was it she couldn't get into her home without hitching a ride? It made me think twice about whether it was my Gran at all. Had someone blocked her, and now she needed permission to enter? She was acting a little bizarre, zipping in and out of rooms looking to see what was where and making comments about things being moved and such.

There was nothing I could do about it now, so we left. It had only been a few days, but it felt odd not to have her with me. I felt kind of lonely and was spending an excessive amount of time wondering about all that had happened over the last few hours. I tried to shake it off and join in the party, which was why we were here. Mike was having a great time, as were the girls.

Returning to Yellowknife had me shifting gears. Things needed to get packed, moved, and unpacked. Settling in was easy with all the extra room. Both girls were now in school, Brett in grade one with a male teacher for the first time. He was great! He had the energy to keep up with her. Since she started school, she had turned into a lovely child; she was no longer a nightmare to handle. Her endless list of questions didn't seem to overwhelm him. I was hoping that would make less of a load for me at the end of the day. Every night since she could talk, after I had tucked her into bed, but before the lights were turned out, she would say, "I have a question." Typically, I would give her three and then tell her it was time to go to sleep.

Taylor, now four, was attending preschool three mornings a week. It was nice for her to be meeting children her own age. There wasn't a mother's club, as there was in Walnut Creek, and we missed that interaction. With both girls at school, there was time to organize the house.

The girls were back in figure-skating lessons, although I was not teaching. I missed watching their progress. They loved their gymnastic lessons, and even with both activities, they had time to have fun and play. It was all about finding balance. That was what I was now working on. I wanted to find a part-time job. An ad appeared in the newspaper, announcing that the paper was looking for a photographer's assistant. I had no idea what was involved, but I loved photography. I was nervous, as this would be my first interview in over eight years. Delivering newspapers hadn't required an interview. My new title would be graphic design artist. What the hell was that?

Not what I applied for, but it was similar to scrapbooking. I would be laying out the news pages from scratch—photos, ads, and copy. I would work Tuesday and Thursday evenings for six hours. Perfect.

My new mantra, "Help me forgive," was still cleaning up things in my life. My first day of work I crossed paths with one of the mean girls from high school who had taunted me. I lifted my head from the computer, and there she was, standing across from me talking to the photography manager, Kenny. I almost fell off my chair. Crap.

Her eyes got big, and she gave me a hug. "Tracy! Oh my God, how are you?" Was she being friendly?

"I'm really good. How are you? You work here?"

"I'm doing really well. I work upstairs." We chatted like old friends. She was married, had a child. Then she said she needed to go, and I was left sitting there wondering what had just happened.

She had been awful to me, but over time I hadn't been a bouquet of flowers in her life, either. It was time to let go of more guilt.

At Christmas my coworker announced that she was pregnant: "Tracy, would you like to work full-time for a year while I'm on maternity leave?" Good question. There was now a degree of balance in my life, and I didn't know whether it would be too much if I worked full-time.

It would mean a lot more responsibility. Seven papers a week that went out to all the communities in the Northwest Territories. One was translated into Inuit. I would be expected to work Sunday and Monday, which would affect all statutory holiday weekends with the family. After-school sitters would have to be found for the girls. It was overwhelming. In a pinch I could bring the girls in to work. Most of the employees on the editorial side were single parents, and I had seen their children at one point or another. Popping out to do a pickup wouldn't be an issue. I did enjoy the creative energy and the camaraderie on the floor. In the back of my mind I realized that, if I really hated it, I could quit.

We had a family discussion to see how the girls felt about daycare. Mike would need to do more around the house, including being involved with the girl's activities on the weekend, which he had avoided up to this point. Everyone said they would help out. The babysitters fell into place, and within weeks I started full-time. This position was more of a supervisory role and would include a lot more meetings, special supplements, some editing and writing. Years ago when I worked in Edmonton I had put together a company newsletter. It became so popular that within a month all sites were asking for additional copies. Perhaps somehow that had prepared me for this.

Spending a few hours a week with people is entirely different from spending full days with the same people. Within minutes the guy across from me, Kenny was driving me insane! There was something about him I found very annoying. Oh my God—he reminded me of Peter!

How could I have missed this? I hadn't thought about Peter in years, and now it was like he was sitting across from me—the same mannerisms, the tone of his voice, his walk; it all brought back horrific memories. Was this what was next on my agenda? Was I to work through all the resentments and regrets connected to that relationship? Was I ready to work through my hate, frustration, and shame? I wasn't ready, and I only knew that because every time Kenny talked to me or I needed to talk to him, or when he was even doing nothing, it annoyed me. How do you let go of so much?

God apparently didn't think I had enough on my plate.

Mike and I hadn't had date night for what felt like forever. He suggested we check out a new restaurant in town. It was during dessert that more memories slapped me in the face.

"Tracy! How are you? It's been so long. What have you been up to?"

It was one of the accomplices of my rapist. He had also been a good friend at one time, and now I wished him dead. What nerve does it take to come and talk to me with my husband sitting across from me? I hadn't told Mike who was involved, but how did he know that or want to take a chance of getting punched in the face?

So many memories came flooding back; my body was reacting to his presence. I wanted to vomit.

I don't recall the conversation. One-sided, no doubt, as he always enjoyed talking about himself.

All right, God, just keep piling it on! Hadn't I just gotten over something of a nervous breakdown?

After I'd worked full-time for barely a month, my mother surprised me—Jane and me, actually—with a trip to Mexico. She was taking us to Puerto Vallarta, for two weeks if we were available. Mike was furious, full of jealousy and wanting to go. But he wasn't invited. And if he went, who would watch the girls?

I could not remember the last time I had traveled alone. A long time. I was terrified. All these trust issues were arising. With memories surfacing about Peter and the rape, could I be trusted? Would my commitment to Mike be jeopardized? I had never been unfaithful, but then I had never had the opportunity. Without accountability, would I fall back into my old slutty ways? Is that really how I saw myself? Or were those just old rumors taking hold in my mind? All these new thoughts brought with them a huge amount of fear. But not enough fear to stay home.

Getting off a plane in a tropical location is heaven on earth. The feeling of the heat and humidity enclosed me, the smell of the ocean; it felt like home. It's intoxicating for my soul.

Our resort wasn't huge but had all the amenities we needed and was located next to the marina. The walking trails, the pool and pool bar, the restaurant, were all great. The massage therapists were fabulous. But I felt like crap! Since the first night after dinner my stomach hadn't allowed me to digest anything properly. My bowels were erupting. Hanging around the pool wasn't too bad. Leaving the resort on a day trip was terrifying.

I hadn't had an extended bout as serious as this since college; maybe that hadn't even been this serious. There were stories I heard about people going on vacation and getting sick because they relaxed. I had also heard people say they didn't take vacations because they felt they always got sick. Shouldn't you be doing something in your life to relax so you don't get sick on vacation? Hadn't I been relatively relaxed before I left? Yeah, not really.

God, I meant it to be sarcasm! I remembered my recent words, "All right, God, just keep piling it on!" Who would take that comment literally? Note to self; no more sarcasm.

What was going on? I blamed it on the chicken from the first night. If I was truthful with myself, however, it was more about the two guys my sister invited over to our table. The situation made me nervous. I was scared to have a few drinks or have fun in case I didn't behave myself. I feared losing control. Have you heard the term "scared shitless"? That seemed to be my life currently.

The more I worried, the worse it got. Would I be okay on the plane? Would there be a lineup for the bathroom? If there was, what would I do? Mum and Jane were staying a week longer than I was, which meant I needed to make it to the airport on my own. Would I be okay? Would I make my connection in Calgary? What if there wasn't food? Would I starve? What if I missed my plane, what if I lost my ticket, what if …

Devising my own personal terror was one thing, but the metaphysical terror in our room was something else. Mum had booked us a junior suite. I pulled the short straw, which meant sleeping on the pullout sofa. A little after two in the morning something dark and scary kept waking me. Time after time, just as I would doze off, it would pull me out of my sleep. It didn't feel like a very nice entity. Normally it was Mum and Jane who saw and felt stuff, not me. They just thought I was full of crap. Which I wasn't, pun intended.

The third morning my sister came running out of the shower wrapped in her towel with her screams directed at me, "What have you brought into this room? There was a guy in there with a sickle trying to kill me!"

"I've done nothing! I told you there is stuff here! It's been waking me up every night."

"Your fear is drawing them to us. Stop it!" She stomped back to the bathroom. Stop it. Was she serious? "If I could get rid of the fear, don't you think I would?" I yelled back at her.

Things didn't improve digestively on the way home or for the month following. It got worse. I finally made an appointment with my doctor to see whether I had picked up a parasite. She ran the usual tests, but nothing came back. My cousin had a parasite, and he ended up in the hospital because he had lost too much weight. That wasn't my problem. I was gaining weight and losing energy. By the end of the work day, it took all I had to feed and bathe the girls. They were living off processed chicken or fish strips and French fries. I would microwave frozen peas or corn and call it a meal. I was appalled with myself for not being able to produce something more nutritional for them. By eight o'clock they were in bed, and I was minutes behind them. I assumed I was letting go of a lot of old stuff, but it sure wasn't a pretty process.

I was still dragging my butt in March when my mother suggested I see a Chinese doctor. He did a strange massage on my stomach area and told me, "Take these pills. They will help strengthen your kidneys." They helped, but it took months to regain my energy totally. Little by little I could stay awake a bit longer. My constitution was much the same. More memories surfaced each day that I saw Peter's look-alike at work. Hadn't all the conversations with Luke when I returned home from college taken care of all the pain Peter had inflicted? What else was left to heal? How many times did I need to go through this? Enough already! I've been married for nearly ten years. Shouldn't I be over this?

At the end of March, Mike came home and told me he was invited to interview for a new job in Townsville, Australia. Here we go again: Edmonton, thirty-nine months; Republic, Washington, twenty-six months; Walnut Creek, sixteen months; Brasil, eighteen months, now—fourteen months! I suppose it was time.

I was a little confused as to why God wanted us to buy a house and then would make us sell it only eight months later to move. After a few minutes I thought it didn't matter, Australia would be pretty cool. But with the state I was in, could I manage another move? We organized the look-see around Easter when my mother planned to visit anyway. She would just end up spending more one-on-one time with her granddaughters while Mike and I were abroad.

Yellowknifers were still fully enjoying winter activities, snowmobiling, skiing, snowshoeing, and tobogganing. Australia was headed into its fall, but it felt like the middle of summer to us. A person could really enjoy the beauty of the country if you weren't overly concerned with jellyfish, bugs, spiders, and snakes! How do people survive on a daily basis with all these threats? Although the Aussies must wonder how we live with bears, cougars, and wolverines. It always comes down to perspective, doesn't it?

We toured Townsville, and I was even invited to fly to the mine site. The landscape was very different and situated next to the ocean, which was a dream come true, but I kept hearing this voice in my head saying, "If you move here, you'll never leave." That was a little disconcerting. But so was the comment that had just escaped my mouth to one of Mike's potential coworkers: "Even if we don't take the job, it really doesn't matter. Mike will be back." Where did that come from, and what did it mean?

The twenty-nine hours of flight and connection time gave us a lot of time to discuss the possibility of moving. The job wasn't exactly what Mike was looking for. I was not pumped up enough to make another transition. My health just could not support it. Our decision surprised me, both in that Mike didn't jump at the opportunity and in that I was picking Yellowknife over the Gold Coast. Did a part of me know it was necessary to do more healing in Yellowknife before the next move? If it had been conscious, I would have made an effort to move. What was to come was most unbearable.

I was gaining appreciation for my family, friends, home, and work. There wasn't a language barrier issue to deal with. Although there was some confusion; I found myself using too many terms from other countries and only realized it when someone looked at me oddly. Then there was the grocery store mishap. Four months after arriving, I realized I was reading the French writing on all the grocery products, not the English. One day I caught myself spinning the can around looking for the Portuguese; French happened to be close enough. I felt a little foolish.

I'm a little different, and that is okay. I hear voices and currently the voices were telling me to have a party before it was too late. *Pardon me? You want me to have a party? Hey, and too late for what?*

The last thing I wanted to do was organize a party. It was exhausting even to think about. But the voice had never steered me wrong yet. I was learning to listen without understanding why. And I had found out that it wouldn't go away unless I did what it asked. It was probably time to pay back all the invitations we had accepted.

My party was a flop. Everyone I invited showed up, but it just felt very awkward. I don't think anyone had fun. Great—something else to be embarrassed about. Well, there was no point hanging on to it. That was my perception, but in truth it couldn't have been too bad, since everyone was reciprocating.

By the end of August my constitution was pretty much back to normal. The fatigue was still hanging on but was way better; I could now stand to make a proper meal. Whatever needed to work its way out of my system had done so. Previously, I had no idea that detoxification could be so intense.

Kenny from work wasn't bothering me nearly as much. In fact we had a couple conversations that were enlightening for both of us. I found out that he was renting a small apartment and paying nearly what we did on our mortgage every month. I told him so and suggested he buy a condo or something. He did. I enjoyed helping him.

His helping me was equally awakening, but more painful. He had been talking directly to his photo assistant, when I made a comment about how it affected me. His reply was, "You know, Tracy, not everything is about you." This comment was shocking. Could this be true, that not everything was about me? For some bizarre reason, at the age of thirty-five, I had thought it was. Not on the same level as when I was twenty-one. I had been living with the feelings that the world was against me. It was not true; it was me against me. Enlightenment is an amazing gift.

CHAPTER 11

Integration

VERY FEW WORLD TRAGEDIES HAVE taken place during my lifetime—worldwide ones, that is. I was at home the day Elvis Presley died. I spent the day comforting my girlfriend who couldn't stop crying. I skipped summer figure-skating school and was glued to the television the day Princess Diana married Prince Charles. And was delivering papers when I found out that Princess Di had passed. Biographies are one of my favorite programs, and I can't get enough of anything historical. I used to contemplate what it would have been like living when King Henry VIII lived, or when Elizabeth Taylor was at the height of her career. How did their lives influence the people around them and society as a whole? That train of thought eventually brought me around to realize that I was currently living history. When history is your present, it really doesn't seem like anything special.

Then 9/11 happened. For the first time I felt like this was a very important part of history. I can't put it into words, but it was just surreal. Even in Yellowknife. Distancewise we are closer to the magnetic North Pole than Vancouver. We are Canadian, not American, but every person

I knew was affected I found it so unexpected in our little corner of the world.

Mike was in Toronto on a course. He was grounded, like everyone else around the world, and couldn't take a plane or train or rent a car. His instructor lost her husband. The stories that came into the newsroom from our community were amazing, never mind what was going on thirty-four hundred miles away in New York City. The television was never turned off. We watched and listened to the destruction and felt the devastation connected to it each and every day.

When I closed my eyes at night, I could see a room full of twenty individuals waiting to be rescued. I listened intently each day to hear the glorious news of them being found. After a week I knew I wasn't seeing real images. It was their spirits that were trapped; they were all dead. Their spirits would need to pass over in order to be put to rest. My sister had started this process a few years earlier when family members or friends would show up in her kitchen. It sounded easy.

"Tell them to turn right, then into the light," Jane explained.

In my mind's eye I made a doorway opening on the right side of a hallway. The light glowed through the opening and into the hall. The Biggest problem was that this room of people didn't know they had passed. A discussion needed to take place to explain what had happened. Not everyone wanted to go into the light; not all were ready. I put in a waiting area off to the left side. Once everything was set up, more souls showed up to cross over. This made the process easier for both of us, as I couldn't always be there to assist them. Most people might not realize that I was doing anything, but I knew that this was helping not only the dead, but their family and friends.

This wasn't the first time I had seen images with no connection to me. In April of 2000 I dreamed about Elian Gonzalez. He was the little boy who arrived in Florida on an inner tube from Cuba. I had seen in my dream the entire process of his being retrieved from his uncle's home by a woman and taken to the hospital and given to a female doctor. The next morning while ironing I listened to the footage on television stunned that it was identical.

The same year, at Mike's company Christmas party, the most difficult situation happened. This one I never spoke about to anyone. Mike introduced me to a lovely young couple who were expecting their first child, practically any day. We chatted for a bit and then drifted toward another group of people. As we left, the voice in my head said in a sing-song tone, "Her baby's going to die, her baby's going to die." I nearly spilled my drink!

"What?"

"Her baby is going to die," the same sing-song voice repeated.

In an urgent manner I started asking within my mind, "Do you want me to tell her? How am I going to tell her? What if none of this is true?"

"You are not meant to tell her."

"Then why are you telling me this?" Frustration and impatience filled my being.

"You're just supposed to know."

"What? Why?"

"You need to remember this."

All evening, every time I saw her, the words would taunt me, and there was nothing I could do. I could tell her, but that seemed ludicrous. What would I tell her? "Your baby is going to die"? It seemed a little cruel. Everything inside me churned. I couldn't eat, but I could drink. So that's what I did. I got so drunk that I was puking in the toilet before midnight. Not a memory of that incident existed in my brain by morning.

Her baby had died in the womb. She found out between Christmas and New Year's. It was March before I remembered the voice, remembered the message. During a meditation I asked, "God, Jesus, spirit guides, angels, whoever is listening: Why? Why did I need to know about her baby? There was nothing I could do. Why is it always death or tragedy that I have premonitions of?"

The reply was not what I expected: "If it wasn't death, then you would think the premonitions were a coincidence."

The voice had a point. Who pays attention when you know who is on the other end of the phone? It is just a cool thing that sometimes happens. Not! It is your intuition working. I needed to start using it more, somehow. I trusted the voice.

On my way home from work, I would ask which route was the quickest: do I turn left or right? Sometimes I wouldn't listen and would take the other route and get stuck in traffic because of an accident or some other issue. I taught my children to talk to their "angels." I didn't want them to be scared like I was when the voice started talking to them, and the word *angel* seemed less intimidating than the voice or an explanation about guides. I felt the voice was one of my guides, although occasionally I thought it might be God directly.

Brett was now seven and Taylor four. We started with simple things like getting them to find missing toys. Then we moved on to listening for answers regarding decisions about gifts for their friend's birthday. They could pick even a popular toy if the answer from their angels told them their friend didn't have one. They never bought a duplicate. It was easy for them; they were so open to listening.

One of the benefits of working at the paper was proofing the paper before it went to press. I knew what was happening in town before anyone else did. The other was that proofing took a significant amount of time, and close relationships grew because of it. That is how Maddie and I became friends. Eventually our conversations ventured into the metaphysical. She was curious about using white light, so I explained it to her. We used it to clear her aura, then to clear our work space.

I had been using white light to clear my energetic body by wrapping it around my body in a circular motion three times. I would do sections at a time—feet to knees, knees to hips, hips to armpits, then armpits to the top of my head. Next I would wrap the light from head to toe, three times. It made my body feel lighter, and occasionally I would get a bit of a head rush. I did my home as well, clearing away all the dark spots. My vision was getting so good I could now see clear or dark areas in my body and in my house. Occasionally I would clear the girls and Mike—well, Mike until he yelled at me one day from the other room, "What are you doing to me now?" He was becoming so sensitive.

Typically, Maddie and I were the last to leave the newsroom at night so we could play with white light by clearing the darkness out. The first time it took several tries to accomplish—big job! There were lots of black spots; actually the entire room was more of a thick smoky color. The next day we sat back and observed. Everyone's behavior had changed. Not that it lasted for long; by noon they were back to normal, rushing, yelling, and swearing. The room would become so corrupt with negative energy that there wasn't much more you could do but clear it all over again.

Maddie was a very good friend with the Arts and Leisure editor, who was always invited to or getting tickets for different functions in and around town. There was a function coming up on the weekend that she wasn't able to attend and asked whether I would like the tickets. The workshop had popped out at me when I had proofread the paper because it was about Forgiveness, one of my mantras. The two tickets were for an intro to the workshop on Friday night. The actual workshop was Saturday and Sunday.

I had no idea there was this kind of strange stuff going on. It was similar to meditation, as the Breathwork put me in a zone, but we were given a topic to heal and were to use the Breathwork techniques to go through the process of healing. It was fascinating enough that I signed up for the weekend.

It was the third weekend in October, and the workshop was led by a wife and husband team. She had written a book about her own experience with the afterlife. She had died in a car accident and, because she was doing such good work here on Earth, was asked if she would like to continue that work. The concept fascinated me. I had never heard before about us signing a contract before birth in regards to what we needed to get done here on Earth or the people we signed on to accomplish that with. I knew there was some sort of soul family, just didn't know it was so organized. If there were certain key points in our life when it was necessary to complete certain tasks, that would explain the huge pull I was currently experiencing about finding my purpose. It was close, I knew it, but not visible yet. It sure felt like time was running out, which made me anxious.

There was lots of information to review first, more of a counseling nature, and all to do with forgiving. Then we were given tips on how to proceed, depending on what information came up for each of us during the meditation. Afterward, it was time to learn how to breathe.

It was not normal breathing. There were techniques to learn, as it was meant to take you to an alternate state. You start by breathing through your mouth like sucking on a straw. After breathing in completely, down to your toes, if possible, you release all your breath with a sigh. This Breathwork technique was developed by Leonard Orr. Metaphorically you are bringing life into your body on your inhalation and releasing what you no longer need on your exhalation. I thought the concept was very intriguing. Each person was to concentrate on his or her breathing and not allow a pause on the transition of In to Out, or Out to In. The breath is meant to be continuous and should take a count of five or six for each inhalation and exhalation. The In breath represents what you allow yourself to have in life, where the Out is about what you are giving away. Balance is needed in all things. You can find the balance by counting your inhalation compared to your exhalation. I didn't only give away all my breath, I then held it for three counts before breathing in again. I was seriously out of balance!

That shouldn't have been a surprise, but it was. What in my life was mine? What did I do for myself? True, things had improved, but it really had been about Mike and the girls for the last ten years. Even our vacations were representations of what everyone else wanted to do. My doing, of course! Always trying to please others! Nothing in Disney World was for me, except to see the excitement on my family's faces. Helping Mike make choices about his career, making a home for Mike and the girls, and making sure the girls were growing up well rounded. It had always been about organizing my time to improve their lives.

Within ten minutes I was in a deep meditative state. Diane set an intention of forgiveness, which would look different for each of us. This work was amazing! Each one of us in the workshop seemed to take turns with our emotional, mental, spiritual, and physical releases. When I reached the emotional and mental release in regards to regret and forgiveness surrounding my mother, father, and sister, no one else in the room was at that point. They were still at the internalizing process stage or well past it. Just as I was ending, someone else was ready to release, and Diane was off to assist them. Both days presented the same way, one person after another, but never two at a time until all eighteen of us were complete. It was an amazing dance with flawless timing. God had to be involved in this process for it to have been in such perfect harmony.

The releases I experienced over the weekend were quite similar in nature. I would see a family member—my mother, father, or sister. All of whom I didn't feel loved me, though the twist was that they did love me. It was not in the way I wanted to be loved, but there was love there; it had gotten all confused. During the breathing process I was taken to a place where I could feel their love for me and see what events had led to the confusing relationship we now had. Our perceptions were skewed, and because of other circumstances, events were misinterpreted. I went through this process with each of them and finally with my husband.

There was so much love under all the confusion. Afterward it was hard not to get caught up in the regret of everything we had lost, including time, because of the confusion, because we didn't have the skills to communicate, or fear had stopped us from trying to communicate. The reality is that sometimes we don't want to know the answer in case it hurts. I spent days afterward thinking about all this and releasing the pain, fear, and regret of the past and how it had hurt all of us. I also found it very hard to accept that I was loved. Within my own family I had always felt like the eternal step-daughter/sister. The truth was starting to emerge.

As each session ended, I would send forgiveness to my family members as well as offering forgiveness to myself. That part was more difficult than all the rest put together. As I verbally said the words aloud, "I forgive myself," huge, uncontrollable, racking sobs released from my body as I sat slumped in my chair. Afterward I was completely drained, but there was such lightness at the same time. Why had I been so hard on myself? Why was it easier to forgive others, but I never thought I deserved to be forgiven? Nothing had been my fault; it had just been.

The image I had of my parents was a fantasy. Typically I was upset with them because they weren't behaving the way I wanted them to, conforming to the image of a mother and father that I had developed in my mind. The question then became, could I love my parents knowing all their faults?

Their faults made up a portion of who they were. To love them meant loving them and their faults as they loved me and my faults. That was unconditional love, and I could love them unconditionally.

So many things changed in my life that weekend. The biggest thing of all was that I felt like I had broken loose of the restraints that had me in a little box. Those restrictions were self-imposed. I had set those limitations within my own mind; there was no common sense to them, they were unrealistic. They were unnecessary in the world I currently lived in. Conditioning had made me believe that I needed to act a certain way as a child, teenager, unmarried woman, married woman, mother, stay-at-home mother, working mother, and wife. Throw in the behavior necessary to be a daughter to my parents and in-laws, and a sister. I had so many rules, and all were different, depending on the relationship. My friends were the only people with whom I was more of my true self.

The time I had spent in Brasil had started this process of unraveling. The limitations to my rules had become difficult to live with, and when I asked for help, the answer had come through a spiritual healing. I now was at a loss. The old rules didn't hold up any longer, but I didn't have new rules in place and wasn't sure how to move forward. I felt so much freedom in my mind. There were no urgencies about "need to's" and "don'ts."

There were a lot of thoughts in my head, but they kept coming back to, *What will make me happy, and what do integrity and honor look like to me?*

Mike picked me up at the workshop an hour before it ended on

Sunday. We had a charity function to attend. I had purchased a long-sleeved silky maroon T for the occasion, something my mother would never have allowed me to wear as a child, "Because it will clash with your hair!" I forgave her for that; she didn't know how great I looked in red!

During the party an acquaintance came over and told me that my aura was amazing and then he asked, "What have you been up to?"

It was one of the nicest things anyone had ever said to me. It came from the most unlikely character. I found it was the perfect ending to my weekend. No more judgment. Everyone has their own stuff, and judgment will only cause confused perceptions.

There had been an issue earlier during the day that had me quite worked up. In class, while sitting in a circle and sharing, one woman mentioned that if she saw any of us outside of class she would ignore us. She didn't want to explain to any of her friends where she had met us or discuss the workshop. Her comment made me frustrated, and my whole body started to shake. "I'm sorry I can't accept that! I've been working really hard at accepting who I am and my gifts. It hasn't been easy, as most people don't understand me, which has made me scared to share. But after this weekend I have accepted who I am and will share what I know with others and will not hide it because of fear!"

This was another level of acceptance. The whole mirroring effect: if I didn't judge others, others wouldn't judge me, and if they did, so what? My relationships needed to be about full acceptance, have integrity. There was this need inside of me to share information; I could no longer hold back.

Judging myself had gotten me nowhere. How I considered a "mother" was to act had made me uncomfortable about having sex with my husband. Some of those rules came from how I had wanted my parents to behave when I was growing up. The majority of the guilt came from my own behavior in regards to my sexual relationships during my premarriage years. I had never given a sexual relationship the respect it deserved. I could see that I had sex to feel close to another person. I used sex to find out whether someone else "liked" me. The truth of the matter is, men will have sex with anyone. They don't need to like you. What a huge revelation!

My husband did love me, yet I was locked into some "rule" I had made up about motherhood and not having sex. What if the girls walked in? When did that fear start? As I sat there in that emotion, I could connect to it and the repeat experience when they were little. Once the romance of lovemaking started, a child would wake up, something would happen, things would come to an end. A new conditioning had taken place, now I stopped us before we got started. How that would be removed was still unknown, but we would have to make an effort.

If I had taken a look years earlier, I could have moved on from this place sooner. Again, judgment was tainting my view. I had never been a priority, and the experience of sitting with my emotions—well, it was very new. Healing truly was a great gift.

Mike and I returned from our night out, and I talked to him about what had happened to me over the weekend. He seemed truly to understand. He was so much further ahead than I was with this healing thing, or perhaps he had little to regret. It was great to have someone in my life who understood. That night we had the most amazing sex ever.

My God, I was starting to feel more like my old self! I was having fun again, laughing more. There was a freedom in my mind. I no longer thought about my indiscretions, and if I did I would let it go and forgive myself and whoever was involved. I wanted to live!

I wanted to bond with my husband in a number of ways. I wanted to spend more time with my children. So I organized it. I started saying no to a lot of commitments that I had felt obligated to say yes to before. I no longer felt I "had" to be part of the board at the playschool or at the elementary school. I felt fine telling the figure-skating club, "No, sorry, I can't help out." And there wasn't any guilt over these decisions because I knew what was a healthy choice for me. My inhalations and exhalations were becoming more equal—not quite there, but getting close.

Telling people "no" was powerful and became easier each time. I had always overcommitted myself and then would spend hours trying to figure out how I was going to pull it all off, which I always did, but with too much stress.

With all the extra time now available, I built snowmen with my children, or we went sledding. Mike and I bought a snowmobile and enjoyed going out with other couples. We attended different functions at the Arts and Cultural Centre, and I was excited about organizing dinner parties. I was having fun. The regret that cropped up was from when the girls were little, and I never seemed to have time for them. "Sorry, Mummy has to do the laundry or vacuuming or dishes." I let the regrets go and decided now that those chores could wait so we could spend more time together as a family.

This caused stress for Mike. He had come from an overly tidy home, and that was one thing he had really loved about me—my anal housecleaning—because I also came from an overly tidy home. To lessen his stress, but allow me to have freedom, the girls and I would clean house like crazy on Thursday before he got home. This of course caused me more stress. Balance was so hard to find.

I loved myself a little bit more each day. Memories of being a nice person drifted to the surface, comments from friends: "What you said changed my life!"

At the end of November I was invited to attend another workshop. This one was on shamanic healing. I had no idea what it was or what to expect, but what I did know was that it would involve more self-healing and I was all in for that. There was a woman in Yellowknife who was currently doing her training and part of that training included a workshop with a certified shaman. To fulfill that requirement, she arranged for someone to come from Calgary to offer this two-day workshop.

On Saturday morning, with my huge, foamy mattress under one arm and my sleeping bag under the other, I walked one kilometer down the street to attend the workshop. Mike was unimpressed. "Do you really need to take another workshop? How much is this one going to cost us?"

The comment surprised me. It didn't have to do with being away for the weekend, which was always my concern, but about money. There was always money for retirement or the children's education fund, and we'd had a sizable down payment for the house. Our bills were paid on time. I was getting better about taking control over my additive spending habits, but the savings account never increased as much as I would like it to. There was this habitual dance Mike and I constantly performed regarding money. It always gave me pause, as he didn't even know how much he made or the amount of our mortgage or bills. Because I always complained that there wasn't enough, he had come to question me about there not being enough.

Would it make things tight before Christmas? Maybe, but I was going. I needed to do this for me, and I wasn't backing down like I normally did. Giving up or giving in regarding something I wanted. If something needed to be given up, it wouldn't be by me this time. The money would come from somewhere. Lately I felt that if I invested in myself, the money would return tenfold. I hoped that was true.

Our cat, Kramer, demonstrated that issue perfectly on the Saturday night of my workshop. After the kids were tucked into their beds, I decided to take a nice, long, hot bath and meditate on a question that had arisen during the day. I had found that talking to my guides in water was so much more powerful.

I was enjoying the peace and quiet when Mike opened the bathroom door and asked, "Kramer is sitting outside here. Do you mind if he comes in?" Kramer loved baths—not personally, but watching.

"Yes," I said.

Mike's reply was, "What?"

"Fine, okay, whatever, let him in." As Kramer came to greet me on the ledge of the spa tub, I had to laugh. There I was again, not letting others know what I really wanted. I thanked Kramer and then called Mike to take him out.

Kramer was one of my spirit animals, and it didn't surprise me. Every night since the girls were little, he would sit outside their bedrooms and look from one room to the other as though he were deciding who needed him most. He always knew.

Saturday we had journeyed with our spirit animals. I was walking down a path when I came across a small rise in the ground. When I looked down, I realized there was a hole. I was told to crawl into this brown hole. It was like being in one of the tubes on a waterslide, turning and looping, and swirling around. Finally I came out the bottom. We were told that once we looked around we would encounter our power animals. The first animal I saw was a mama bear. She looked scary, and I wasn't sure why I was seeing her. Then I saw her cub and watched the relationship between the two of them. It was warm and gentle, not what I expected from a bear. It made me realize that I didn't need to be so strong and firm with my children. I could hug them and feel that love and compassion. As I walked along, I was introduced to a variety of animals, one transforming into the next. There was some type of cat, perhaps a panther. As it jumped, it transformed into a hawk, and I was flying. Up in the sky is the only place you can really see everything; it was such a new perspective. As the hawk dove into the river I became a salmon, swimming upstream. It was difficult, but never once did I consider giving up; it was necessary for all of us salmon to get where we were going. There were many more transformations, but some were so swift that it was hard to gain an understanding before I changed again.

During the journey meditation I would get an impression of what each of them meant, their strengths and weakness. With that, the realization arose that weakness was not a negative thing; for all things to be in balance, both sides are necessary.

Sunday we learned how to release soul-parts. We started the day, again, with a group prayer. We had done the same thing at the previous workshop, and I still didn't find it very comfortable. Nor was the chanting or closing prayer. The sharing was voluntary, and at least it was interesting. All of it was necessary, I guess. I would do it and learn to gain comfort in these situations if it meant more self-healing.

The discussion led into the taking of other people's soul-parts. How, in wanting something that someone else had, and if they were in a place of weakness or vulnerability, they could let go of a part of their soul. Was this stuff real? If it was, it was pretty freaky!

We were guided on a journey to find out whose parts we might have. After we found out, we were then guided to give them back. During my travel I found out that I had taken two soul-parts. One was from my friend Cynthia from high school and the other one was from a childhood friend from Bissett with whom I was no longer in contact. To give back the soul-parts, we didn't necessarily have to tell them about it verbally, but we needed to have the intention to give it back. The childhood friend's soul-part I could return during the meditation. That was easy. For Cynthia, it was necessary for me to call and try to explain. Then I was to blow into the phone with the intention of releasing the soul-part back to her. That would complete the transaction.

Cynthia's soul-part was in my head as a snapshot of her with her head back, laughing. I remembered the moment clearly. We had been out at a small gathering, her and her boyfriend, me and some guy, sitting across from each other. I remember her being so natural, laughing without holding back anything and wishing, intently wishing, I could be like that. Had I taken her laughter or the innocence behind the laughter?

Even during my time out of the country we had stayed connected, although our relationship had become more of a struggle since I had become engaged. Not a struggle in the sense of getting together, but within our conversations with one another. Some were snitty, others just mean, more her toward me, than I to her. I had wondered where it had all come from. It was now clear to me. We kept in contact because we were friends, but also because of the soul issue. At the very least, unconsciously, she was angry with me. I called her that night and returned her soul-part. What was interesting was that a few months later Cynthia found her soul mate. Coincidence? I think not.

As we discussed this transfer in the early afternoon, the topic of age came up. Apparently some parts have a hard time returning because they remembered you as you were when they left. As we continued to talk I became progressively more agitated. By three o'clock when we stopped for a break, I decided to speak with the instructor about my feelings. I was full of anger and was quite positive Peter had taken lots of my soul-parts, and I wanted them back!

With my intention stated so strongly, she asked me to stay after the workshop finished, and she would do a treatment on me. Although I knew this was necessary, I was terrified. What would they do to me? What would happen? Once the room cleared, the two shamans set up a table in the middle of the gymnasium that I was to lie on. I closed my eyes and hoped for the best. They danced around me, shaking their tomahawk things, playing the drums and chanting. I felt nothing, except foolish. When they stopped, I was told that Peter did have pieces of my soul—eleven pieces, to be exact. It was all my good stuff, too! She had also found one other piece from when I was four that she integrated back.

It had been more than fourteen years since I had seen or spoken to Peter, and I was pissed that he was still affecting my life. I was told that he didn't want to give my soul-parts back and that it took some serious negotiating. He would not give them up without something in return. Apparently he was still the selfish jerk he'd always been.

I thanked both of them and was warned that Peter might feel weird and try to contact me, unconsciously needing back what he felt he'd lost. The one good thing about moving around so much was I didn't think he had a clue where I currently was. I walked home with my mattress under one arm and my sleeping bag under the other. It was around six p.m. and pitch-black, except for the streetlights shining overhead. In the glow of the light I could see sparkling snowflakes falling. It was magical. I might have been wearing my long winter parka and Sorel boots, each weighing about five pounds, but I felt lighter and happier than I ever had. I didn't feel like I was living in any part of that dark cloud anymore; light had finally entered and surrounded me. With pure enthusiasm for the first time in my life, I just kept thinking, "What's next?"

I was told that change would come, and I needed to be gentle with myself. Monday morning on my way to work that was perfectly apparent.

I was driving, stuck in morning traffic and feeling extremely anxious. My nervous were on edge, and I was completely confused. I remember being told that some soul-parts have a hard time returning because they stay the age they were when we lost them, and it takes time for them to reintegrate. Most of my soul-parts would be between the ages of fourteen and twenty; this particular one felt about seventeen and hadn't had her license very long!

Feeling no sillier than I had felt over the past month, I decided to talk to my newly acquired soul-parts. I told all of them that we were relaxed while driving and there was nothing to be anxious about.

I made the intention to keep all my parts in case Peter ever contacted me. I had them back, and I wasn't going to fall into a place where I felt sorry or anything else that might jeopardize losing them. I thought I had everything covered. I was getting back on track and felt safe and secure until my sister Jane called a few days later to tell me she was meeting Peter for drinks. I didn't even know they were in contact with one another.

"What? You can't do this!" I continued to explain what had happened over the weekend and that it was important that she not give him any information about me. "And please be careful."

Why did Jane have to do this to me? Just a minute, was it about me? Why was I still so frightened of Peter? He didn't have control over me and couldn't affect me or my family. It was only my thoughts about the situation that were creating problems. I had to trust my sister.

Trust.

Wow. Did I know how? I micromanaged everything because I didn't fully trust anyone. Had I ever? Perhaps trusting myself was the first step.

CHAPTER 12

Slowing Down

THE HOLISTIC HEALING COMMUNITY IN Yellowknife was huge. There were eighteen people at my first workshop, and more than sixty attended the second one. In February I was invited to attend another Breathwork seminar, this time given by Dan Brulé. The introduction was made through Brett's piano teacher, Ardith Dean, another breath practitioner. I never would have guessed she was into this stuff. I reminded myself: no judgment.

Dan had visited the previous summer. I remembered reading an article in the paper about him teaching people to walk on fire, which I thought must have some magical qualities to it. Now I didn't know; nothing seemed voo doo-y, just different. Dan was returning to do a week of workshops. This would not be about walking on fire, but about breathing. I planned to attend Saturday.

Mike was away on business in South Africa, so I needed to find a babysitter. It meant that the weekend would cost me that much more. I'd tried not to think about it or the comments from Mike when he returned home.

Saturday was amazing. Instead of sitting in chairs and doing Breathwork, we were lying down on air mattresses. This time the degree of my healing was very different. I went deeper, and my whole body went numb at different stages during the process. The numbness had me freaking out, but then Dan was there to guide me though my breathing. Breath wasn't entering my chest; it had gotten stuck along the way.

During the lunch break I felt something big was going to happen in the afternoon. I was fidgety and nervous. When I returned after lunch my bedding had been moved, and both Dan and Ardith were lingering nearby. I trusted my intuition enough to recognize that something transforming was about to happen. Knowing this did not help my nerves. I could feel electricity in the air; oh my, what was this all about?

Both of them worked with me for the entire afternoon. I was able to breathe in through the top of my head and down as far as my waist. I know this won't make much sense to a lot of you, as my understanding of it is limited. It definitely had to do with my chakras. Although I balanced them often, this part was on more of the physical plane. The breath was opening my energy centers on an entire different level. There were dark spots, like in my house, and the breath was dissipating that darker, heavier energy from my body. I could feel energy moving within my body. I could breathe out my chakra centers, front and back. It was fascinating.

If you sit as you are and pay attention to your breath, instead of breathing in and out of your nose, try to breathe in through your nose and on the exhalation, push the breath out your crown chakra. You can try each chakra separately. Then try to push that breath energy down and out your feet. You may find that it gets stuck, but if you keep doing this exercise, you will eventually remove "blockages" from your body. You will feel lighter, and your breathing will deepen in your chest and the circulation will increase throughout your entire body.

At Dan's and Ardith's insistence, I returned on Sunday. They did make it sound like it was life or death. Nothing could have prepared me for what transpired.

First everything in my body went numb, which I had become

accustomed to. I was able to breathe out the top of my head and out the tips of my fingers. I was working on breathing past my waist and out my toes. As I was doing this, I was overwhelmed with so much love; the feeling was overpowering! It was the purest feeling you could possible imagine. I so wanted to share it with everyone! To share it, I transformed it into a cloud of pure, white light, then it expanded, getting bigger, eventually filling the room, and then the whole city of Yellowknife was encased in this cloud of love. It continued to expand to enclose the entire world. It was so vast and so pure, it brought tears to my eyes. The sheer essence of it was overwhelming.

It was so beautiful, explaining it could never do it justice. I basked in the wonder of it and then it changed into pure rage. I became the white light that engulfed the Earth. I felt like God. I was huge in size, encompassing the Earth with my arms out as I looked downward. The anger kept growing in magnitude, expanding out to incorporate the entire universe. It felt like I had given nothing but love to the world, and the humans had twisted it into something ugly. The world had turned to evil and no one could feel the love I shared with them any longer. The question in my mind became, *Why has this happened?*

The rage became stronger, to the point where I literally started beating the floor with my hands and feet because of its intensity. I wanted to scream and let everyone know the pain I felt, the pain God felt. Then, as fast as it had arrived, it departed, leaving a deep sadness in its place.

The sadness came from the anger and confusion of the world. There were feelings of hurt and misgiving for all human beings. It had me in deep, gut-wrenching sobs that were no longer controllable. I continued crying for a long time until there weren't any tears left. Then change came again. I started to bear down like I was about to give birth. The need to push was overwhelming! My mind was saying, *This can't possibly be happening to me! What is going on?* Another part of me decided to let go of the ego and do what needed to be done.

I had given natural birth to two beautiful little girls. Without that experience, I would not have had a clue. I went through the entire process of delivery. I felt the pain, had the urge to bear down, felt the delivery of something, than knew the placenta was right behind. It was the strangest experience of my life.

I was exhausted and shaking, much like in natural delivery, but I was also content. I had heard of people being reborn, but never did I imagine the process to look like that!

I was ready to begin another chapter of my life. I was ready to move forward. I was ready to trust the process.

I asked Dan what it all meant. "Don't think so much about it; just enjoy life as it comes." He pulled an Osho Zen tarot card for me. It was a picture of a turtle. "You need to slow down." Then he tossed the card toward me.

I looked at him in confusion. Hadn't I already done that?

Realization came a week later when Maddie and I were walking through the grocery store. I was picking up a few things for Brett's birthday party. Maddie was going to help me with the party until Mike returned home later that night from South Africa. There would be eight little eight-year-old girls.

Maddie had a few of her own things to purchase. We headed off in our separate directions, coming back together minutes later. She had her basket over her arm and was sauntering along as she always did, looking like she hadn't a care in the world. I was walking beside her with my basket, but seemed to be taking three steps for each of hers! True, she was taller than me, with longer legs, but not to that degree! It probably looked like I was running along beside her. I was the hamster on its wheel, running like mad and not any further ahead. No wonder I was always tired. Had I been doing this my entire life? Running like mad and getting nowhere fast?

I didn't think so. When I had been on one of the walks with my Mother's Club in Walnut Creek a dad—yes, occasionally we had dads— told me that I walked with purpose. I had questioned him about what that meant, exactly. He told me that I walked like I had somewhere to go. My question to him was, "Doesn't everyone?" He told me, "No." Hearing that was a surprise. Maddie didn't walk like she had somewhere to go. I was walking like I had too many places to go; Know the saying "Hurry up and wait?"

I started to pay attention. The feeling was more like impatience, and it was a common occurrence, even when I was driving. Everything was on a deadline. Being on time meant being ten minutes early. My body and mind push one ahead of the other. If I wasn't going fast, I would get emotionally overwhelmed that I'd be late. This action was not getting me anywhere faster; it was just causing a disruption to my emotional state! But with conscious awareness, change can take place. I decided to change my behavior: I walked with longer strides, drove in a calmer state. The exercise was like a mantra. I had fewer issues with road rage, there were more green lights, fewer careless drivers, and I traveled from A to B effortlessly! Think "turtle."

As I relaxed more and more with all things in my life, I began to realize that my place of work was very unhealthy—toxic, even. Maddie and I had tried to clear the yelling, screaming, swearing, and fighting away countless times with white light, to no avail. But one does get used to any situation over time. I had become complacent, but now I realized that this noxious environment was affecting my turtle state. I couldn't continue to relax and improve my life outside of work if I had to deal with this chaos every day. Maddie had recently moved to Edmonton. I hated working holidays. I missed my children too much because of this full-time position. I couldn't attend their school activities during the day or pick them up after school. I wanted to spend time with them. The previous summer my in-laws had visited for three weeks to watch the girls while I worked. It was lovely of them, but too much to expect every summer. I wanted to be included in more of the girls' lives. Maybe balance does not come every day, but from year to year?

Mike had received a significant promotion, and we were doing much better financially. By allowing myself to heal, giving myself the time necessary to do the work, it felt like the Universe was now rewarding us, rewarding me to continue this work by finding better balance. I wanted to quit and gain some additional balance in my home life. I knew it was healthier mentally, emotionally, and physically, but my ego kept interrupting my intuition process, saying, "What about the money?"

During the summer I worked to pay for daycare or day camp. That realization was all I needed to make my decision. My sister was also getting married, and I was having problems getting the time off. My redheaded temper flared up as my mind kept repeating, "Really? Try to stop me!" I wasn't going to miss my sister's wedding.

Mike and I talked, and we decided it was feasible. I would take six months off, April until October, then look for work. I handed in my resignation with glee. My boss had a difficult time with it, "You keep thinking that your life is more important than work, Tracy. Your priorities are backward." No, no they weren't. The Brasilian mentality of work to live seemed like a healthier choice. Now I just needed to find the job that would give me all of it.

Woohoo! I was unemployed and going to spend time with my kids, my husband, and my friends. Life was going to be great!

The best-laid plans have a way of changing. And change was something of which I was starting to take note. Over the last several months, I couldn't manage to keep my coffee from spilling. It happened at the workshops, in the car, at friend's houses, everywhere I went. I knew I was being told something, but what? I used to have a terrible caffeine addiction when the children were little. If I didn't get a mocha on vacation, all hell would break loose! It got so bad, I started traveling with my own espresso maker. When we moved to Yellowknife I had cut myself down to one a day and removed the chocolate, making them into vanilla lattes. Did I need to cut out the caffeine? I couldn't drink regular coffee without getting sick, but that wasn't happening. Maybe decaf would make the universe happy.

Oh my God! Extreme pain, for four days: caffeine withdrawal! How could caffeine be good for you if it hurt this much to stop drinking it? What I found out after the first week was I felt more awake all day long without caffeine. Interesting.

If accidentally I was given a shot of caffeinated coffee, instantly I felt supertense, anxious, and agitated. I wanted to scream because everything aggravated me! Quitting caffeine had taken my life down a notch; there was fewer high highs and low lows. Amazing.

My life had been in a transitional phase ever since moving to Yellowknife. But now there was time and money to reorganize my home from top to bottom. We had been in the house almost two years and hadn't done much. For years my mentality had been to paint walls white so they would match everything, and the house would be easier to sell. It didn't look like we would be moving any time soon. It was time to pick out paint colors, starting with the girls' rooms. Then Mike and I would decide on something other than white for the rest of the house.

My life was busy with the house, tea parties, and luncheons. I went to the gym every day and out for coffee afterward. I was available to help in the girls' classrooms, attend field trips, and be more alert during their gymnastics classes. Finally I had energy to do the stuff I wanted. We were eating healthfully again and going for walks or bike rides in the evening.

Intuitive moments would sneak up on me. I was at a luncheon and thankfully, before I blurted out, "How far along are you," I bit my tongue. She hadn't announced her pregnancy yet, so that would have been a major faux pas. And I hadn't really announced my coming out of the psychic closet entirely; I was easing them into it. Several times I had "guessed" the sex of the baby and due dates for various friends. Only I know what it was really confirming.

One night a girlfriend brought over a few other friends for me to read their cards. There were five of us, and three of the readings had gone rather well. The fourth woman didn't want to share her question. She held it in her mind, and I shuffled and went to deal. Then I shuffled again and went to deal. The third time I stopped, looking over at her, and asked, "Do you keep changing your question?"

"Yes, I'm not sure exactly how to word it."

We sorted her question out and then I was able to deal.

With my weekends free, I was able to attend Brett's gymnastics competition in the neighboring community of Hay River. This sent my nerves on edge. Brett would be staying with her teammates and coaches at a local school gymnasium. I opted for a night in a hotel, hoping this night alone would at the very least reduce my fear around infidelity. It was tightly connected to trust. Last time, on my Mexican vacation, I had made myself violently ill, or it had at least triggered my illness or cleansing, which lasted months. I couldn't imagine cheating on my husband, but I needed to know that.

A lot of this was coming up again because a friend from school in The Pas had recently moved to Yellowknife. Karen and Peter had dated briefly before Peter and I had dated. But because she was gorgeous, with that Farrah Fawcett hair, had loads of confidence, and had actually been capable of dumping Peter for cheating on her, I had disliked her immensely. Emotions get so confusing as a teenager. I now accepted the truth and was impressed by her abilities and confidence. We were now very different people and, well, Peter was not a part of the equation, at least not in regards to our relationship with each other. But her presence had brought back so much insecurity that still needed to be healed or released from my body. Infidelity and trust were only part of the issue.

Spending the night on my own was enough to release my fear. Having my own space for twelve hours was a pleasure I hadn't experienced, ever, or at least for what felt like forever. I had a long bath and read a book. Why had I made this into such a huge deal?

Perhaps this wasn't about Peter at all, but about Mike? Was I falling out of love with him again? Possibly. Now he was caught up with this new promotion and had not put forth any great effort to improve our relationship. He seemed distracted or disinterested.

Summer was here, and it was wonderful, except for the rash that showed up at one o'clock every afternoon across my arms and chest. Occasionally it would travel down the front of my legs. The sun seemed to make it worse, and I had no clue what was causing it. It needed to go away, with my sister's wedding taking place outdoors. I didn't want to be spotted for the photos!

I went for allergy testing, and the results offered no explanations. My next choice was to stop eating and drinking, all things, and slowly introduce items back into my diet. I tried a couple of sessions of BodyTalk, which is a holistic healing technique, I didn't get the results I wanted. I didn't completely understand it, but it was supposed to get parts of the body talking to each other in order to allow healing to occur—in this case, my rash to disappear; that was my expectation. My body must be trying to tell me something else. This was turning into the summer of "no fun!" Thank God the rash wasn't itchy. But boy, it was annoying. At least my doctor had offered me a backup plan for Jane's wedding. If the rash appeared, I could take cortisone pills to clear it up. It was not the answer I was looking for; I wanted to get to the root of the cause, not just medicate it away. It was like the doctor who wanted me to medicate Brett with Ritalin. Weren't answers forthcoming regarding her behavior issues? The problem had been resolved rather than covering it up?

Mike took pleasure in my plight. Being a big Seinfeld fan, he compared my "Summer of Tracy" to the "Summer of George" and laughed.

The umbrella and I became very good friends, as I did with long-sleeved shirts and hats. Staying covered up from the sun seemed to help, some.

Mid-August we packed the car for the fifteen-hour drive to Edmonton to attend my sister's wedding. Mike and I would be celebrating our eleventh wedding anniversary the day after her wedding. I was fearful that we would be dealing with the same weather during our wedding, plus thirty-five Celsius! That would be my worst nightmare. The lack of food in my system seemed to have alleviated the problem, for now. It had been days since my rash had erupted.

The sixteenth was overcast and it lightly showered on and off. Not a day the bride wanted, but it was a perfect day for me. No set time was made for the vows—sometime around 1:00, she had said. People had been arriving in my mother's backyard since noon. The tent was set up, and all the chairs were in place. The guests were indulging themselves with a glass or two of champagne.

I looked at Jane and told her to start walking out the door at 1:23. As she stepped out, the rain stopped, and the sky opened up—lovely, blue sky! The service was beautiful, and the weather cooperated. The pictures were done, the caterer served the food, and the reception was in sight. Relief washed over me. I could now have some fun. Except, of course, that as the matron of honor I needed to give a toast to the bride. Can anyone say "stage fright?" Before the age of sixteen I never had a problem standing or speaking in public. I could read in front of the class and play the lead in the school play, but now I could barely stand in front of my family and give the toast. Jane told me not to worry, but what else was there to do? I had been worried since she asked in April. There was some relief in May when, during my morning shower, I finally found the right words. My problem was that I kept reliving an incident from seventh grade. I had done fine until the punch line, then nothing; I forgot it completely. I shouldn't have said, *God, don't let me forget*, rather, *God, help me remember!* Words are powerful, and I was just starting to understand how precise we need to be with them.

There was a longstanding joke about my sister that started at my wedding. Her boyfriend at the time had asked her to marry him. Her reply was, "If you're around in ten years, I'll marry you." After she broke up with him, we were concerned that we'd have to wait ten years with one individual before she married. The kicker was, it was the very last day of the ten years since that comment, and now she was getting married.

My legs were shaking as they had at my own wedding. My voice was squeakier than usual, and there was a little hesitation at the punch line, but I managed to pull it off.

There are moments when we have insight into our future; it is just a matter of paying attention. These premonitions are about what will happen in the future, not about us making the future happen. That is something else; that's manifestation.

My sister had accidentally encountered Mike's parents at the airport two weeks prior to her wedding. She felt that my father-in-law was ill. This concerned us, so we decided to extend our vacation three days and drive the eight hours through the BC Mountains for a visit. The area where they live is one of the most peaceful and beautiful places on earth. They have twelve acres on a huge lake surrounded by mountains and trees. It always feels truly like a vacation; there aren't any chores, we get to watch the girls run around and have fun, and we're treated to his mother's amazing cooking. But I forgot how hot and humid it could be in August. The rash started before we even arrived. *What did I eat now!*

The rash disappeared during the night, so I ruled out environmental factors, plus this was a different environment, and I didn't think it could be something in the air. By three o'clock the next afternoon my entire body was covered, including the spaces between my toes. Staying indoors was as hot as being outside, so I found no relief. It had gotten to the point where it was starting to itch. It was time to take a pill, but then I stopped and started thinking about what I had eaten over the last day.

Lattes had been one of the first things to go over the last few weeks, because coffee had been the culprit several times during my life. What I hadn't considered was dairy. I had been consuming ice cream every day with the girls at the beach. The tea parties and dinner parties always had dips made with sour cream or cream cheese. There was always a bean dip loaded with cheese. Actually, most foods seemed to contain some dairy. My mother-in-law covered her salads with whipped cream; covered her oven-baked perogies in a cream sauce; cheese was laid out for sandwiches at lunch; and cheesecake with fresh strawberries from the garden had been dessert!

I had consumed more dairy in the last twenty-four hours than over the past month! God didn't need to give me any more messages. The answer to my plight was obvious. Of course, hindsight is always twenty-twenty. All the answers had been there; I had just ignored them. It was after that second latte of the day that my body's tolerance level evaporated, and the rash would occur; add in an ice cream, and it got worse. Jane had even given me a milk body wash which she said would help. It had made my rash worse, so I threw it away. No light bulbs there.

Dairy hadn't even shown up as an intolerance on my allergy testing.

But people said that many intolerances didn't. Removing dairy from my diet was extremely difficult, and it made me angry. Eventually I was able to narrow it to whey, specifically. Whey is found in everything, including most breads and margarines. It was also used to coat my allergy pills; it's what makes things shiny! My diet changed significantly, which didn't improve my mood. No milk, cheese, yogurt, no cereal because of the milk, no toast because of the margarine. No Kraft Dinner—a quick, fast, easy meal.

I was angry with God. Why didn't he use his voice and tell me, "It's dairy!" That, on top of everything else, left me frustrated and annoyed. It was impossible to go out and eat, not only in public, but also at other people's homes. No cream sauces meant no more yummy pasta. No tzaziki sauce, lasagna, pizza, or cheese and crackers! Cheese is prevalent in our society. I didn't want to question everything my host was serving, but was there milk in the gravy? I was now finding it in foods outside my radar.

I started drinking decaf lattes with soy milk and learned to like them. It was my only vice. I did manage to lose seven pounds, which was the upside, if I was looking for one. It took a long time to come to terms with my loss. People may think it is easy, but changing your diet for any health reason is still a process and not always an easy one. Grieving became part of my process.

Eventually the universe told me why this had happened. It was all about greed.

"Greed?" I asked, not understanding at all.

"If there was a cup of milk left in the fridge, you hoarded it for your coffee. If there was only one piece of dessert or a chocolate bar, you hid it or ate it before someone else noticed."

I'm embarrassed to say, but it was all true. I had become greedy. I always felt bad about hoarding or taking the last bit of something. Releasing greed was another part of finding balance. I would do what I needed to; I wasn't about to go through another large lesson like that again. Healing seemed easy, but not understanding the universe's messages was frustrating. I needed to get in touch with more of my senses to understand more quickly, if there was to be a next time.

The dairy thing took up quite a bit of my time. Okay, being angry about the dairy allergy took up a lot of time. After two months it was time to move past it. It was time to find a job. I was looking for something part-time that would be fun. Then the paper had an advertisement for a job at the local photography shop. That would be fun. I had a keen interest in photography and wanted desperately to learn more. I had started taking a course through the New York Institute of Photography and was really enjoying what little I had learned.

I knew the manager from high school. She and I hadn't talked a lot, but were more than acquaintances. I received a call two days later for an interview. Yeah, I was going to learn more about photography. As it turned out, that was not the position I was being interviewed for, again. The current bookkeeper was leaving. They were offering me a part-time bookkeeping position. When they told me, I just laughed. The first year in Yellowknife I had sent out tons of résumés for an accounting position and never heard a word. I had gotten past the fact that I would never work in the field again, and here I was being offered something I had never even applied for. *God, I don't understand!*

I didn't "need" a job, so the choice was mine. If I didn't like it, I could quit. After a bit of discussion, it was decided that I would work two days doing bookkeeping and two days in the front learning about sales. I'm not a salesperson. I even hate bartering. This would be challenging, but they dangled the opportunity to learn how to develop print copy down the road.

It was the Christmas season and selling came easily. Most people knew what they wanted. I also loved doing the bookkeeping. How I had missed working with numbers, figuring things out, making the columns balance, and doing month-end reconciliation. Even calling people about their outstanding account receivables wasn't tedious.

By February life was in a really nice groove. There were a few issues with my girls, but time and discipline had sorted things out. I was still meditating every morning directly after my shower. I wasn't using a mantra, but rather listening to the voice in my head, which kept me centered throughout the day. My mood had improved noticeably, and I found that I now walked with my head up and smiled at the people passing by. Not many people had their heads raised when they walked; the ones who did, smiled back at me. It was like we shared a secret.

One particular sunny morning while the air still had a nip to it, I was crossing the main downtown intersection to work when my head boomed with a new voice: "No matter what happens today, you will not quit your job!"

What?

"You will not quit your job today!"

Okay! I replied within my mind, with a bit of agitation.

Stranger things had happened, so I never gave it a second thought. I arrived at work, turned on the lights, and set up the till for the day. Everything was in place to open the store. At noon I would put on my bookkeeping hat and work until two. The owner, a large man, made even larger in such a small shop, arrived at work in one of his "moods." I had seen him like this several times before, seething at the seams and then he would have a temper tantrum that would have put a two-year-old to shame. This morning his rage was aimed at me.

It started over an outstanding account that I was handling. He became unrealistically upset that it wasn't paid and started cursing and swearing at me and about the clerk in charge of paying the so-called account. He called her names that I will not repeat and that were not necessary. Losing his temper was one thing. I had seen this all before with my father and had dealt with verbal abuse from Peter, but what really got me was the fact that my husband worked for the company he was attacking. Although I wasn't, I could easily have been friends or acquaintances with the clerk in question. That is what really upset me about the inconsiderate, rude, arrogant ass!

It always surprises me what I will put up with and what tips the scale. He ranted all the way into the back of the store, where he began to throw things—the fax machine, the telephone, probably a stapler. I stood in stunned silence at the front of the store, seconds away from walking out the door, when I was reminded, "No matter what happens today, you will not quit your job!"

Under my breath escaped an exasperated "You have got to be joking!"

The manager came over to me. I could see the shame and apprehension in her eyes. "Are you going to quit?"

Resigned that I was not going to, all I could say was, "Apparently not today."

I wasn't given a reason for staying, and I never asked because I had begun to trust the voice in my head. The Universal plan for me was bigger than I could ever have understood, but evidently my purpose in life was not to be a photographer. There had been too many roadblocks. In October, when I had come to terms with that, I had wondered, "Why am I working here, then?" After experiencing the first outburst, I thought it was to help my boss heal from whatever trauma he was holding inside. After this most recent blowup, it occurred to me that perhaps I was just attracted to unhealthy workplaces.

Peter had never physically abused me, but he was extremely good at mental abuse. It was harder to recognize and seemed more difficult to heal from. Was this work environment all about me not running away and instead recognizing what was healthy and what wasn't? But I had done that at the newspaper. There had to be another reason.

I had changed my situation multiple times, improving my life each time whether it had to do with employment or my relationships. I was now living life with fortitude and an awareness like never before. Previously I had made life happen and now it was time to decide what I wanted in a job, what was the next stepping stone until my true purpose presented itself. I didn't want to sit next to the bathroom, that was for sure! I wanted to be sitting next to a window with fluid sunshine embracing my work space. So, I started imagining a window next to my desk and the bathroom far away. I saw and felt sunshine, and it was glorious! Some might think it was daydreaming, but I learned it was all about manifesting.

A few weeks later there was an advertisement in the newspaper looking for a part-time accountant at a travel agency. Perfect! My résumé was already prepped, so I added a cover letter, walked it over, and dropped it off. An interview was set up a few days later. A real interview. I was very nervous. I hadn't had a real interview in years, and not one that would actually ask me accounting questions. My friends suggested I wear my glasses instead of my contact lenses, dress in slacks, and make myself look more professional. Did I look so unprofessional? All their advice was just making me more nervous!

The interview took a little more than an hour, which I thought was a good thing. But I have a tendency to overthink things after the fact. She asked a lot of questions about various scenarios that could happen during the workday. The one glitch was that they were looking for a full-time employee for the first six months; then the job would become part-time.

The next few days were torturous; my mind wouldn't stop its assaults on my inadequacies! Wondering whether I had said the wrong thing, or perhaps was too personable, or perhaps not personable enough? Finally the call came, and I was offered the position. A family meeting was necessary so we could all consider this option. Could everyone handle me working full-time again, and this time through the summer? More helping hands at home would be necessary. After-school care would have to be found for Brett and Taylor, who were now going into grades four and two. As a family unit, we all agreed we would work together to help Mum out where necessary.

Mike and I had finished painting the entire house during the winter months. Brett had picked purple, and Taylor had picked blue for her room. The rest of the house was called Lamb's Wool. The earth tones were grounding, soothing, and surprisingly, blended incredibly well with all our furnishings. I hadn't decided on a color for three walls in the kitchen or the one wall that traveled around the corner into the dining area. Nothing seemed to match the oak cabinets. Every room had been reorganized, and the clutter had been removed. With all that work complete, taking on a full-time job didn't feel overwhelming. What they paid was adequate, the job seemed interesting, and it would include free travel to Edmonton, which was a bonus! I—so proud of myself—negotiated a week off in June to visit my new niece or nephew, as Jane was expecting.

My desk was next to a large, south-facing window. The bathrooms were far away. I was very happy.

CHAPTER 13

Experiencing

WHEN I LEFT THE HOUSE, everything ran effortlessly. I did what I needed to do and got where I needed to go. Occasionally, I was given a gift—directed to the perfect pair of shoes on sale or I bumped into an old friend to catch up. Working through a lot of my stuff had brought a real calmness to my life. But when I walked through the door at home, I had no control. It was difficult to live in these two worlds, which were so different. I meditated to bring them together, to blend them, to make them easier to manage.

Be careful what you ask for. *Hadn't I been?*

In the fall Brett asked me if we could start attending church. I believe that attending a Catholic school and knowing that all her classmates attended church every week were the factors that made her present the question. She hated to miss out on anything. My reply was, "Sure, we can attend church."

I had experienced God's miracles many times, not only in my personal life, but through requests. Last summer he had responded to my request for help when trying to set up a gazebo on my own and wasn't quite tall enough. "God, help me!" A breeze moved in and lifted the tent, which allowed me to move the pole into its correct place. "Thank you, God!"

During my meditations I was having strange visions about the crucifixion of Christ, and I thought I might be him. The visions were so exact; the details of the ground, the buildings, clothing, all of it seemed so real. I knew I was not Jesus Christ, but it seemed then that all of us must be made up of parts of him. This thought seemed to hit home and felt more real. Then I started questioning the statement "He died on the cross to save all our lives." What did that mean? My need to find the answer to this question was persistent. I didn't remember any discussion around it in Sunday school. I knew the answer was somewhere in my soul ... then one day, out of nowhere, I was on the cross, I was being crucified; my belief in what I was doing was so strong. I was dying for what I believed in. There was no fear, only peace. My story was meant to help people around the world, but over time it was used to cause wars. It was supposed to be about releasing fear and opening our hearts to love. Trusting.

This entire vision and the emotions attached to it only took seconds to allow my soul to resonate an understanding. There was more information that I accepted at an unconscious level that I have no memory or understanding of, but a sense of peace hit me like nothing else had before.

So when Sunday came, the girls and I attended worship at the United Church of Canada. Mike wasn't brought up in any religion. I'm not sure whether he entirely believes in God, although he believes in something. We had married in the United Church and had the girls baptized; he was supportive of that. He was even supportive of us attending, but he would not join us. He said it made him feel like a fraud.

Spirit did not encase me in this house of God. The service was not inspirational. After the service I went to retrieve the girls from their classroom, and I asked whether there were any forms that needed to be filled out. Their teacher's response was, "You're coming back?"

What a strange thing to say. I could not contain the look of surprise on my face. The first thought floating through my mind was, *Apparently not.*

The following Sunday we attended the Church of Christ, which was just around the corner from home. It was a better fit for the girls, who knew children from school. They had also attended Bible camp over the last two summers at this church. I hadn't considered it as a first choice because I was United. Such a difference! This church was friendly, upbeat, and very welcoming. Within a month we felt like we had always attended. Spirit was here. The pastor was an amazing speaker, and I found useful information in every sermon. All of it was so pertinent to my current evolution. I had been wondering why God had picked me to talk to during my meditations and spontaneously during the day. Many of the sermons discussed how regular people had been chosen to do God's work. I was a regular person. Was I being called to do God's work?

We were having so much fun and started staying for coffee and tea afterward. It was so many years since I had last attended church; I was surprised at how comfortable I was. I had only sporadically attended after the age of thirteen. We had never attended once we moved to Yellowknife in 1982. In Edmonton and Republic I had only started to attend to get the girls baptized. I had checked out a few churches in Walnut Creek, but they, too, lacked spirit.

Then the church made an announcement about a six-week class to learn more about the church and God. I felt that I had gotten to know God pretty well, but it would be nice to amalgamate my spiritual studies with religious ones. There were eight of us from the congregation being directed by two church leaders. We met every Tuesday at a different person's home and would bring potluck. Afterward we would discuss various subjects. I found it very informative and could easily ask anything I was unsure of. I was assimilating religion and spirituality nicely. When we met in church, I felt a closer connection to God. I'd never experienced that in any other church. I was invited to the baptism of one of our group members, and it was a holy experience. I wanted to jump in myself!

Our fourth meeting was phenomenal! We talked about people

speaking in tongues. I had never heard of this before and found it fascinating. We moved on to how God has a plan for each of us, and in his own way he will speak to us. I decided to mention that he was already speaking to me, that I heard his voice in my head. Everyone stared at me, jaws dropped, except for one. He told me and the rest of the group that he also heard God speaking to him.

"Really?" I asked. No one else I had ever spoken to had experienced this—not even my meditation teacher. I was intrigued and excited not to be the only one hearing voices. I had accepted all my other gifts after reflecting on James Redfield's novel *Celestine Prophecy*. He hadn't heard voices but had been guided by bright lights or gut instinct.

I couldn't wait until our fifth meeting. That excitement was quickly put aside. This meeting was different; it was more about business, and we were asked to become members of the church. Then the rules were stated. There were two I found ridiculous: "You will not be allowed to read the horoscopes or use tarot cards."

"Why?"

"They don't come from God. They are the work of the devil."

"Doesn't everything come from God?" I asked. I was told no.

Jane had given me a deck of cards for Christmas one year. They weren't formatted like a tarot deck, which I also use periodically, but were called Fairy Cards and were developed by Doreen Virtue. The connection I had with God while using those cards was real. God spoke to me through those cards, because I had asked him to! I used them in the morning. "What do I need to be aware of today?" I would ask as I shuffled them, then taking one card to see what I should work on. If I was worried about money, I might get the card "Financial Flow," and this would help me remember not to worry. Some of the other cards that appeared were, Honoring Your True Feeling, New Opportunity, Self-Reliance, Rise above Problems, Laughter, and Family Harmony. Each one had something personal to say to me, improving myself and my day. At night I would pull a card asking, "What did I learn today?"

Perhaps I relied on the cards too much, but the inspiration that came from those cards had gotten me through some really tough days over the past two years. How could that be bad or considered the devil's work? How could they not come from God?

I didn't return to class after that. I asked the girls whether they wanted to continue going to church. It didn't matter to Taylor, and Brett said she'd rather spend Sunday with her daddy.

Spirituality and religion couldn't amalgamate, not here, anyway.

I finished painting my kitchen and dining room. There was this amazing color that had popped out at me called Sangria. It leaned toward a vibrant orange/red in the dimmer light and a brilliant orange when the light shone in. For two weeks I was home painting while the girls were visiting their grandparents and Mike was working at the mine. The space couldn't have turned out any better. It looked amazing!

Now, with the top three floors complete, with new paint and free of clutter, I moved to the basement. The storage area in the basement had never been touched—added to, yes, but not organized. With the purchase of the house, we inherited half a dozen solid wooden upright lockers. For me to start this project, they needed to be moved so I could make better use of the space. The first two I managed, with great difficulty. The third one came back on my left ring finger, and the blood started gushing. My first reaction was to go to the hospital to get stitches. But I had gotten a piece of wood from the baseboard stuck under one of my nails, and there was nothing to do but remove it naturally. If they couldn't freeze me, I wasn't going through the pain of stitches.

This left me with plan B—wrapping it and applying pressure to stop the bleeding. As I sat there, I started contemplating, *What was I thinking about when this happened? Is there a connection to my thoughts and injuries? I was letting my mind run wild, agitated about something.* I had been mulling over my marriage and how much more work did I want to put into it. That was all I ever seemed to be doing, trying to get my marriage back on track with little to no help from my husband, who was always consumed by his work.

Thinking about this new concept—the connection between my mind and my injured finger—had me drifting back to the last time I had stitches while I was attending school in Winnipeg. What had I been thinking about that time? How to move past my relationship with Peter. When I was hit by that car while crossing the street at the age of eighteen, I was cursing Peter for all his inadequacies.

While vacuuming, and if my mind was running rampant with negative thoughts, I usually broke something, dented the baseboard, or occasionally injured one of my toes. There was definitely a connection between what was going on in my mind and these occurrences. Each time I was upset when the injury happened, but what else did I need to learn about this connection? Was there a connection between organizing my house and organizing my life? Did the color I'd used on the walls have meaning, too?

Why were we going to buy a red car? What did that mean? I had seen a vision of us in another Ford Explorer, but this one was red. The vehicle felt different. I told Mike I was pretty sure it had a third row of seats. "I'm not buying an Expedition!" he said.

"It's not an Expedition!"

"I'm not buying a red car!"

"Too bad we are going to buy a red car."

He negotiated with me that if I painted the kitchen Sangria, we wouldn't buy a red car. "Sure," I said. It was a win/win for me, as I knew we were going to buy a red vehicle. Some things couldn't be changed.

All summer Mike looked at cars—white, blue, black—but there was always something it didn't have that we wanted. Then the call came to me at work, "Our vehicle's here."

"What do you mean?"

"There is a red Ford Explorer with a third row and everything else we wanted. I'll pick you up after work, and we'll take it for a test drive." It didn't surprise me that we bought it that night. My kitchen was already painted, so win-win!

I still wasn't sure what to do about my relationship with Mike. We were doing all the things a married couple does—buy a car, fix the house, have dinner parties with friends—but we as a couple had lost that connection. Every Thursday evening after the girls were in bed we sat up and talked, well mostly he talked. That wasn't truly us connecting.

He was a good man, ambitious, provided well for us, and was a wonderful dad. But sometimes he could be so anal about things that it made living together near impossible. It became very challenging to have people over, especially friends for the girls. Mess and noise drove him nuts. Sleepovers, forget it! "But they're kids!" I would say.

When I was growing up, there had been people coming and going to and from the house all the time. I was used to it. Mike's household had been quiet. Very few people intruded on their home life. So I realized where this came from, but wasn't it time to let it go?

I preferred having the toys and activities at my house with the neighborhood kids over, rather than having my children at someone else's house, where I didn't know what they were up to. Not everyone had my values or kept an eye on the children. None of that made sense to Mike. I had worked really hard on letting go of the "small stuff"; I even read the book. I had trimmed down the list about what I needed to get on the kids about and what I could let go. As I became healthier, there was a realization that letting go of some of the extra work and relaxing about it was liberating. Everything wasn't as important as my mind had always told me, or as I had been conditioned by my family. Going to the beach on a sunny day was much more rewarding.

When Mike was at work I would see how many days I would go without cleaning up the house. I could go three days without washing dishes before I would cave. It was the reverse of anal, but the exercise allowed me to find better balance. There was fear attached to having a messy house. My mother's voice floated in my mind: "You don't want people to think you live this way!" And Mike was no better, hollering about a sock or toy left out of place, a cup not put away on the counter. He seemed to be getting worse with age. I was tired of it. Before he came home from work, I was a mess, screaming and yelling at the girls to clean up their mess. "Your dad is on his way home, let's go!" We couldn't find a middle ground, so I wasn't sure what I was going to do. Our house wasn't just a showpiece; it was meant to be a home.

His reply always was, "I'm not living in a pig pen!"

A pig pen, are you serious? No one in their right mind would consider our home a pig pen. Then, when I asked him what was wrong, he would tell me that the windows were dirty or there were items in the laundry room not put away. Someone's perspective was totally askew!

He was becoming too much work. I was tired of carrying the load. For over three years I had pretty much been the sole parent taking care of and organizing both the girls' lives. It was me who had to deal with any issues at school and attend the parent-teacher interviews. I signed the girls up for their activities and made sure they got to them. I organized the playdates and sleepovers. I organized our lives as a couple; never once did Mike come home and suggest an outing, dinner, a movie—not even a walk around the block. It was too much.

He was great at taking orders, but I was tired of years of doing that! I wanted a partner. I wanted him to relax. I wanted him to be happy, happy to help out, happy to share, happy to participate in this family. Right now he seemed to be an outside entity.

I needed to see a psychic. Nothing to do with Mike and me—even with all my frustration I knew our relationship would work itself out as it had numerous times before—but the universe, my guides, kept telling me, "You need to start writing a book."

"Me, are you joking?" I failed twelfth-grade English the first time around. Not by much, but really, me write? The second time around I had an awesome teacher who inspired me to the point that I enjoyed writing. But, really? This is what I needed to ask the psychic. Maybe the voice was having fun with me; perhaps it really wasn't my guide. Maybe they had tied up my guide and were giving me false messages. It could happen!

Mike and I drove to Edmonton to retrieve the girls after their month of visiting various sets of grandparents during summer vacation. I called my mother and asked her to book me an appointment. The psychic told me I was going to write a book. I stared at her in disbelief. "What am I going to write a book about?" She just looked at me and then pulled out a book with lists of publishers in it. So, she couldn't or wouldn't give me all the answers.

Before leaving I had come to terms with the idea. The universe had guided me thus far; I supposed it would let me know what the book was about. As I was on my way out the door, she yelled, "Oh, and you and your husband are going to go through a rough patch, but you'll get through it in the end."

My mind was preoccupied, and I was barely listening. "Mike and I? I'm not worried about us. We'll be fine. Thanks!"

We returned home, and life continued. My job was monotonous, but I had won a trip for two to anywhere in the world and had started planning where Mike and I would go. My choice was Greece. I had wanted to get married there, but my father had kaboshed the idea, wanting a huge wedding where the entire family was present. Not really realistic, as in November it would be cold. We discussed Fiji! But it just took too long to get there; we would lose four days to travel. Finally we settled on Mexico. I couldn't wait, but Mike just kept repeating to everyone, "I'll never survive spending a week alone with Tracy."

We arrived in Cancún the last week of November, without Mike's luggage. I told him it was because he was in a rotten mood. That of course didn't help his mood. I had been playing with the concept for the last few months, and there was a definite connection between mood and how events played out around you. If you wanted to feel rotten, your day would be rotten. If you found your smile, your day would improve.

A lot of these new ideas transformed after reading Dr. Wayne Dyer's book *There's a Spiritual Solution to Every Problem*. He talked about how everything has a frequency, and if you place yourself in the company of higher frequency, you would pull yourself up and into the realm of more happiness. Placing yourself in a lower-frequency environment would keep your mind cluttered and your life a mess. That is what I took away from it, in conjunction with all the work I had been doing on myself. I had let some friends go because they dragged me down. I definitely felt

TRACY MAKARENKO

it! I felt the difference when I was out of my house and flowing with the energy of the universe, compared to when I was at home having to blend and meld into the roles of mum, wife, and housekeeper.

If Mike never smiled, he would have a horrible vacation. He cheered up slightly when he found out there was a market where he could buy the necessities until his luggage arrived. The rest of our vacation continued much on the same note. The thought of writing was still on my mind, so I had brought a pad of paper to see what would develop. I was pretty sure it was about the healing journey I was going through, and giving insight and sharing my experience to allow others to move in the same direction. Thirty pages was a good start. Mike spent his time drinking margaritas and doing Sudoku. The drinking got worse after we returned home.

Something was up, and I would have to have been an idiot not to notice. He had made a comment after returning from his parents' home when he dropped off the girls during the summer: "I missed you. I didn't think I would." I never replied to it as it had left me rather stunned. I knew he was working through something and waited for him to talk. But that conversation never took place.

More often than not, when he was home he would stay up late listening to music, drinking. Occasionally I'd find him puking in the bathroom at three in the morning. A week before we got married, I had asked him whether he was sure he wanted to marry me. I thought it took a lot of courage to bring up the discussion. It was about checking in to make sure we were still on the same page. We had been back a few weeks, and I now needed that courage more than ever to ask, "Mike, do you want a divorce?"

Shock played across his face. "No."

"Are you sure? What's going on?"

"Nothing, I'm fine." End of conversation. The dryer bell went off, so I wandered upstairs to complete the laundry.

December brought transition within my company. Our owner was retiring and had sold his company to the competitor. My position would change. Good. What it would be I did not know. Interviews were

198

performed and people assigned. I would be working from nine until three. Perfect. I could get to the gym before the girls got home from school. I would be responsible for the account receivables. There were now four of us in the back room. There was a window, but it faced the main office. The bathroom was not as far away. Hmm.

To amalgamate the new and old employees, the owner flew us all to Edmonton for an all-expenses paid Christmas party. So nice! Mike was furious that he could not attend.

The few days away gave me time to reflect on the year—actually, the last few years. Life was really good. My dairy allergy was under control. My gym routine was firmly in place, my house had been painted, we had purchased a new vehicle, my new job was currently challenging, my family was healthy including my father-in-law who had made it through chemo brilliantly. I had a lot to be thankful for. I had just returned from Mexico and was now in Edmonton for a wild and crazy girls Christmas party!

Everything was so much better than last year. Well, of course, except my marriage, but that seemed somehow minor. Something had changed in me. I no longer wondered about our future. I knew we would be together forever.

Life was a gift, and I seemed to have figured out a whole chunk of it. We had so many reasons to celebrate. All of Mike's family had come for Christmas, and I couldn't have been in a happier place. I felt good about myself. It was deeper than that … somewhere inside I had fallen in love—with me. Love emitted from me to everyone, including my girls and Mike. This realization came out of nowhere mid-December.

Mike seemed confused by my sudden joyfulness. I hoped it was contagious; he needed to find his happy place, love for himself. Instead, he booked himself to work at camp over New Year's Eve. What was going on? I only hoped that a few days alone at camp would help heal whatever plagued his mind because I was starting my Happy Ever After!

What Now?

CHAPTER 14

Patience

"YOU HAVE GOT TO BE joking! What now?" were the silent words being spoken to my guides, angels, God, and anyone else who was listening! Personally I felt I'd done all my work and thought I had gotten to the "Happy Ever After" portion of my life.

Well, isn't this ironic?, was the next thing I thought when my husband came home from working New Year's, sat me down on the sofa, and told me, "I don't love you anymore."

I actually laughed, out loud, at the irony of the situation. I had found love, not only for myself but for him, and now this? What could be funnier? He looked at me like I had lost my mind. It was still too new for me. I found it amusing. Is this what the Universe had been preparing me for? Hadn't I done enough work? Had I asked for this somehow? When I asked for more serenity, was this the beginning of it?

I looked intently into Mike's eyes. "I just went through this. It isn't that you don't love me. You just can't feel that love right now. It's locked away. You need to find love for yourself. Then you'll feel love for me." I said this as I placed my hand over his heart.

"I feel nothing for you. I haven't for a long time." This hurt a little, but I trudged ahead. The truth was he didn't feel love for anyone—not his children, his parents, or his brother. He'd had no reaction to his father's cancer, or his brother's recent issues.

"Are you moving out?" I held my breath as I waited for his answer

"No."

"Where are you planning to sleep?"

"In our bed," he said with a straight face, which added to my confusion.

"Okay. So you want to try and figure this out?"

"Do you think we can?"

"Yes, I do." We continued sitting on the sofa and talked late into the night.

It really did hurt, but it wasn't like there hadn't been clues to what was coming. I had just let them slide while I was working on my stuff. A part of me believed he still had me placed on a pedestal, but that no longer seemed to be the case. At least now I knew what was bothering him. There was something to work with, and I was committed for the long haul.

Surprisingly, I was able to sleep through the night. I knew everything was going to be all right. It would, wouldn't it? The next morning after I woke up, I sat beside our bed and meditated, asking, "Will Mike and I get divorced?"

"No."

"Will we separate?"

"Yes." Well, I didn't like that answer.

"But will we divorce?"

"No." That was good enough for me, so off to work I went.

By March I was no longer treading water, but bobbing up and down trying to get air. His stating repeatedly, "I don't love you," had taken its toll. What had me holding on this long was that in February during the middle of the night, Mike reached over and grabbed hold of my thigh. He held it like I was his life preserver, the only thing keeping him afloat. He hung on for hours. I lay perfectly still while he slept.

The counseling wasn't changing anything. We hadn't told anyone outside of our family. Well, I told Jennifer. We had met within the BHP wife realm and formed a connection after Betsy, Kevin, and the kids had left for a two-year stint in Peru the previous year. Mike and I just kept pretending that everything was normal. But then, what is normal?

We were still interacting socially, and when we were out, he followed me around like a zombie. His personality had completely disappeared, and all he would repeatedly say was that he didn't love me or, "This is wrong. We shouldn't be doing this." "What's wrong? All the great sex we've been having?" Which we were and which also confused things! One night after being out at a function, I sent him to the spare room to sleep. He couldn't understand why.

Was this a clinical midlife crisis? Did I need to check him into a psychiatric facility? I was seriously considering it.

Dan Brulé was returning to teach a Level I Breath Practitioners course. It was seven intensive days, and I signed up. I booked time off work, and Mum promised to come and watch the girls for the week. This class was expected to run from eight in the morning until close to midnight. My intention in taking the class wasn't to offer treatments to others, but to help myself heal from the damage Mike was causing to my soul! I was losing patience with him and wasn't sure what I would do next.

The workshop taught me different breathing techniques, how to work with clients, and gain confidence, while assisting others during Dan's evening seminar healing sessions. The entire time, even while working on others, we were releasing our own stuff. One particular day I thought the pain would kill me. It was a full day set aside for each of us in the class to have a private session. The pain during my session was tremendous! And it all had to do with Mike.

That shouldn't have been a surprise, but the reasoning behind it was. I needed to let him go, release the need to control his healing process. What I thought would help was only an illusion. I needed to let him go so he could take control of his life and make the decisions necessary to regain it. The pain was coming from, not wanting to let go, around the fear I felt that if I did, I'd lose him forever. That he would leave me.

I didn't know what I would do if he left! It was the gut-wrenching pain of lost love. My mind knew release was the only answer. Even at a soul level I knew it was necessary in order for us to move forward. My heart just wasn't ready. A big portion was ego. The trophy wife couldn't even hang on to her husband. That had become my nickname among the BHP wives. I had gotten over judging others, but I didn't want to be judged, mostly by myself.

The fear attached to letting go was enormous! The anger about this being the next step in my life was overwhelming. I cried, I yelled, and I pounded the floor during my treatment. Then I cried some more. Finally all the emotions rolled out of me, and I curled up into a ball and sobbed uncontrollably for hours.

The huge release didn't make me feel better afterward, like so many other sessions had. This time I just felt raw, empty, and detached from the world. The work was very similar in nature to the shamanic work I had done. I was holding on to Mike's power, parts of his personality, and needed to give them back to him. There had been an energetic power struggle between us I had not understood consciously until now. I compare it to the Italian mama who does everything for her son, even after he gets married. She never gives the power of information over to him, not even to his wife. When she dies, he's lost. She has died with all his stuff, and he doesn't even know how to fold a pair of socks.

We had caused such damage to one another, not only in this lifetime; I was coming to realize it also came from many lifetimes before when we had been man and wife. Over time we had become one person and now needed to be separated into two beings in order to move forward. Was this necessary in order for me to find my purpose? If you love something, set it free; if it comes back, it is meant to be. The reality of that sentence sucks!

It had been more than two months, and I was tired. I had meditated, read my Fairy cards, did tarot readings, and used my pendulum, and all had said there wouldn't be a divorce. All had mentioned a separation. The sooner that happened, perhaps the sooner this nightmare would be over. The cards said it would be settled by Easter, which was only a month and a half away.

It was time to kick Mike out. I gave him a heads-up on the phone before he came home Thursday. He'd need to find a place to live. I did up a one-page contract listing information about the house, our girls, the finances, and had him sign it. There was nothing legal about it, but it needed to be done to make things real. Mike needed a reality check. After he signed it, all he said was, "I didn't think it would feel like this."

How the hell did he think it would feel? Had he given it any thought? His counselor had said the only way to know whether leaving would make him happy was to do it. Did he really think leaving would make him happy? What was wrong with him? Then I realized I should be happy he was finally feeling something.

We now needed to speak to the girls. We told them we didn't know what was going to happen, but we would continue seeing the counselor. Brett, having just turned ten, understood what was going on and had questions she wanted answered. Taylor, at seven, was beyond devastated. She turned on HGTV, plugged her ears, and stared at the television the entire time, crying and repeating, "This isn't happening, this isn't happening." Reminding myself that all things happen for a reason and that she had signed up to be a part of this family and therefore a part of this experience didn't help me get over the idea that we had just seriously damaged our child, our children.

Mike moved into a hotel until he could find more permanent accommodations. No one was thinking finances; all expense attached to this situation was minimal compared to what was happening to our family. After he left, the girls asked me whether we would be getting divorced. I told them to check with their angels. Brett said, "No! Daddy will be coming home!" Taylor told us her angels had gone on vacation.

I cried all night, then for days, which turned into weeks. I rented *Something's Gotta Give* and felt like Diane Keaton after her breakup with

Jack Nicholson, full of uncontrollable sobs. Mine usually took place in the shower, ending with me curled in a ball on the floor until the water ran cold.

Mike had the girls on Saturday nights. When he dropped them off on Sunday, I would still be sobbing. "I hate seeing you this way. Maybe I shouldn't take the girls overnight," he'd say.

"No! You need to spend time with your children!" As much as it hurt, it was so important that they remain connected.

Easter came and went, and nothing changed. The girls saw their dad once a week, and occasionally we would have him over for Sunday dinner. Things felt awkward. All the songs on the radio talked about breakups; it wasn't encouraging.

My thought process was, "If I have a night off, I should use it!" But I fell way short of actually enjoying myself when I went out. Staying home without the girls in their beds was terribly depressing. I was exhausted, emotionally, mentally, and physically.

I continued healing work with my group of practitioners and one-on-one sessions with Ardith. The week with Dan had been powerful—so much so that I decided to take my certification. Part of that included four sessions with a certified practitioner. The first two sessions allowed me to let go of a lot of little things—brain clutter, mostly. During each session my body's temperature turned to ice! No matter how many blankets Ardith piled on, I couldn't get warm. Old is cold, old being something from early on in this life or from another life.

The third session was with another student. We sat across from one another and did a mirroring exercise. We were to look into each other's eyes. Ardith had placed a mirror facing the two of us. I believe it was to give the space more energy. Initially looking into her eyes I could feel her kind heart, see gentleness in her face. My mind wandered. Could I ever be that loving? She was in the midst of moving and had brought her white cat. It began to wind its way between my legs. It was so pure and full of love, like its owner. It was odd to see something so white, since both my cats were black.

The image of my black cats took me to a dark place that existed many centuries ago. It felt ancient, similar to *The Lord of the Rings*, and I was the evil sorcerer! The image flashed back to a little old lady who lived in a cottage. She, me, was stirring her cauldron, adding a little of this and a little of that. She helped people far and wide, offering healing herbs. I could feel her contentment. Then a transformation occurred! She was no longer a little old granny, but a tall and powerful force to be reckoned with. She, now a he, used this new power for evil and killed thousands of people. With the population of the Earth much less, thousands would be more like millions now. The remorse that poured out of me was tremendous, and a continuous stream of tears began to flow.

Consciously I knew I had been holding back on my healing treatments. I was scared to work on others. I had a fear of having too much power, and I was scared for it to come to the surface. Now I understood why. Then the voice told me, "Everything happens for a reason." *I killed all those people for a reason!* That was even more terrifying to accept.

Everything happens for a reason. I did believe that. Then the most bizarre thought entered my mind. How many times had I heard murderers say, "God made me do it." If we were all here under contract and needed to fulfill a purpose, are murderers fulfilling their purpose? Even knowing all that is in store for them during their lifetime? Evil needs to happen in order for us to offer forgiveness, learn trust, and release judgment. Oh my God, this changed my entire belief system! I was eternally grateful that in this lifetime I was on the other side, healing and not harming.

It took me to another level of understanding with regard to unconditional love.

My grandma expressed unconditional love all the time. She was my role model. At fifteen I had gained a five-year-old step-cousin. The love my grandma offered him surprised me. Of course my only basis for step-anything was through fairy tales. She loved him as she loved me. How could that be? Was it to fill a void he had from being bounced from one parent to the other?

Grandpa's memorial was the first time all of us cousins had been together since our teens. The conversation at one point turned to our grandmother. I told them I was her favorite, because I believed it. They all turned to me and insisted they were her favorite! Even Emily, who was a grand-niece, believed she was the favorite! I was stunned that Grandma could love us so abundantly and equally. Later that weekend some little neighbor kid asked me to move so he could talk to his grandma. I just laughed and said, "Sure." Where did she find all that love and compassion? It was something to stride toward.

Mike had moved from the hotel into a company townhouse, but now he was being asked to find another alternative. It was Father's Day when he asked whether he could move back, but into the spare room. I had great hope that this was the beginning of the end but didn't hold my breath. Easter had been wrong. We discussed it with the girls, hoping they would understand, but I barely understood. I prayed that this situation wouldn't cause permanent damage to their grown-up relationships. Clearly, my parents had affected mine.

That weighed heavily on me. I had done so much work on myself to help improve my children's lives, by releasing fear and finding a happier place within myself. I didn't want them to fall into the same patterns. I had been told that the work of clearing cellular memory from my body and soul would help heal seven generations forward and seven generations back and all those connected. I had done and continued to do the work to help everyone. I just hoped the confusion we had caused our children was minimal. In my heart there was just no other solution. My cards and pendulum told me the girls would be fine. If the girls were damaged, I just hope we could repair it so they didn't take this mess into their own lives and the lives of their children.

Mike and I started sleeping together a couple of weeks later. The first time was like the "first time!" It was electric! It seemed like there was actual voltage flying between us. It was amazing. Afterward there was so much confusion, mostly Mike's. He couldn't understand how I could still love him or even support him in this process.

I did still love him. But it hurt me to see the pain and confusion on his face. I wished there was a way I could help alleviate his pain, but I now understood that this was his journey and his alone to figure out. Later he told me that on the January morning after he had told me he didn't love me, he thought I was going to stab him to death.

"What?"

"Well you were just sitting next to the bed. I thought you were going to stab me."

"I was meditating." This was more confusing than I thought. He shared with me all the nightmares he had where he was covered in blood. He told me that they had started long before Christmas, and he was scared to stay in the house in case we came home and found him dead. The fact that he thought I would be the one to kill him didn't make sense, but there were a lot of disconnected thoughts.

A part of him had been protecting us from what he felt was the inevitable—his bloody death. In my shamanic class the woman I had been partnered with experienced a traumatic death. Birds—ravens I think—taking her body high into the sky and letting her drop out of her skin. It had traumatized her, but it represented a rebirth. Metaphorically, that was what Mike was experiencing. Even the Death card in a tarot deck usually means rebirth, the end of one thing so the beginning of another can take place. This was easy for me to see, but not always as easy for the person living through it. I had dreamed of our house catching on fire, and the dream book said the same thing—rebirth.

Mike had been having a lot of other dreams that had come true. He would dream about meetings at work and would prepare for that meeting because he knew what was coming. His third eye was opening, which was a good thing, but only if you know how to use it, and you don't allow fear to supersede. I had also found that out the hard way.

Now I had something else to work with. But by the end of June he decided to travel to Australia to look for a job transfer. He told me he needed a change. "All the way in Australia," I questioned him. Change has been going on between us for years, you didn't need to go somewhere to find it, just wait a few minutes!

He may have been sleeping in the spare room, but we were attending company functions together. Both his and mine. I didn't know whether Australia meant both of us or only him, and I don't think he knew, either. I didn't ask the cards; I was tired of their answers. Easter? Really?

Perhaps time away would give him the perspective to figure out what he needed in life. His counselor kept telling him he needed to leave, to "find out if you miss them." I had one word to describe her. Mike had left, and he was still no closer to any answer. I knew letting him go was necessary, no matter what our line of credit looked like. In truth, it was only money, and there would always be more of it. We always seemed to have enough when I sat back and thought about it without my emotions getting involved.

I was over the fear of going to the bar and having drinks in case I became slutty. I'd been hit on and wasn't interested. I was committed to my husband through thick and thin. There is always a silver lining if you look for it. There were still only a select few who knew our relationship was in the "complicated" category. I thought. Small towns gossip loudly but only behind your back.

After three weeks of job hunting, Mike returned without an offer. "Tracy, it's time to put the house up for sale. We can't continue like this." He shared this information with me by phone while I was on holiday with the girls at my sister's home in southern Alberta.

"You don't think we can resolve this." Selling the house in my mind meant that we were done, our marriage was over.

"Even if I don't find a job in Australia, we need this situation to change."

His statement tore my heart to bits once more. I knew the reality of the situation, but everything I was hearing from my guides and my mother's voodoo friends all said the same thing. Mike needs time away, he is really confused, "and it seems he's doing this for you."

"Doing this for me? Are you joking?" No one saw us getting a divorce. Maybe we would be one of those couples that stay married but didn't live together. That would be so sad. *Fine, I'll live with him needing time away.* It wasn't like I could stop him.

For me it was now about acceptance. I wasn't ready for the next step, but sometimes there isn't a choice. Timing is what it is, and so I talked to Brett and Taylor: "Daddy wants to get a job in Australia, so that means we will be moving. Not with him, but on our own. How do you feel about moving here, nearer to Auntie?"

"When will we see Daddy?" Taylor asked with tears in her eyes.

"I don't know, honey."

"When would we move?" Brett asked.

"I'm not sure, honey. We have to sell the house first. Maybe October or early November."

"Where would we go to school?" Taylor asked.

"There's a school down the road from Auntie. Maybe there, if we found a house nearby." Silence took over as we all contemplated our own thoughts. My job and friends were in Yellowknife, but my heart wasn't there if my husband wasn't there. Moving wasn't an issue for me; I was moving.

When we got home after the September long weekend, I put on a strong face and decluttered the house for its impending sale. It was ironic how the past year—the painting and organizing—now seemed to be about preparing the house to be sold. I was hemming and hawing about moving closer to my mum or sister. The day I finally made the decision to move nearer to my sister, Mike told me he had received a job offer.

He was leaving to work in Australia. I needed to support myself and the girls, emotionally and financially. What in heaven's name was I supposed to do? I had a lot of skills that I had acquired over the past four years, and then some, but none of them were appealing. Perhaps I could offer some form of holistic healing, even part time. I really did love helping people through Breathwork treatments. It was powerful healing if you were committed to breathing.

To obtain my certification, I needed to offer treatments to a dozen people. Colleagues and friends were interested in what I was doing and signed up eagerly. The astounding benefit for me was that I continued to heal as they experienced their treatments. Maddie and I had received free Reiki treatments through an offer in the newspaper, but neither of us felt much. Many of my Breathwork classmates had Reiki and told me it complemented the sessions beautifully. A Level I & II class was being offered later in the month, and I questioned the cards and the pendulum. I spoke to my guides, God, and the angels, and it was meant to be. With a big sigh, I gave in: "All right, let's see where this takes me."

I found that the healing work I did during the Breathwork sessions was Reiki—well, a form of energy work. What I liked about Reiki was that it gave me more guidelines to follow, as currently I had none. A prayer was given, and protection was asked for. I learned how to cut my cords from my clients, so neither of us would take anything away from the other. I had been doing a variation of cord cutting with family members and others. When lingering negative thoughts continued to occur in my mind, I would chop away with my imaginary chainsaw. Working in the Reiki energy was also less exhausting than trying to get the energy to flow; with Reiki it flowed naturally, automatically.

After my attunement to the Reiki energy, it was necessary for twenty-one days to cleanse my body of meat, sugar, caffeine, alcohol, flour products, and television—all considered negative influences. It was like the frequency that Dr. Dyer has spoken about in his book. It was also necessary to do treatments on myself daily during that period. The cleanse was necessary to remove toxins from my body, which in turn would help improve my frequency levels. Increasing my frequency levels would increase my ability to communicate better with the universe and my own body. Looking back, I realized that my body had been preparing for this moment for the last three years.

Have you ever walked into a room and wanted to leave because it felt yucky? Have you ever walked into a room and just knew you were going to have a wonderful time? Those are examples of two very different frequency levels. Yucky is low, and uplifting is high. Frequencies can be attached to buildings, rooms, people, food, plants, television shows, and books.

Everything has a frequency level. If there are a lot of lower frequencies surrounding you, like naysayers, they will drag your frequency levels down. Remember the saying "sucked dry"? Being around them might make you tired and put you in a bad mood and usually causes a lot of drama in your life. To get your third eye and your crown chakra to open, which allows your intuitive abilities to heighten, you need to raise your frequency levels.

Normally, I wouldn't have been able to stick to a twenty-one-day meal plan because it would have affected Mike. He is a meat and potatoes guy. Currently, I didn't care what affected Mike. He was doing what he felt was necessary; now, so was I. Surprisingly, Mike encouraged this new line of work. Or perhaps I should say he was no longer discouraging it. He had done some Breathwork with Ardith in March, as I didn't think I should work on him. Now, in September, he allowed me to perform Reiki.

This work continued to amaze me.

The first treatment was completely textbook. The second treatment was not something we had even discussed in class. It should have sent me running in the opposite direction, but it didn't. It had me hooked, I wanted to do more. It was the hook, line, and sinker: I had found my purpose!

I started at Mike's feet and worked my way up his clothed body the same as the last time. When I reached his head there was a lot more "stuff" trapped in there. It felt thick, like when you move your hand through water, and you feel the pressure. Then it turned gunky, like the texture of tar. I closed my eyes and took a look. My hand was attached to a dark, black mass. It was trying to hide behind something, but there wasn't enough something to do so. The Reiki energy had released so many blockages, allowing the energy to flow and now this "thing" was visible! I could make out a little gremlin-looking thing—yikes! It became a tug of war, me pulling outward and it wanting to stay! Weird. Finally, using all my effort and sending out a couple of prayers to the angels for help, I managed to pull it out of Mike's head, just as he sat up and yelled, "Enough already!"

I didn't have time to pay attention to Mike. I needed to get rid of this thing! I visually wrapped it in a burlap sack so it would be easier to hold on to and then offered it to Mother Earth. She didn't want it; she pursed her lips! Normally she took whatever blobs needed dumping. Although this wasn't a blob … it was an entity? My guides didn't want it. Frantically I yelled inside my head for someone with God's love and light to come and remove this thing from me. An angel appeared and removed it from my hand. It was only through claircognizance— that knowing part of my mind—that I knew what had happened. I wasn't listening to direction, which is clairaudience; no one was talking to me—it was more of an understanding of the situation, a feeling. The entire event took under a millisecond. It may have been the archangel Raphael who assisted me; he helps with passing others over or dealing with entities. Did he offer the knowing information? Is that the way he communicated?

Mike was sitting on the floor holding his head between his hands. I asked with concern, "How are you doing?"

"My head felt like it was ready to explode! There was all this pressure building up, then it disappeared."

After explaining the entire event and gaining insight into the situation from my guides, we were able to gain some understanding. It was an entity that had inhabited his body. After another look, I found two smaller entities hiding in one of the dark places left. As the Reiki entered Mike's body it removed the blockages, allowing light in, and these entities needed dark to survive. The dark had evaporated during the treatment, and there was nowhere left to hide. I knew that they had either attached themselves or were "given" to Mike while he was in Brasil. My guess was that it had happened during the month he was on his own, and the girls and I were still visiting Canada. Was there a connection between depression, old countries, and hitchhiking entities.

Could this be why my husband had been acting bizarre? These things had been sucking the life out of him, turning him into a zombie state. Or did they just contribute to everything that was going on in his life?

Possibly a little of both? Within two weeks Mike was almost back to normal, but he still planned on moving to Australia. *Why?*

The girls and I planned to visit my sister and her family in Turner Valley in October for Thanksgiving. Turner Valley is just a little bedroom community twenty minutes outside of Calgary, nestled in the foothills of the Rocky Mountains. If we had time, a day trip to Banff was only 150 kilometers away. We did not have time this visit, as it was the opportunity we needed to find a house. Our home was on the market and was getting lots of action. We would be moving by mid-November at the latest. I was grateful to be working for the travel agency, as our flights cost us only a fraction of the normal fare. Our line of credit had almost reached its limit and I didn't want to add anything more to it if possible. Although I hoped to rent, my mother had agreed to cosign a mortgage for me if the need arose, and my only option was to buy.

Mike did not want to be involved. I had invited him in early September, but he was having none of it. Partly he was embarrassed to face my family. "Get over it." After his last Reiki treatment, he changed his mind and booked a ticket to join us.

My sister's house was busy. Her daughter was sixteen months old and her new son only a month. I had forgotten what it was like to have little ones around. Beds were in short supply with the girls and my mother there, so Mike and I were bunked together. Because of this I was able to give him a third Reiki treatment before we went house-hunting on Saturday morning. The girls and I arrived on Thursday to narrow down our search. We mostly looked at rentals, and they were scary. The ones in better shape wouldn't take pets, and we were not getting rid of our cats. I didn't want to be picky, but there were some things I wouldn't budge on. The girls toured the school. It was much smaller than what they were used to, but it had all the essentials. It was a block from my sister, so when I was working, the girls could easily walk to their Auntie Jane's after school.

The two houses for sale nearest my sister were old and needed a lot of work. Our furniture wouldn't even fit in one of them, and the other had only two bedrooms and one bath. We had the option to develop the basement, but I felt that would be a long time in coming. It was the better of the two choices, if I had to choose. Just before we were dropped off, the realtor suggested we take a look at a newly built spec house. Mum and I both chimed in "Yes!" Mike just looked at me with disdain. Perhaps the Reiki wasn't working.

The house was a one-story bungalow with a walkout unfinished basement. It was $12,000 over my budget, but it had everything I wanted. Everything I wanted, at least for now. I could also use part of the basement space to run my healing business part-time. There was a beautiful porch across the front of the house, which faced south. The backyard wasn't much more than a parking pad, but there was a deck off the kitchen at the back of the house. When the basement was eventually finished, most of our furniture would fit. I found myself checking walls to see whether my china cabinet would fit and then berating myself that it was too expensive! My mind then wandered to, "How can I make this work?"

We thanked the realtor, and she dropped us back at my sisters'. I was resigned to living in her basement until we could find something more suitable. Mike pulled me aside and asked if we could grab a coffee and talk. I asked Mum if she minded watching the girls. "Not at all. Take your time."

We ordered a vanilla latte and a decaf vanilla soy latte and took our seats on the outdoor patio. He looked so serious; there was definitely something on his mind.

"When we walked into that last house I saw myself living there."

Surprise flashed across my face. "What? Like a vision?"

"Yah."

"What does that mean? Does it mean you're staying? Do you see us in that house with you?" I knew I needed to tone it down; my excitement was bubbling to the surface.

"Yah, I see myself living there, but I don't know if I'm staying. I have a responsibility to the company. I signed a contract, I have a start date. But we're going to buy that house together." Well, I hadn't seen this coming.

But then I rarely saw anything coming lately. My comment to the universe had recently evolved into unpleasantness.

We took the girls over on Sunday to have another look. We talked to our bank and signed the papers. In the realtor's papers Mike included finishing the basement within four weeks of our move-in date. Yes, Reiki worked.

Over the next month our house in Yellowknife sold, and we finalized the house in Turner Valley, Alberta. Mike couldn't—or didn't feel he could—get out of his contract to go to Australia. Some work ethic thing. We had discussed it in every possible direction; at one point I even suggested that we all take a year off and spend it in New Zealand. He had been talking for months about just sitting on a beach in New Zealand to regroup. It was a dream; the reality was reckless. More reckless than this past year? Really? Perspective.

He told me he would work three to four months and then come home to us. He was sure he could find a job in Calgary, but if he really liked his Australian job, we would join him there. Things had changed dramatically in the last few weeks. There were still holes in his plan that bothered me, but so much had been sorted out, I could live with them for now. He was much better, but he never talked about us joining him immediately, never considered changing his status from single to married. Somewhere in his head, he had gotten his commitments confused; the job was coming ahead of his family. Where he wouldn't relent was when his employer pressured him on an earlier start date. He told them he couldn't start before his family was settled in their new home. That was something.

He drove with us from Yellowknife to Turner Valley and helped us unpack. Then he spent a few days with his parents. The day before he left, he looked ill. I felt ill but was ignoring it. None of us knew when we would all be together again. Every time I brought up booking a Christmas flight he said, "*No*, it's too much money."

"It isn't about the money," I told him. "It's about being together for Christmas."

Mike left. The girls, both now in the English program, adjusted to their new school. Brett was handing in homework in French that was supposed to be in English. Taylor's teachers all thought she had a learning disability, as she couldn't read or write in English. I told them repeatedly that she had just transferred from French Immersion. I didn't say it, but perhaps they were the ones with the learning disability.

The job hunt was on. This task should have been easy; I had oodles of experience in various fields. I could work at a newspaper or a travel agency, or do bookkeeping. The economy was booming, and I couldn't find a job. I practiced Reiki and Breathwork on myself and anyone else who was willing.

Mike was miserable. He wished he was coming home for Christmas. "It's only money. Come home." He finally agreed. It was wonderful to have him back. My problem was, I didn't know whether he was home because he was lonely or because he really missed us. I'm sure he missed the girls, but did he miss me? He said he did; he said he loved me. He still felt a lot of guilt for what he had put us through over the last year. I could see it in his eyes and in his expression. When he left this time, I wasn't sure whether he was going to come home. He said he was, but I just didn't feel it.

Brett broke her leg—a double fracture to her lower left leg—two days before Mike was to return to Australia. Taylor had fractured her wrist before we moved from Yellowknife. After Brett's break, I kept pondering how broken bones were linked to their dad's departure. I found out that bones are connected to the foundation of our body. If the change is large enough in a child's mind, or adults for that matter, it can have a detrimental effect on their bodies—specifically their bones, in this case. The foundation of what their household looked like was changing. It's not just the mental well-being we need to be concerned about. There was so much to learn.

I was still meditating every day, but rather than using a mantra or talking to my guides, I spent that time being thankful for all the wonderful things I had in my life. I felt it was important, as I was certain my frequency level had been damaged in a multitude of ways. At other times during the day I visualized seeing Mike and me together, or all four of us as a family doing different activities. During these visualizations I would feel joy and laugh out loud and be sincerely grateful.

When I talked to Mike on the phone, he couldn't wait to come home. He loved me. It still thrilled me to hear it. By the end of January, he didn't know when he was coming home; the company needed him. He had to figure out how he would tell them, and he felt like the progress he was making on some of the projects needed to be seen through to the end. "But it won't be long."

Then he started calling at odd hours and just wanted to talk to the girls because he was running out the door to one thing or another. By the end of February I was pulling tarot cards to find answers. The card that kept appearing in my readings was "female friend." I didn't want to be a friend, that's not what I wanted at all. It was time to meditate. I pretended that I showed up on his doorstep as a surprise for his fortieth birthday. I saw myself sitting on the top step to his house with my suitcase. He pulled into the driveway with a female in the front seat. Well, that was a bit of a surprise. I reached for my pendulum.

"Is Mike coming home?" Undecided.

"Is Mike wearing his wedding band?" No.

"Is Mike having an affair?" Do I really want to know the answer to this question? Relax for the answer to show … no. It was the answer I was looking for, but was it true? I couldn't bear this anymore. Jennifer, my rock during this whole ordeal, had reconciled with her husband and moved from Yellowknife to Australia to be with him the previous summer. She was living within sixty minutes of Mike. A phone call was in order. I needed to know what she knew. Yes, she had heard a lot of rumors about Mike having an affair. They were seen together constantly—evening BBQs, then running early in the morning, shopping for furniture, and out at different events. He had helped her hang curtains and taken things to the dump. This was not something Jennifer wanted to share with me; she was very upset. She told me that if he was lying to me, perhaps it was time for a visit.

I had become a Reiki Master the previous weekend. I sat and meditated in the Reiki energy until I calmed down enough to call Mike and discuss the situation. I called him at work; there was no way I was waiting until he finished for the day.

No prelude. "Are you wearing your wedding ring?"

"Why are you asking?"

"I want to know. Are you wearing your wedding ring?"

"No. It's too hot here, and it pinches my finger."

"Are you having an affair?"

"What?"

"I know about her. You've been seen all over the place with her. Are you having an affair?

"You have your friends spying on me?"

"So you are."

"No, she's only a friend."

"You need to decide if you're coming home or not. I'm giving you a month to decide. After that, we're done."

"What do you mean?"

"I'm done, Mike. I've been waiting around for a year, supporting you during this entire ordeal. You're supposed to be figuring things out and setting a date to come home."

"I told you I have this work commitment."

"Yes, and now I'm telling you that in a month's time if you don't come home, your commitment to us will end."

"I can't face any of you. I've put you through so much."

"Well, you have two choices. You come home and face us, and we move on with our lives together, or I come over there, and you face me when I serve you with divorce papers. Your choice." Click.

Oh my God, I was done! One more month, and there would be an answer one way or the other. I curled up in my closet and cried until the girls came home from school.

He waited until the very last possible day to make his decision—Easter Sunday. There was a lesson in this: the guides and angels thought they were so humorous? I hadn't asked, "What year?" Mike would give six weeks' notice. I felt like I had been holding my breath for a very long time.

It might not have been a love affair or a sexual affair, but it was an affair nonetheless. Mike never admitted to anything, but there were lines that had been crossed. Truth be told, I had anticipated that something would happen while we were apart. I actually thought that would be the one thing that would eventually bring him home. In a way it was. My girlfriends asked how I could take him back if he had had an affair. In the beginning of our marriage, I never would have tried to forgive. Now, fifteen years of relationship seemed worth saving. I had matured into a person who was willing to forgive. It didn't mean it didn't hurt. There was another level of trust for me to get through—and, of course, forgiveness. Aren't some relationships worth fighting for? But of course both people need to want the same thing; that's the kicker.

Was this work never-ending?

My mother supported me on a daily basis from the other end of the phone. My dad had been a huge support during our separation, visiting me several times in Yellowknife and visiting over Christmas. I had never seen so much of him, ever. This time he'd brought a different girlfriend. Her comment to my father was, "Why is she fighting to keep him? There's nothing special about him."

"The person you met isn't Mike," he replied. That really did sum it up. Mike could be self-absorbed, maybe more than some, but he was also sensitive, supporting, a great father, ambitious, helped around the house, and we both loved to travel, eat good food, and drink red wine. And we loved each other.

We briefly discussed moving to Australia. In the end I couldn't do it. I didn't want to move again. In February I had lain on the floor in front of our huge living room window, basking in the sun with the cats, and come up with a name for my healing business, Healing Possibilities. I was now a Reiki Master and a Breathwork practitioner. During the month of May and June I would become a Karuna® Reiki Master and certified reflexologist. I was also attending a weeklong diploma course in psychosomatic therapy.

Karuna® Reiki was about compassionate action, finding unconditional love through opening the heart chakra. Wow, did I ever shift after that class. So much more understanding for human nature arose in me. Releasing myself from resentment and judgment and offering forgiveness moved me to another level of awareness. All the individual angels were introduced to me in more depth, but I felt most connected to archangels Michael, Raphael, Ariel, and Gabriel. Usually I saw the angels as sparkles: Michael was indigo blue, Raphael was green, Gabriel was yellow, and Ariel was orange. Now I could feel their energy when they were called on—Michael light and airy, Raphael heavier and more protective, and Ariel made me feel like I was being stretched, moving more energy into my head. Now if I concentrated I could bring them into full view; their wings were massive!

What I didn't know is that the archangels were omnipresent; they could be everywhere at once. This was wonderful to know, as spirit guides and past spirits could only be in one place at a time, and sometimes I needed to wait for them to show up when called on. Now when I got into my car, I drew the power Reiki symbol for protection, wrapped my car in white light three times, and placed an angel on all four corners of my car. Very weird things started to happen. I swear, once my car merged and melded into another car that had entered my lane. It was like the particles of both vehicles became one and then separated again. Not a scratch or any damage was noticeable on my vehicle; it was as though we had never collided.

Because of everything going on in my life, I was glad that Mike was happy to come back to Canada to live and work. He had felt that living in Australia would be much the same as it had been earlier on in our marriage, when we had moved every eighteen to twenty-four months. He now understood that the girls needed to be settled in one spot. Family was coming more into balance with work. Many of us have gone through the same thing; we get caught up in our work and lose perspective about what is real and true.

Conditioning is a hard habit to break. There are so many ideas that our family and friends have planted in our minds that we take on as truths. When the reality of those truths start coming apart, our lives can get rather messy before the rebuilding takes place. The chakras on the front of the body connect us to our emotions. The chakras on the back of the body relate to our free will, which really comes down to our conditioning. The base chakra is about our foundation— where we live, how we live. When we start breaking through how our parents expect us to live, struggles come into play. People who chose a profession because of a parent, who live in a certain house or area, or who fulfill the expectation that they will marry and have children at a particular age are all examples. I had broken through much of my conditioning, Mike was now doing the same. The front of the heart chakras is the emotional balances and imbalances of love, the back is the conditioning around love. If you grew up with conditions placed on your love—"I love you so much when you're good," or "They're family. You have to love them!" Do we?—there ensues a series of struggles to get to the other side of what we have been told and what we truly feel about the situation.

While I was still living in Yellowknife, it became evident that when I spent time with my mother and sister together, it was toxic. A visit with them left me exhausted for weeks. My frequency had been seriously affected, and recovery time was necessary to get back to where I had been before the visit. For seven years, while we were so remote, I never saw the two of them together. I had been away from them for so long that now experiencing their abuse astounded me. I had not recognized it before. Mike had, but I hadn't understood it because it was natural for me to be treated a certain way by them. Now, with us all together, they fell back into old habits of ignoring or teasing me, acting like thirteen-year-old girls when we got together. Mike had seen it for years. I was conditioned to the behavior, but now my boundaries had changed. I spoke with them separately: "The two of you treat me badly when you are together, and I'm only visiting with you separately if the abuse does not stop." They had a hard time seeing their behavior as abuse, but our next visit together was very different.

In order for the conditioning on all sides to change, action is necessary. I wasn't excited about having this conversation and was filled with fear of reaping more abuse because of it, or losing a relationship with them entirely. That is why I spoke what I needed to from my heart. When you speak from your heart, people feel it and react in a much calmer way. They consciously—maybe unconsciously—feel truth in your words.

Now that I was working more from my heart center, I remembered truths from the past. Words from when I had been in Australia four years earlier: "Even if we don't take the job, it really doesn't matter. Mike will be back." How could I have forgotten? There were other conversations I had forgotten. When I finally called Stephanie to talk about my last year, she reminded me, "You knew you were going to separate years ago."

"What?"

"Remember you told me when we both lived in Edmonton, 'Stephanie, I just got this flash that ten years from now, Mike and I are going to be separated.'" I'd forgotten.

And they kept coming: "Mike is doing this for you. He needs to leave, it's in his contract." That crazy contract we all sign before we're born. That comment now made sense. I never would have followed my path into holistic healing if he hadn't left. I never would have given myself the opportunity to pursue it so adamantly. He never would have given me permission to spend the excessive amount of money necessary to certify and set up shop! I would have relented and continued my life by supporting him and his work, following him around from site to site. When he decided to leave, I needed something of my own to support my children, support my soul. Although the guides said he was coming back, there was a part of me that needed to be realistic. Maybe I couldn't have stopped any of it from happening; perhaps it was all destiny. With this new information, I was able to find gratitude for the journey I'd endured over the last horrific eighteen months. It would take me longer to heal, but I had something positive to grasp on to while I did.

Thank you, Michael, for your generous gift.

He returned home the second week of May 2005. There was a rebuilding of our relationship. We had nothing to lose, so we spoke our truths about our dreams and our feelings. When we came back together, I felt like it was a cosmic rebirth, an "Until death do us part" thing. I felt it in my heart, in my soul. Mike felt the same, and there was more of a commitment than when we originally married. We'd had a polite marriage for the first twelve years, all about trying to please the other person. It was an internal pleasing, something that came from what we thought was best for the other person. This new union was more about truth and acceptance; it had boundaries, and the control we had both wanted in the end was now relinquished. Partnership wasn't about control; it was about love. And our love for each other had changed; there weren't any conditions on that love. Neither of us was on a pedestal, expecting the other to fulfil a dreamlike quality, so we accepted each other for who and what we were. And of course what our hearts wanted. I had spent months manifesting seeing us together. When I looked ahead at our future, I now saw us as an old couple sitting on a bench swing, watching the sunset.

We all have karma to clear in our lives, for that is part of the reason we are here. I now understood that everything that had happened along the way, in my childhood, teen years, as a young adult, had influenced my life by placing obstacles in the way so I could eventually learn how to release those past disputes, mentally, emotionally, spiritually, and physically.

While Mike was gone, I kept seeing myself in the late 1700s as an old bag lady sitting on the side of the road across from what I believed was my home. I had been gone a long time. Mike stood in the front of this manor house, in a proper English garden, playing with our girls. Then a young lady showed up, taking his arm. They all headed toward the gate.

For months I punished myself by replaying this past-life vision. "Perhaps I deserved this, him leaving me as I left him in this past life. If I had left him, no wonder he left me now." It wasn't until he came home that I pressed Play on that vision.

I stood up and crossed the road toward my home. The girls caught sight of me and raced toward me, yelling, "Mum!" Mike released the woman's arm and reached for me. We all entered the house together. I had been gone for a year, and it didn't matter; everyone was thrilled to have me home.

We felt the same way about having Mike home.

I had learned so much about myself, and I was willing to concede to the mistakes I'd made. Working through the regrets of my past before I met Mike had been necessary to get me to this point. Now I would have to forgive and move on from the regrets that had accrued during our marriage. I had a pretty clear idea of what needed to be done. Balance would have to be found between the girls, Mike, and my new business.

Mike continued to heal, struggling still with the idea that I loved him and wasn't just using him for financial support. How could he not know I loved him? It had to do with his regrets and embarrassment over his behavior. He had commented multiple times that he didn't understand why I didn't just file for divorce and leave during this whole mess. He apologized profusely to the girls and me. I kept reassuring him of my commitment and my hope that that was enough for him to find forgiveness in his own heart. To forgive oneself is powerful.

Mike made it up to me with diamond earrings, a diamond pendant, and a BMW. If that would ease his guilt, so be it. There were lessons for me too, learning how to accept help and learning to say "Thank you." Much of my life had been about making excuses when people gave me something. Positive or negative, they were all excuses: "Oh, you shouldn't have!" Quite frankly that's rude. In saying thank you, you allow the giver to feel your gratitude for their having done something thoughtful, and you allow yourself to learn how to be gracious. Not thank you, blab, blab, blab, just "Thank you."

Mike also agreed to take me to Greece for our fifteenth wedding anniversary, which was a childhood dream! There hadn't been a time in my life when I hadn't wanted to go to Greece. My sister agreed to watch the girls for three weeks. Athens, Mykonos, Santorini, and Crete— ancient civilizations, but where were my past-life memories? The need was so great, I was sure there must have been a few past lives waiting for me to discover. The lives I discovered were not my own but spirits left behind. A boy of about eight being chased by his dog ran me off the path at one ancient ruin. Mostly they were peaceful, quiet, ancient artifacts. And Greece, with so many years of civilization behind it, produced excellent red wine!

The trip was healing for Mike and me; we could spend an extended amount of time together and really, really enjoy each other's company. I prayed that healing would enclose the girls. It seemed to me that since I had started this healing process, everyone in my family was being affected. It was like they were being dragged behind me whether they wanted to or not. I suppose they had the choice to cut the cord and be on their own way, but it seemed we had all been affected in some way or another. That included my parents and my sister.

There were a few hiccups. One when Brett had to do a project on Australia, and then the entire household became tense. Maybe we needed to book a trip to Australia to clear the effects it still had on our lives. It was a bit overwhelming for Mike to get used to all the activity in the house again. And he didn't have four days to relax from our pace by working away from home. One of our problems had been that I had always organized everything and made all the decisions. But that had evolved from his lack of interest or his comment, "You decide." That habit had to be broken, and it took a lot of work for me to remember to consult someone else on matters I had been dealing with for so long

The miracle of life is holding love in our hearts and making time for all that is precious; that was now what we worked toward. All my concentration for the last year and a half had been directed at supporting all of us without doing all the work. About trying to walk with the energy within my household, and somehow my health had suffered because of it. Working on one item did not balance all the modules that made up my life.

I was no longer going to the gym or practicing yoga. I hadn't gone cross-country skiing and had only taken my bike out a few times. I had gained fifteen pounds. I wasn't eating differently, but the stress of my situation was not allowing my metabolism to process properly. I had been hanging on too tightly, mentally, not allowing the weight to release. Because I am only five three and fine-boned, the weight had added three dress sizes. My boobs had expanded from a B to a DD! I did not like it.

The girls were in activities. Brett attended art class and gymnastics, and Taylor was on a soccer team. In kindergarten she had come home from school and asked to play soccer. She had played indoor and outdoor every year since. There was nothing in Turner Valley for activities, so we traveled fifteen minutes to the next closest town. If I'm being truthful, the traveling directly after school without proper meals worsened my weight-gain problem. While I waited for one child or the other to complete her activities, we would eat take-out. Three days a week we juggled food and schedules, and my body wasn't used to it. There was an upside that had encouraged me to ignore the problem; it was nice to not cook and clean up in the kitchen.

Whether it was the weight or the situation I had endured, my lower back was killing me. The pain was so bad at times, I could barely walk more than a few feet; the need to sit down would become so overwhelming. The only thing that relieved it a bit was sitting. I would bend forward and stretch out my lower back. Usually there was enough activity by noon that it felt better, unless I was standing for any period of time. Typically nothing hurt when I worked giving treatments; the Reiki flowed through and released it all. I love doing energy work.

CHAPTER 15

Transformation

WHEN I COULDN'T FIND A job in any of my acquired fields, and a sign was displayed in my chiropractor's office, "Room for Rent," I knew it was time, and the Universe wanted me to step up and start my healing practice officially. I would become a holistic healthcare practitioner, which was much more complicated to explain than any other job I had performed. Although rent was minimal, the entire idea of needing X number of clients to cover my rent and expenses overwhelmed me. What if I never got any clients? And then I needed to think about what steps were necessary to run a business! Oh my. Daily, sometimes hourly, I worked on letting the "What if's" go, continually connecting with my power and moving forward!

I jumped in feetfirst on June 1. I stopped thinking and just followed guidance from my guides. I set up shop, got business cards printed, took out ads in the local newspapers, and attended trade shows to offer free treatments. Truthfully, I was having more fun than I could possibly have imagined! I now knew why I had worked at the photo shop; it was to refresh my accounting mind about budgets, bank reconciliations, and bookkeeping in general. I was digging into the recesses of my brain, remembering information from business school about marketing and advertising.

The advisements were working. People around town were recognizing me at the dry cleaners, bank, grocery store, and drugstore. I hosted informative evenings where I talked about the work I did, offering demonstrations. Then I was invited to speak to the Cancer Society. Business wasn't booming, but I did have clients. Confidence came slowly about being a healer, but also about running a business. I wasn't used to putting myself out there. It was 2005 and what I did was difficult for most people to comprehend; it took a huge leap of faith—not only for me, most days, but especially for potential clients.

To gain more experience, I'd travel to Edmonton once a month, offering sessions out of my mother's home, mostly to friends—hers and mine. One particular Saturday I left early to run a few errands before the first of three clients was expected at 11:30. I arrived back at Mum's house at 10:30, feeling exhausted. For a few years now, while still sitting in the car, I practiced what I called a transition breath—breathing in, then exhaling down into my toes, and grounding myself before I moved on to my next task. I also found it filled me with additional energy to get on with my day. As I sat doing this now, I wished I didn't have to work today, wished I had the day off to just visit with my mum. Life had gotten so busy.

Ten minutes later, I didn't have to wish for anything; my three clients canceled. Now, how did I accomplish that? Ahh, I had felt it. It hadn't just been words; very strong emotions had been attached to my statement. I had accomplished changes like this before but had gotten confused when it came to attracting more clients. How did I change it around to gain more clients?

Gaining something seemed more difficult. There were many times, once I reflected, that I wanted something, and it had happened. Currently, my biggest problem was that I wasn't entirely accepting of my gift; in some small way I felt the universe had coerced me into doing this work.

Why did other people just get to live their lives, while my life was full of so many challenges and tasks?

I decided to do a healing around my anger with the Universe. It took me to bardo which is our in-between-state. I was visible upset.

Next to me was a table with papers on it, my contract to come back to Earth. In front of me were quite a few people, but really only three were clearly noticeable, the rest were in more of a mist. The three in front were insistent that I return to Earth, "We need you down there to do this work." Their instance just aggravated me more.

"I don't want to go! It is so painful to be a part of that process. There is so much hatred. There will be so much I need to work through before I get to a place of peace." I felt it in my soul, I knew this to be true.

"You will help millions of people." That statement, of course, was all that was needed to be said. How could I pass on helping millions of people?

Even without that knowledge I couldn't have stop doing this work if I'd tried. Although some days I felt like a square peg in a round hole, it was so exciting to see healing happening in others. The effects of my work were so amazing, though people still saw some of it as a coincidence: their doctor had changed their pills, they had gotten a new bed, the pain had just gone away. It was so exasperating at times that some people just didn't get it! It was the Reiki! Or their bodies would start to detox, and then they became scared that the sessions were bad for them. My experiences weren't so vast that I could put all of what was happening into words, but I knew it was all good.

There had been people clinically depressed who within ten weeks were living amazing, fulfilling lives. People who couldn't walk because of injuries, now hiking mountains! They believed, and that had helped build my confidence. But how was I to get the people who hadn't experienced these miracles into my office?

Every day was a learning experience and, quite frankly, sometimes exhausting. It was fascinating, but exhausting.

My cousin Emily's mom, Aunt Beverly, had pancreatic cancer. By the time they found it, she had very little time to live. I spoke to her, and she was more than willing to accept long-distance Reiki treatments. I spent a lot of time giving her treatments to heal. She died. I did not understand. Why hadn't I saved her life? The healing was supposed to go where it was needed.

And the voice said, "The healing went where it needed to."

"It went to her death?" was my response. The strangest reasoning entered my head. Reiki could be used to help people die peacefully. That started a flow of tears. Then I remembered we had done a breath exercise with Dan. Our partners pretended to be dying, and we were to breathe in unison with them to bring calmness during their passing.

I'm healing people, not killing people! It was all so confusing. Understanding came, acceptance was a bit slower. The relaxing energy of Reiki could benefit people in the end, especially the ones afraid to die. Then my thought continued. It could help by relaxing them and allowing death to occur by their letting go of those cords that might otherwise have held them here on Earth longer than necessary. There was so much depth to this healing.

Truthfully, I wasn't healing anyone; I was only a conduit for their healing process. I needed to stay in neutral and take myself out of the healing process to allow things to happen. By removing my ego, I could just be with them, not in my own process, not attached to my own stuff. I entered their energy field, and miracles happened, but if the client didn't want to be healed, little to nothing would change for them. They never fully let me in, so the work was much slower. I had seen where within days they were back to whatever ailed them. Talking to the cancer support group was another good example. They all lived their disease; it was their life. I had done miraculous things for them during that evening, but not one of them had called for an appointment. Change in their lives would have been too difficult for them to accept: what would they talk about? Their mood would have to change; their frequency would have to change. I could see how healing might be scary and might seem too overwhelming for some people to accept. The idea of people not being able to accept such a positive modification in their health was horrendous to think about.

It was so evident when people sent their spouses or partner to see me. Typically nothing changed if they were only there to please someone else. When it did, it never lasted for long. Sometimes I could get deeper and make changes happen in a thought process, or they would get so excited about some pain leaving their body. Those people kept me doing my work. Now I knew my purpose was to inform people, from my heart center. The more people who knew about this work, the more people would know about this work.

Every day of work was changing my life. New information presented itself every time I worked on a client, and with this, my contentment with the work grew stronger. One client, when I put my hands on her, felt as though she were full of anger. "Were you allowed to show your anger as a child," I asked.

"I was raised Catholic; we are never angry, only loving and kind."

"You were recently run over on your motorcycle, you can barely walk, you're having migraines, and all you keep saying is how you forgive this man for hitting you."

"I do forgive him."

"Are you not angry at him at all?"

"No. It was a blessing for me. God has a plan."

So much conditioning. "Your body is full of rage. I can feel it overflowing. Part of the process to get to forgiveness is releasing anger."

Her anger was now starting to surface. I could feel it from where I sat, see it in her face. I tried to explain that until this anger released from her body, it would be difficult to release her physical injuries and allow them to heal. The injury and the emotions were trapped in her cellular memory. She left, angry at me, but at least she was now angry. When I started this work, this wasn't what I thought it would look like, but now I realized that it didn't matter whether she came back. I had done the work from my heart and knew the universe would support me.

She spoke to a colleague of mine, told her I had no business stepping into the counseling side. I had only let her know what her body was telling me. The comment made me happy because she was still working through that anger. Six months later my colleague commented that the woman had spoken with her again and wanted to thank me for what I had said. She had started therapy and the first thing she was advised was to start working through her anger.

This additional confirmation was enough for me to put to rest the question of whether or not I was improving people's lives in some way. I didn't need to know everything that was going on. I trusted the universe in all things and knew I was walking in my energy and was securely on my life path.

The body tissue at a cellular level has a story. The body wants to heal but can't seem to do so entirely on its own. I am thankful for twelfth-grade physics because of this one concept. When a car impacts the wall, the arrows pointing toward the car show how much force is causing damage. Physical, emotional, and mental damage can affect the body, and that force stays dormant in our cells until a hands-on healer releases the force from the body. The tissue can then return to normal, once the pain, anxiety, and mental anguish is released.

It is all so amazing.

In February 2006, a year after opening my practice, I moved into a bigger space within the same building. My clientele had increased, but I was still stressed about money and the commitment; the responsibility to perform weighed heavily on my shoulders. Mike covered all our household expenses, but I so wanted to contribute. I was becoming obsessed with money.

Every morning I'd wake up, and, while showering, I'd balance my checkbook. In my mind I'd subtract all the purchases I had for the week and see what was left over. There was money left over, but I couldn't relieve myself of this annoying habit. To get rid of it, I would pretend to pour all that information into my hands, then, holding my arms out, I would say, "God, I no longer want to think about this issue any longer. Please resolve this for me." I could feel the weight lifting from my hands and shoulders. I knew the universe would guide me in the right direction. Now I visualized seeing my laundry basket full of dirty sheets. That had to manifest additional clients?

Then a client told me about a course she had just taken called a *Millionaire Mind Intensive* by Harv Eker. They promised that, if I attended, my financial blueprint would revamp into something healthy. It worked; certain negative thoughts were disappearing from my mind. Every morning during my shower I now thought, "My day is going to be great." And I'd think of all the ways that could happen. This change didn't occur overnight, but I felt progress was happening. I encouraged Mike to attend the course. Afterward, he kept getting promoted. Why did it work so much faster for him to gain financial prosperity? Something was still blocking me. I added a citrine crystal to the wealth corner of my house and business; I would try everything. I had rose quartz crystals in the shape of a heart in each window of my house: "Please bring in more love and harmony."

A memory revealed itself. I was twelve and had just won first place in my figure skating competition. I was so happy and proud of myself! The next day my best friend wouldn't talk to me. I hadn't competed against her, so I didn't understand why she was mad at me. Then came, "You didn't deserve to win. My cousin should have gotten gold!" She was upset that I had beaten her cousin? Her cousin was three years younger than me. But the scenario now made sense in my current life. I had never gotten gold again—silver, yes, but I had never allowed myself to excel past that in case I lost another friend.

A meditation with my spirit guide was in order for direction and healing. His name was Jonathan, which I found interesting, because when I was a little girl I had planned on naming my son Jonathan. I lay down on my massage table and asked him to make an appearance. Through my mind's eye, I could see his full form five feet away from me. He was at least six feet tall and dressed like one of the characters from my romance novels. Dark skin, dark hair, billowing white shirt, and tight black pants tucked into black, knee-high boots. Yum, could I be so lucky? I asked whether he could come closer so I could see his face. A second later we were nose-to-nose and then his image was gone. It felt like we had crossed a line. It was very unnerving.

He was only one of a group of guides who were here to assist me on this earthbound journey. I had been given a few names over the years. Once we pass over, others from our soul group have the opportunity to experience life on Earth, and we become the support team. Jonathan and I had lived lives together, but I couldn't recall more than that. I knew Mike and I had spent a minimum of five lives together in the past because images continued to crop up.

There was also a little man I kept seeing around me who was only four feet tall. He was perfectly dressed in British attire, although from very long ago. I thought maybe he was some type of forlorn brownie, although he seemed a little too tall for what I knew about brownies. Okay, I really knew nothing about brownies.

One of our local metaphysical shops hosted a variety of workshops. There was a guided meditation being given around "Meeting your Guides." It didn't take long, and I was connecting to this little guide of mine. I could see his mouth moving but couldn't hear him speak. I brought in archangel Ariel to help translate. We had an interesting conversation, but when we finished I couldn't remember a thing. This had happened numerous times during my own healing sessions; it was like I was placed behind this wall, everything was downloading clearly, and then when I woke from this state, it was all ... gone.

There were about twenty of us sitting around in a circle. When it was my turn, I mentioned my experience and asked, "Who is this small man?"

"Have you ever miscarried?"

Strange question. "Yes, actually twice."

"Hum, well you are seeing your son from your second miscarriage," and there were the tears again. Nothing could have been more shocking. Why hadn't I seen it? Of course he was a perfectly formed little boy!

"I'm having problems hearing him," I said through all my emotions.

"That's because this work is so new for him. Over time the two of you will be able to communicate."

My first miscarriage released a year later as a large, white ball of light from under my rib cage. Another son. Children born on the other side grow in accordance to the age they would have been on this side. Sometimes it is necessary for them to be born on the other side to help family members on this side. My first son had gotten scared and decided he could not do it. He felt a lot of guilt for disappointing me. This type of forgiveness was easy to give.

Brett and Taylor both saw their brothers. In fact, one morning I entered Taylor's room and both girls were standing in front of the chin-up bar, laughing.

"What's going on?" I asked

"Our brothers are trying to do chin-ups and can't."

My sons weren't the only thing I was seeing. On a trip to Banff, I stumbled across a fairy glen. Could it be real? But I could see them— fairies flying in and out of one spot on the side of the river's edge. I sat and watched for over an hour.

My reality was so different than a year ago. How many dimensions existed in this world?

There were other dimensions living simultaneously with us. In Yellowknife I used to get a glimpse of different sections of bodies. The floor of the dimension's home was on a different level than our home, so I might see the upper half of a body on a rocking chair. At the age of six Taylor told me she saw heads on her floor moving around. Poor girl. I always wondered why she threw a blanket in the middle of her room and jumped from one side to the other. She was seeing people from another dimension as well.

Both girls had seen the dead and knew how to pass them to the other side. They knew how to protect themselves with white light. They had learned to look for auras on people's cars before they took a ride. They would be more prepared than I, but still things surprised all of us.

A client came in; it was her first appointment. Halfway through the treatment, I went into a very deep trance where my treatment room transformed into someone's kitchen. I was standing at one end of a long table. There were seven older people sitting around the table playing cards. It reminded me of a mixture of my grandma's kitchen and the one at our cabin, rustic in nature. There was red gingham curtains above the farm sink at the far end and a door off to the left. A man got up out of his chair from the head of the table and walked over and stopped in front of me. He looked to be eighty, with a large nose and very little hair. He looked old, but his body didn't move like it was old. He stood in front of me and slammed an energetic portal, Bam! Both my client and I jumped! Could they see us too? They could, and they had the power to lock us out. So very interesting.

My client started to share her vision, and it was the same as mine. We had both seen another dimension together—riveting.

This Reiki stuff was like magic. It took me back to the book I read in Republic called the *Mists of Avalon*. I felt as though I could control the weather like Vivian or Morgaine had. In fact, I remember lying on the beach as a teenager in Yellowknife and trying to control the wind. Sometimes it did feel like I made it stop. It was also at the beach that I stood over a girlfriend lying on her towel looking up at me. As I looked down at her upside-down face, there was a moment of familiarity, but I didn't understand from where. Now, every day I worked on clients and saw their faces upside down. When I was eight or nine, I would doodle during our long car rides. The images I drew were similar to the Reiki symbols I now used—so much synchronicity.

My déjà vus had become so comforting to me; they meant I was on the right path, but recently they had eluded me. "Jonathan, why am I no longer déjà vuing?" I asked my guide.

"Your entire day would be a déjà vu." That was good news.

I had finally said yes to the universe and my gifts. I now enjoyed this interesting ride and was open to learn everything offered to me. Not usable stuff in normal society, but really good stuff to help my clients. They weren't just people looking for healing; they were also looking for answers. Many were starting to listen to their own intuitive abilities. Many told me they were drawn to come to me for healing work. Things were changing in the world.

Some were scared of what they couldn't see. I was able to assure them nothing was going to harm them. I offered them tools to alleviate their fears. I remember being scared coming up from the basement as a child; it had felt like people were always chasing me. Now I knew it was my guides. "But why do I only notice them when I'm running up the stairs?" I asked Jonathan.

"Normally your spirit guides are in an open space with you. When you move up the staircase, they become more compressed and therefore more noticeable." Okay, that made sense.

Many people asked why I wasn't a vegetarian in my line of work. Other than loving meat, I had no answer for them. It had me pondering the question, though. I decided to talk to a cow: "Doesn't it upset you that you're raised to die so we can eat you?"

"You don't eat my soul; you only eat the flesh I leave behind. My purpose is to feed you."

"Thank you. Then I will only eat you if you are killed in a humane way." I started purchasing only organic meat. I wasn't going to eat any angry chickens, either.

There was a certain balance to the universe about which I was gaining a deeper understanding. Originally it started with the concept that parts of souls were transferable. Knowing that everyone should keep their own stuff made sense. Next, I started to recognize an imbalance between myself and my clients. With some clients, I traded house cleaning, babysitting, treatments, and various other things. There were times when I felt that I wasn't getting my fair share. Those moments made me realize that the trade was probably out of balance, as with my babysitter in Brasil.

Is that why the energy wasn't flowing properly at home? Outside, the day flowed beautifully. Inside my house, it wasn't chaos any longer, but the serenity I was looking for wasn't quite there. An equal exchange of energy was necessary. But was it possible? How could I get an equal exchange of energy from the children? I needed to do less, and they needed to do more; ahh, love could also be used as an exchange. If I could truly feel love from them, or receive a beautiful hug, I'd be happy to do something extra for them.

There were no longer high highs, and low lows; it was all more of a rolling hill. Up, then down, my day was spent in more of a meditative state.

Then I taught a Karuna® Reiki workshop out of my house. There were an uneven number of students, so I was trading treatments with one of them. As I stood over her torso, I felt an unusual energy enter my home. It raced upstairs, then down to the basement, stopping just outside the doorway of the room we were in, filling the space. The behavior reminded me of my Gran, but the energy was very different.

There were three of them, tall and white, much like Eva in *WALL-E*, a smooth surface and large round eyes, although they were closer to seven feet tall! Then one stepped out of its alien form, and walked as a five-foot, seven-inch man into our room. Our energy was much too slow for him to stay in his former form. He stood across from me and poured liquid similar to mercury into my hand. I then proceeded to pour it into my student; his gifts were for her. He then placed an old-looking cap on her head—something that would have been used under a chain mail hood dating back to the 1200s. We felt that it had something to do with the Knights Templar. He then outfitted her with a pair of sandals that tied back and forth on her lower leg. Last, he handed her a staff with the most spectacular orb on the end. The crystal was amazing.

He then turned to leave. *Wait!* I exclaimed in my mind. *Do you have anything for me?*

He turned and looked at me. I now felt bad for asking. He reached toward me and placed something into my chest, into my heart chakra. Then he reentered his body and the three beings whisked away, instantly. The amount of love, unconditional love, I felt now was tremendous. I couldn't judge anyone, because each of us was on our own path, just trying to make the most of it. If that was the case, there was nothing to judge. When people around me became upset, I could see that it was only their stuff they were struggling with; typically, it had nothing to do with me or anyone else. I now sent love their way.

Opening my heart had been a continual process. My heart had opened, and, umm, my breast had grown from a B cup to a D cup. I had lost the weight, and they hadn't changed in size. Could love have to do with that expansion?

But of course it had. The courses I had taken talked about the connection between the body and mind and said everything was connected. Each toe had a purpose; so did the fingers. In Yellowknife I had cut the top of my ring finger on the left hand. That finger was all about relationships, which was where my mind had gone while I tried moving those lockers and was cursing Mike! The wedding ring originally was placed on what is considered the throat of that finger, to keep the wife silent. Louise Hay's book *Heal Your Body* was even more detailed, naming body parts and diseases along with positive affirmations to make changes in your life. Those positive affirmations, in conjunction with the body work, had changed my life completely. Words were so very powerful when action followed.

All summer I had asked for a little break and then I fractured the fifth metatarsal bone on my left foot. I had received just that—a small fracture, or a little "break." I took my four-week holiday with my leg up, reading all the copies of *Twilight*. Brett had taken to them, and now I had the time to find out what they were about. I had clients who, when they needed a break, broke a leg. If life wouldn't let them have time off, they found it the only way they knew how. Teaching them that they were important and therefore allowed to take time for themselves was necessary to change the cycle.

When I dove deeper into what my break really meant, I was met with a lot of answers. First it was the same ankle I had repeatedly sprained during my childhood. It occurred to me that with so much damage, or blocked energy, when I rolled my ankle, this time there was nowhere for that energy to go except deeper into the bone. I believe everyone has a weak point in their body, and currently mine was my ankle. Thoughts and emotions could get trapped in this space and, over time, with less and less room, ailments would arise, becoming worse with time. Sprains would turn into breaks, headaches into migraines; stomach issues would become chronic issues. And if we never looked at what was going on in our bodies, it could eventually turn into cancer. That was enough to scare me into getting more bodywork done.

I was doing lots of self-healing but hadn't seen my own practitioner for a long time. As I started healing the energy trapped in my ankle and foot, I became very aware that my ego had also been involved. With all the "miracles" I was performing, I somehow thought I was above everyone else on the healing journey. Now all I was thinking was, "What will my clients think of a healer with a broken foot?"

The truth was we are all on the same journey. What made me so special? This realization was humbling, and that is really where anyone in service needs to come from. I had always been empathic; now, sitting in a humble state took me to another level. I could sit with my clients, wherever they were, and allow deeper emotional releases to happen.

In the fall I attended another course, this one in Albuquerque, New Mexico. I arrived a few days early, as I was drawn to visit Bandelier National Monument. As I walked along one of the paths and contemplated the rock walls and all the petroglyphs, I stopped in my tracks. There on the wall was a carving of the head of my alien. I now realized that he, his civilization had been part of the ancient Lemurian culture and had visited the ancient Puebloan people 10,000 years ago. Or were they more connected than that?

CHAPTER 16

Releasing Fear

OUR LIFE AS A FAMILY was also changing. We needed to move. Was it just the rhythm of moving every two years? I meditated; it was more than that. The school board planned on moving grades seven and eight out of the elementary school and amalgamating it with the high school. Brett was already boy crazy; there was no way she was going to attend a school with boys up to five years older than she was. Mike and I were also very tired of driving the fifteen minutes into Okotoks for the girls' activities. Waiting around for up to four hours sometimes was getting tedious.

The house-hunt began in November 2006. Our house sold quickly, and we found a lovely two-story walk-out close to both the girls' schools. I could move my business into the basement with ease, and there was more than enough space to start hosting some of the Reiki classes I had begun teaching.

Now I had to get the girls into the Catholic school system, which I had been told could be near to impossible. The year and a half of public school had me turned off; there was no accountability or celebration of the Christian holidays. To me those were important parts of the school system.

Jonathan's voice had repeated all week in my head, "Talk to the principal at the junior high about admission for Brett first, before going to the elementary school."

I never questioned it; when it was time, I went there first. I spoke to the principal. In a roundabout way, he asked me if she needed any assistance; they weren't looking to spend more money on aid. "No she doesn't need any help. Her marks are in the nineties and everyone loves her." The excitement rolled out of me, knowing he would admit her. She'd start after Christmas.

I crossed the street to the elementary school and spoke to the secretary. "Hi, I was hoping to talk to someone about registering my daughter to start in January."

"Are you Catholic?"

"No."

"I'm sorry, we don't have any room."

With complete sincerity I said, "Oh, that's too bad. I really wanted both my girls in the same school system, and her sister will be attending JPII."

"Oh. What grade is your daughter in?"

"She's in grade five."

"Let me look … look here, we have a class that only has seventeen students. We can place her there."

"That would be great. Thanks!" Thank you, Jonathan! Thank you, God! It paid to listen.

Both the new schools were fabulous, as was the staff. Taylor's new school really got her back on track. Her old school hadn't provided any additional work to get her reading up to grade level. I was unaware of this until Taylor's new teacher called me to implement a plan to improve her grades.

Before our move, we lost Fitzgerald to colon cancer. We had noticed him slowing down at fifteen years old but didn't realize how sick he really was. The house felt like it was in mourning until we were gifted with a little ginger kitten, Max. He lessened our grief, a little, and added a lot of new energy into the house. We had hoped he'd pull Kramer out of his depression. He did, but only by making him mad. Kramer was not fond of his new brother. I tried to do Reiki on Kramer to assist him in his healing. For months he avoided me. Then one day I found him on my healing bed. "I guess this means you're ready," I stated and then went to work.

We were all dealing with some emotional baggage. I had moments of utter sadness; it made no sense to me. My husband had returned, and we were getting along wonderfully, the girls had settled into school and had found new friends, I had a lovely new home, my business was doing well … what was there to be sad about? Rather than avoiding my emotions as I had for so many years, I sat there and connected to my sadness. It was definitely real. "Tracy," I asked, "why are you so sad?" It didn't speak to me, but I could feel its loneliness. Are you lonely for me? That realization startled me. "Lonely for me," I repeated aloud. Then it dawned on me—I had been so busy, I hadn't been taking time for myself. Even after the "break," I had jumped back on the bandwagon. This thought seemed to provoke sadness into a better mood, like a small child who is happy you've finally figured out what she really needs. I promised "it" that I would make more of a conscious effort to spend time with myself, take baths, do longer meditations, read a book, go for a walk, and in general bond more with myself on a daily basis.

Making more time for me would be a balancing act, as I was registered for so many courses over a two year period. CranioSacral therapy was calling my name, and I didn't even know what it entailed. In October 2005 I attended a holistic conference in Banff, took a one-day workshop, and fell in love. I signed up for the first level in February and then over the next two years planned to take another four levels!

Dr. John Upledger, an osteopath, had developed an amazing, hands-on-treatment. CranioSacral, skull to tailbone—but it encompassed so much more! It was much more medically based, and I had come to realize that if I wanted to attract even more clients, something more concrete, something more medical was necessary. That "leap of faith" wasn't always an easy sell.

CranioSacral released tissue on all levels—skin, fascia, nerves, muscles, and bones—and improved circulation and released all that nasty cellular memory. It did all this by using a compression, decompression technique that brought the body back into a perfect anatomic state. Eventually. There is no miracle pill, and there is no miracle treatment. Everything takes time. I'd come to realize that forty years of damage to my body couldn't be repaired overnight. If it did, perhaps the remedy looked nasty like chemotherapy and radiation treatments for cancer. Maybe all that was, was a quick fix? I preferred it this way, doing the work and allowing things to unravel and rebuild naturally.

I was thrilled to be doing more work on myself but was also so surprised how much more there was to work through. Hadn't I done so much already? I had worked through shame, guilt, fear, anxiety; offered up forgiveness and learned how to trust; let go of judgment and released my ego; accepted others and myself for who we were; relinquished control; found helping others humbling; removed the limitation on my conditioning and opened my heart to unconditional love ... there was more?

Apparently. The first day of my CranioSacral class, my neck released. I wasn't aware it had happened or that I had a problem with my neck. It was the following morning while blow-drying my hair with my head upside down that I caught myself stretching my neck out. Why was I stretching my neck? Did I do this every morning? Surprisingly, I did. Why did it feel awkward this morning? Because my neck had been released the previous day, and now it didn't need stretching out. Fantastic!

More physical adjustments took place in my body as time progressed, the bones in my ankle and foot were straightened like putty; all the strain in my lower back disintegrated; my TMJ disappeared! In the third-level workshop, all the deeper emotional stuff started rising to the surface. In the fourth level we started visiting our birth. I had dealt with some of it in my breath classes; going through my birth gave me an understanding as to why I slept all the time. When I was born prematurely and placed in an incubator, the nurses came around and checked me every two hours. My expectations of coming to Earth to share love had been shattered. I hadn't even seen my mother for five days, as she was recovering from severe hemorrhaging. Every time I opened my eyes there were these dead people leaning over me, staring. I didn't like it, so I closed my eyes and tried to ignore them, but then the nurses would come and touch me to wake me up, and there the spirits were again! I wanted to go home, to heaven. I didn't want to be here; nothing was working out the way it was meant to.

Experiencing those emotions and thoughts was huge for me. So much of my life had been confused because of this event. Again, I gained an understanding that certain experiences needed to take place in order for me to fulfill my destiny, in order to be set on the correct path here on Earth. Avoidance was no longer necessary, so my naps disappeared.

So while a lot of students were dealing with their birth, my sessions took me to childhood and past-life events.

We worked in groups of three, and it was my turn to lie on the table. Instantly I floated back in time to London, somewhere around 1870. I was a little man, maybe five feet, six inches, fine-boned and scholarly-looking, perhaps in my late twenties, early thirties. It felt like I was at the least, upper-middle class, and my clothes confirmed it. They fit well and seemed relatively new, not of a dandy, but of a proper, learned gentleman. I was on my own, and it didn't feel like I had any responsibility for anyone other than myself. I had just exited a little bookshop and was enamored of the book I had purchased. The book was open, and my nose was only inches away from the text, my eyes intent on reading. Without looking up, I stepped off the cobblestone curb and was run over by a team of horses and a carriage; the driver had lost control.

Next thing I remember is that my eyes opened, and I was laid out in what I thought was a doctor's office, no ... it was the morgue. On the right side, standing over me were two men who had just cut me open above my nipples from the right to the left, then down and from left to right above my pelvic bone. They were standing there observing my organs function. There was a brief minute when they looked at me and I looked at them, all of us with shock on our faces, and then I died.

In this lifetime, no one has ever been able to convince me to sign my donor's card. I have always been scared they would take organs from me before I died. Now I knew where the fear stemmed from—a past life. I was able to let go of that fear, although I still won't sign my donor's card. I also have a fear of horses, and when I was around them as a child, they'd kick me breathless.

Directly I went into another regression, to another time. I started uncontrollably making funny faces, twisting my face around, stretching it this way and that, raising my eyebrows, and making mad eyes. My two colleagues were killing themselves laughing. It took me more than a few minutes to figure out who and where I was. It was a current life experience from around the age of eight or nine. I was sitting in front of our bathroom mirror making faces. I was trying not to laugh because that would make my mother angry. She didn't like to laugh on a normal day, and today had not been normal. I had been to the dentist and had caused a lot of problems.

Mum told me, "Stay after school today, the dentist will be there waiting for you." No one prepared me or told me what a dentist was. Dentists are scary. He had this crazy chair and this big, long metal thing he wanted to poke me with, inside my mouth! I started yelling and screaming. They brought my grandma from work in the Variety Shop across the street to calm me down. That didn't work. Finally they were able to contact my mum. She came over and told me, "Sit down, be still, and stop making a fuss!" So I did; you don't cross my mother.

I'd forgotten that part. I remembered the dentist being mean, giving me a needle in the front of my mouth above my teeth. I know a lot of people my age had horrible dental experiences as a child and now get sedated. I always wondered why I sat perfectly still when I went to the dentist; it is because my mother told me to. That cellular memory was still intact.

What I started remembering during the regression was the dentist gave me five needles. My entire head was frozen right down to my clavicles. That was why making faces in the mirror was so funny: I could see movement but couldn't feel a thing. As I came out of the regression with this new knowledge as an adult, I realized that the dentist had given me that many needles so I wouldn't bite him; it wasn't that he hated me. With this realization, the anaesthetic started releasing from the cells in my skull. My entire head went completely numb, and I could taste the anaesthesia in my mouth as it released from the trapped cells. It took three days for the freezing to release completely.

When I tried to get off the table, my legs wouldn't hold me; they had turned to jelly. I now remembered sitting in that dentist's chair with every muscle in my body taut. Acknowledging my experience had also released the tension I had carried in my arms and legs all these years. Many people had said I walked like a stick was up my butt. I thought they were just being mean! I had sat in that dental chair like a plank for over an hour and a half. Now my lower back was a bit relieved of pain, but what I noticed most was that my belly felt so much better. For years I was never able to lie flat on my back without getting intense pain in my stomach—at the beach, in bed, especially at the dentist. Within a half hour I always needed to pull my legs up toward my chest to help alleviate it.

I was open to healing, and it was happening!

Past-life regressions are a difficult concept for some people, especially if you don't believe in rebirth because of your religion or conditioning. What I tell those clients is it doesn't matter if what you see is real or not, it is more about the lesson you learn from what you've seen.

I have seen so many diseases release and dissolve through the process of past-life regression work. One client saw herself as Snow White, the one in the cartoon. Was this a real past life? When we got to the part where the witch offered her the poisonous apple to eat, it got interesting. She knew it was poisonous, but she also knew she couldn't do anything to stop herself from taking that bite. She didn't want to be rude.

This had been a big part of her life—doing things she didn't want to do because she didn't want to be rude. Recognizing how detrimental this was really hit home, and she was able to let go of that belief system and make the necessary changes in her life to fulfill her dreams.

Sometimes clients go back to the womb, where they took on a parent's belief system. This was the case with my youngest daughter, Taylor. She didn't do the work; I did it for her. I revisited the time in our lives when I was pregnant. Mike and I so wanted our second child to be a boy and believed it was going to be. I know those hopes and dreams affected her in my womb. She is such a tomboy—she played rough, loved to burp and fart, her room was painted vibrant boy colors, and she never played with dolls. She did have Princess, her beany buddy cat. Doing the release would only change the part of her that was a belief system, not the true core part of her personality. I spoke to her in this regressed place and told her how sorry we were to have inflicted the idea that she needed to be a boy rather than a girl. She told me that she just wanted to make us happy and would do anything to accomplish that. I told her we were happy, and if she wanted to do more girl things, we would be happy to assist her. Again, I told her we loved her, and we just wanted her to be happy. I also redelivered her in a kind and gentle way to release any trauma that had occurred during her aggressive birth and that might have affected her neck and head.

Within a few weeks, she started paying more attention to her hair. Then she asked to change her room from orange and green to pink. She still loves soccer and prefers to wear jeans, but she has added pink to her wardrobe, whereas before it was all blue. She also mentioned to me that her neck no longer hurt.

Then I was introduced to visceral manipulation, and reflexology took a back seat! To work on the organs directly rather than through the feet—remarkable! Name an organ, we covered it. Every organ represented a different emotion: worry and negative thoughts come from spleen issues; the stomach is more the social stresses of life—for me it also included changes and what people would think of me. I worked kidneys, liver, pancreas, intestines, heart, lungs, bladder, prostate, bowel, thorax, thyroid, and adjusted diaphragms! I could talk to the organs as well and find out why they weren't doing their job. Our discussions were remarkable! My client appointments increased tenfold.

So many different things could affect the organs—a car accident, surgeries, a slip and fall, even gravity could be a contributing factor over time. Dysfunctions could arise like chronic abdominal issues, acid reflux, kidney infections ... the list is long.

All the organs move in unison, like a pendulum, one beside the next. If that rhythm is interrupted by one organ, the other organs around it can be affected in a domino effect. After surgery, nothing is put back the way it was before it came out. One client had anesthetic sitting in her bowel years after surgery, and it was now causing severe issues because the area had become numb, and the muscles no longer responded. Or a stomach could close up on itself from a trauma, making digestive issues worse, to the point of no return as far as the medical community was concerned. Twenty minutes of unwinding, and these organs were back to normal. There was always a follow-up appointment to see if there were day-to-day stresses also causing problems, or if it was only an old issue. But the client could eat again!

After getting my lungs and bronchial tubes worked on I was actually concerned for the first time that perhaps it wasn't a healing crisis or healing transformation, but a medical condition. My old conditioning cropped up. I'd grown up with bronchial asthma as a child—ages two through nine. All the physical and emotional traumas connected to my lungs and bronchial tubes had released from my body; spiritually I was sure of that, but mentally I was positive I had H1N1! I swore that I was on death's door. It took some doing to stop my mind from floating to the H1N1 scenario. After a day two on the couch, not moving or eating, I relented and saw a doctor. I didn't have H1N1. My body took a bit of time to heal, but afterward my lungs felt amazing!

Healing can be ugly. Many people quit during the process because they think they feel worse. It is only the large amount of toxins being released that exhaust us. The internal organs are working to clean things up and tend to use up the majority of our energy supply. We need to rest so we don't take anything away from that healing process. After you get through that chunk of healing, you will feel better than when you began.

Then a new trend began in the ailments I was seeing. Arriving at my office were not people with bad knees, whiplash, or migraines, but victims of rape. I was able to assist them from a neutral place because I had let go of my own anger about being raped at seventeen, but not the confusion around the event. I still didn't know how it had occurred; the evening didn't make sense. With each new client coming through my door, I realized that I needed to deal with this issue on a much deeper level. It was starting to bring up issues around the safety of my girls, who were now entering their teen years. I needed to get rid of the residue so I could release the fear around their well-being. If I didn't, I knew that I could manifest it in their lives.

There was one woman who had assisted in my CranioSacral classes, so I called her to book an appointment. Typically treatment was easy for me; I never struggled—it was all about getting it done. In class the teachers always used me as a demo because intuitively they knew I was quick and efficient. I knew how to connect with whatever it was that needed to be released. Did it surprise me at times? Always. This was no exception.

Belinda was stabbing me in the left side of my back with her finger. Realization set in: it wasn't her finger, it was … part of my belt buckle, and it hurt intensely. The pain was pulling me out of a deep, deep state of sleep. I could feel a penis on my lips, but I couldn't move or say anything to stop it. I felt a penis in my vagina. That actually made the pain in my shoulder lessen, but where did the penis come from? Whose penis was it?

Then I remembered every detail of that night. I had been invited to a friend's house, along with two of his male friends. They had come to pick me up from a party, but when I entered the car, it felt like death. Everything told me to get out. Consciously, I told myself, *You're crazy. Everything is fine.* When we arrived at his house, I sat down to watch a movie, and they started making drinks. It was close to midnight. At the party I had one, maybe two, drinks all night. On an unconscious level, I knew they were trying to crush up a pill—two pills, actually—but the pills kept making the drink look funny. One mentioned to the other, "Let's tell her it's an aspirin, and if she takes it now, she won't have a headache in the morning." Unconsciously I knew they were trying to drug me, but consciously I didn't believe it. Perhaps I had Snow White syndrome and didn't want to be rude.

All three of them stood around me and offered me the pill and popped one of their own. I looked at it and then popped it into my mouth. Over the next hour I tried to leave several times but was told to sit down. Nothing felt right. Then I passed out. Not my friend, but his buddies, carried me to the bedroom. One dropped me, saying, "I've done my part. Now it's up to you." The rapist dragged me the last eight feet to the bed, dropping me again. Then I bounced off the bed before he raped me.

Now the words escaped my lips, "They drugged me. The pills were his mother's. I remember him telling me once that she needed them to sleep."

"Yes, they did," Belinda confirmed. I started to cry. For years I was sure it was my fault, that I had fallen asleep on one of their shoulders, and they had taken it suggestively. The only thing I had done wrong was getting in the car in the first place. They had drugged me. The tears kept coming, more from relief than anything else.

There was freedom in this knowledge, and, with so much shame now gone, I wanted to reconnect with my old high school girlfriends. I had kept in contact with a few of them over the years, but it was time to get us all together. I started with Kathleen, Cynthia, and Olivia and then worked my way out from there. This year we would all turn forty. It was time to reconnect, for all of us to heal. Ten out of thirteen girls, now women, celebrated over a long weekend in Banff. We had the best time. Twenty years dissolved, and we talked endlessly and laughed heartily. It was exactly what I needed to continue moving forward. We all decided to get together semiannually.

I'd applied for the Advanced CranioSacral class, sending them a photo and two pages of details about myself, my practice, and my healing experiences. The selection was done intuitively. The class would last five days and was considered more intensive than anything else I had taken. I had heard that some students worked late into the early-morning hours, letting exhaustion take over so they could no longer hang on to those boundaries; everything would then be revealed. Healing the nitty-gritty would happen. At least that was how I saw it. With another level of fear releasing from my life, I realized it was time to contact Peter. He was a loose end that still brought on a tremendous amount of fear.

I was aware that he now lived less than an hour away from me, and my concern was that I'd bump into him at the mall, or just about anywhere in the city. I didn't want him to know where I lived, or have the opportunity to meet my family. I had run away from the relationship at twenty, and somehow he still had a hold over me. I managed to find him on Facebook. Thank you, Mark Zuckerberg.

I contacted him, and we arranged to meet for lunch.

Mike didn't want me to go; he was worried that Peter would hurt me again in some way. But I was persistent about needing this meeting. We picked a quiet café, and I sat down across from him. I just kept staring. I could only imagine what his ego thought I was looking at. He had taken care of himself, he told me, through rock climbing. Had his head always been so large? Where was my mind at fourteen? This is what I found attractive? Was there nothing to choose from? Or was my self-esteem so low that I never looked for anything better? *Acceptance without judgment, Tracy,* I reminded myself. *You were only fourteen.*

His vulnerabilities and insecurities were apparent to me now. I had misinterpreted them completely for something else—confidence? Perhaps I never noticed them at all because my vulnerabilities and insecurities were more severe? Now for me there was no connection, no fear, no need to please. There was freedom in that awareness.

"I want to apologize for how badly I treated you."

This brought my head up from my plate. "Really?"

"Yes, I was terrible to you, and I'm really sorry."

"Thank you, Peter." All my pent-up emotions evaporated. It amazed me, yet again, how such a small statement could release so much. Afterward there was no longer a charge when I said his name or thought about the past; in fact, more positive memories surfaced.

Not my rapist, but the boy, my "friend," contacted me on Facebook. There was no apology. The discussion only produced an "I'm different now; I'm not the same person" response.

"Yah, well neither am I." Letting go of this would take a little longer; there was still so much anger because of his betrayal of our friendship. All I had to hang on to was that karma would take care of the situation. I didn't hold the same amount of animosity against my rapist and that fact had me pondering why. Then I remembered that we had been at a party together, and I had threatened to reveal the truth of the situation to his peers. The fear revealed in his eyes gave me back my power. "He no longer has anything of mine; that is why there wasn't any dysfunctional energy between us," I asked Jonathan. I felt his agreement, rather than heard it.

Resolving these old relationships had me thinking about John. There wasn't anything there to resolve. We had broken up amiably and when I returned to Yellowknife, we had visited a few times over coffee, having met by accident, if you believe in such things. They had been nice visits.

My relationship with Luke was also trigger-free. While I was still in Yellowknife, I had attended the funeral of his fiancée. She had died of some rare lung disease; it was so sad. The church was standing-room only, on both floors. I hadn't known her all that well, but was there somehow for Luke. I waited a while before exiting so I would have a chance to given him my condolences. He thanked me and then continued to hold my hand for ten, maybe fifteen minutes. Originally it felt awkward, standing there as other people offered their condolences. Then I realized that if he needed my hand to support him in his grief, I could just be with him during those few minutes. Something dissolved.

And the high school boy who broke my heart? Well, I never did get an apology from him, but the clarity around our relationship eventually revealed itself. I had blocked so much. Now I felt grateful for not having endured that relationship beyond that moment. He had given me a great gift.

Why did some of the same issues come up time and time again? I had figured out that some things needed to be healed on different levels— physical, mental, emotional, and then spiritual. I hope that meant that then we were done.

Moving past all these old relationships and releasing all the fear attached to them opened my availability to continue writing my book. They were all connected to my fear of succeeding. It had in some way also closed the door for my healing practice to expand. I hadn't wanted anyone to find me, and now it didn't matter. A former student, now friend and feng shui expert Mia Staysko mentioned that my website didn't post my name. Unconsciously that had not been an oversight; consciously it surprised me. Now I could post my name. People would know who I was and where I was located.

I took the Advanced CranioSacral course, released another level of earthbound fear, and was able to tap into a deeper place of loving myself.

CHAPTER 17

Resolution

I WAS ON THE RIGHT path. I believed in God. I believed in my purpose. People could stray from that purpose, but then they would always feel incomplete, as I had for so many years. Occasionally, while looking for that, we sometimes divert, learn a few lessons, and then eventually get back on track. Others might think we're on the wrong path, but in Mike's case, he had been on the right path. He learned what he needed from his experience. His career was no longer Number One on his list. Now he was slowly gaining the understanding that *he* should be Number One. If he didn't do what he needed to make himself happy, then how could he follow his life path? He took up fly-fishing, and that really took him to another level; it was meditative for him. His intuitiveness had always been built in, and he ended up at the right place at the right time and was offered a job he loved. Now he would split his time between working at home and traveling to different projects around the world. He loved it; passion ignited him again! We could accept it, for when someone is doing something they love, how can you not? It all made him happy, and that allowed for more time to be spent with us.

All my wandering had me exactly where I needed to be, and still revelations showed up.

When I was little and someone asked me what I wanted to be when I grew up, I told them, "I want to know everything about everything." I was always told, "There is no such job!"

Then, somewhere along the way, probably in my midtwenties, someone mentioned the Akashic Records. They contain all the knowledge of the universe—my information, your information, current lives, past lives; it was all recorded in the Akashic Records. They had been coming up more often, and now it was time to tap into them. Of course there was a part of me that believed I already knew that information, but ... I wanted to connect to that ancientness, the old magical part.

This time I lay down to meditate, setting the intention to find out where they were located. It didn't take long for an image to appear. It was as though I had always expected it: big, solid wood door opening into a circular tower area made of castle bricks. There was a set of circular stairs to the right, but they didn't interest me. I wanted to head forward through the large, brick, arched entrance. On the other side was a large-size room, three stories tall with amazing windows at the top. The walls were covered in shelving full of books, and the center space was filled with tables stacked with books. Turning more to my left, I realized that the room continued; the end was not in sight. What gained my full attention was another set of stairs on the far side of the room to my right. They led up to what looked like a loft and more books. As I crossed the room heading toward the stairs, I let my hand glide across books along the way, but I never opened even one.

I reached the single wooden staircase, each step forward taking me into a darker space than the last. Glancing up, I realized that the loft was enclosed in darkness. Now, at the top of the stairs, I could only see slightly; there were shadows encompassing more tables of books, but seeing deeper into the space was impossible. I was used to walking through my house with the lights off. I was capable of getting around, feeling for the corners of the tables and not knocking over any of the stacks. As I continued through this space, I noticed a small glimmer of light across the way on my left. There was a door slightly ajar. I focused on the light and continued to move toward it. Slowly I opened the door and was surrounded by the purest, brightest, white light I had ever known. It was as blinding as the pitch-black, but I was used to the dark; I knew there was floor to feel my way along. What did this white light encase? Could I ease my feet along? What would I find in front of me? Did it matter? Did I not trust? Could I only trust the dark and not the light? Taking a big breath, I took a step in and closed the door.

The books had been a guise; the pure white light was the Akashic Records which held the collective unconsciousness. I knew it was an important step forward, a new beginning. I had moved into the light and all the knowledge it held.

Mike and I had been asking for more prosperity, not only financially, but with regards to our health and our relationship with our girls and extended family. By asking, we also found friendship with a few families from Brett's volleyball team. With all the traveling to tournaments, the moms had come together and shared hotel rooms multiple times. When the season ended, we continued seeing each other socially. Our friendships had grown over the last few years. Sara's daughter and Brett also had French class together and both had signed up for a school trip to France during Easter break of their eleventh-grade year. The teacher felt they needed two more students to make the trip feasible. I mentioned to Sara one night while we were out for dinner, "If this trip is canceled, Mike and I have talked about taking the money and going to Mexico or Hawaii or somewhere."

Three days later it was canceled, and the following day Sara called and said, "We just booked flights to Hawaii. Want to come?"

There was a moment of silence and then a "yes," escaped my lips.

Oh my God, did I just say "yes" without confirming with Mike? Financially, we were doing very well; prosperity expanded daily. We could afford it with a little bit of effort. Fear had taken hold, though ... too many dreams were coming true. Mike and I had booked a sixteen-day trip to London and France for the fall of 2011 to celebrate our twentieth wedding anniversary. And we booked a week of skiing over Christmas. Could we really afford to add Hawaii in April? Actually, we could. "All my dreams are coming true," I repeated, yet again trying to come to terms with everything I had manifested.

Our other volleyball mom, Barb, also decided to come, so in total there would be thirteen of us! Everyone was so excited.

By January I was overwhelmed. Volleyball was over, so that freed up some time. Brett was now driving, so that was also a plus—less driving for me. Taylor's soccer was keeping me busy, but after ten years I was used to that. Mike was traveling more, so he wasn't much of a help. Mentally I had prepared myself for that, but perhaps emotionally and physically it was taking a toll on my body. My business had kicked up another notch, and I was booking appointments months in advance. The downside to this was that if something came up—a sick kid, unscheduled appointments, a change to Taylor's soccer schedule—I wasn't available at the last minute. And with Mike traveling so much, neither was he.

There was also this weight on my shoulders telling me to finish my manuscript, revamp a couple of workshops I had developed, run those workshops, add the Angel Card Reading service to my website, revamp my entire website ... Hawaii seemed still so far away. I needed a holiday now, and Christmas break had just ended.

Running the business and dealing with all my personal commitments was becoming too overwhelming for this one-woman show. During my lunch break in early January, I tried to figure out what to do. There was really only one choice: quit taking client appointments. "That's your solution," I repeated out loud. And answered with a "yes."

Fine. I'd be done by early March. I started letting my clients know.

Everyone was shocked, as was I, but it felt right. There was a student I had mentored to whom I was pleased to hand over my clients, without that, I might not have made the decision to quit. The healer in me couldn't leave my clients hanging. Not having clients every day did not slow me down any. Revamping my workshops and website was a full-time job.

Taking on personalized Angel Card Readings added to it. I also organized a more professional newsletter and started doing a free monthly Angel Card Reading on YouTube. I never questioned why I was doing all this; I just knew it needed to be done.

The girls also filled in what space I didn't have available. "Mum's not working, so she must have lots of time to run around and do things for us!" was their thought process. In truth, it was nice to be more available for them. It seemed to me that when they were little they needed me and then there was a period of time when things flowed. Now, in high school, they needed me again. To ground them in all ways, set additional boundaries, counsel, and love.

Maui came quickly and was absolutely amazing. Mike and I had been to Mexico a few times. Mike had actually worked on and off in Mexico over the last two years. We had started going away during Easter break with the girls a few years back, since they were getting so big, and we felt that family time was running out. We had been to Vegas, and yes, it was a tremendously good time even with a twelve- and fourteen-year-old; their eyes got so big over everything. And there is nothing better than a Cirque du Soleil show. Another year had been Disneyland and then next the Dominican Republic. Nothing drew us like Hawaii. With all the traveling Mike and I had done, we knew this would one day be home. I was sure people sold their soul just to return. But I wasn't putting that out there, as I knew it was possible!

It wasn't until I quit work that I really noticed how fatigued I was. Following a daily schedule had me in a perpetual motion that hadn't given me time to notice the pace I was keeping. Although over Christmas break I had gotten a bad cold, so I knew something was up. I usually didn't get sick unless I was run-down or needed time off. That whole broken leg thing again—thankfully, not as severe! Returning from Maui brought some of my energy back. I had upped my yoga practice from three to four days a week. Every class I now noticed some minor change taking place within my body—one thing opening more than it ever had, something closing up, a new ache. But change is good; it means movement is happening.

By August, energetically I felt much better. All my projects where completed, and I sat for a day in silence. That was all my body could handle, or was it my mind? I sent out an e-mail telling my clients that I was back, and quickly I was booked into September. It was great to know that the business I built could take a time-out and recover so quickly. Work for me in the past year had all been about service and had flourished. Now I understood a balance needed to be found so I wouldn't burn out again.

In September Mike and I traveled to Paris, Normandy, and London to celebrate our twentieth wedding anniversary. My first night in Paris had me waking up in a cold sweat. In my mind's eye I could see and feel rats eating me alive. What was this all about? I started thrashing around and then realized I needed to get to the bathroom and turn on the light to release this vision. The rats followed me. I flicked the lights on, and the rats disappeared. I knew they weren't real, not in this life, but they had been real. I would have to deal with this experience to release the cellular memory attached to it.

In Normandy on one of the World War II beaches, I experienced red water up to my waist, with dead bodies scattered around me. So many bodies. I turned and left quickly, clearing the space as I went, sending any lost souls to heaven.

At the Normandy American Cemetery there was only peace. The dead had been laid to rest.

After our return from what was a wonderful trip, I booked a doctor's appointment. After months of seeing my chiropractor, acupuncturist, CranioSacral therapist, Reiki specialist, naturopath, and masseuse, nothing was changing. I had a few ideas about what was going on in my body, but I needed to rule out Parkinson's. The tremor, specifically in my hands and head, was a major concern. Thankfully the family hadn't noticed it yet.

Initially it felt like my frequency was off, like I was taking something in that wasn't in unison with the universe. Other days it felt like I was hypoglycemic. Some days were worse; other days were better. Occasionally it didn't feel like it had anything to do with me at all. After quitting work, my shoulders had dropped two inches and no longer sat up around my ears. Had the strain between my head and shoulders created pressure in my neck? The muscles were sure tight, and my neck was as solid as a cement block. So much damage had been inflicted on my body when, at eighteen, I had been hit by a car while crossing the road. I was sure there were residual issues there that had never cleared.

My doctor didn't do any tests. He was convinced that it wasn't Parkinson's or any other disease. Truthfully, I didn't think it was, either. I told him I'd be back in six months if it didn't go away.

I continued with my therapies. In December I flew to Seattle for a Brain Speaks class. It was so weird, as I hadn't attended a workshop in over three years; could it really have been that long? There were two women from my Advanced CranioSacral class there, and, with the diverse group of practitioners on the floor, we decided to work together. Knowing each other's capabilities and hands was important to us and our brains. That was not ego but intuition.

I had been having problems with my right elbow during yoga class for what seemed like forever. The first day of class, in a silent room with over sixty students, I let loose a scream that would have woke the dead as my elbow was snapped back into place. It felt so much better afterward. It had felt weird, but I had never imagined that it was dislocated. The thought now floating through my mind was, "Since when, and how?" Was it during a fall when I was figure skating?

On day two, many of the major components of my brain were put back into place. For some reason, energetically they had fallen down into my neck. Again, when had this occurred? The car accident? So much stemmed from that event.

Day three. Oh my God! Belinda, again, was shoving her fingers into my back, across the entire left side, mid–shoulder blade. It had nothing to do with my rape this time. "Tracy, what is this?" she asked gently. We were rooming together and had become good friends and associates over the years.

"I don't know."

"Yes, you do. Connect with it."

I didn't want to, which wasn't like me at all. *Relax into it Tracy, feel it. What is it?* The words slipped from my mouth without conscious knowledge: "Some stinky little boy hit me with a rake across my back!" Instantly I was so angry.

"How old are you?"

"I'm eleven, he's fourteen! He was mad I was making him leave our yard. Jane and I didn't want to play with him." The lost memory was floating into my conscious mind. "I don't remember any of this. I don't even know if it is true," came the second part of the statement in a different voice.

"Just stay with it. What else happened?"

I drifted back to the event, "He came up behind me and took me by surprise. When I fell I scraped my left hand, and that is when I dislocated my right elbow. I think that was also when all my brain parts whiplashed into my throat. I never cried but got up and turned to face him. He took one look at me and, although he had a good fifty pounds on me, started running. I was faster and jumped him, got him to the ground and started hitting him with my fist until my arms and fists ached. After that I stood up and started kicking him with my bare feet. I told my sister Jane to give him a couple good kicks too. He had tried to choke her a few years earlier with a hockey stick when we had been at the local rink."

"It was the summer my dad was working while he was on break from college. He wasn't around, and it was actually why the boy was angry. Dad had kicked him off the clean-up crew because he wasn't working hard enough. After the incident, my sister and I then went over to my Grandma's house and she put a balm across my back and gave me a baby aspirin. We hardly ever got baby aspirins, and they tasted so good. I remember that being the best part. She then sent me up to my uncle's bed to rest. I couldn't lie on my back or my front because my head wouldn't turn. So I ended up on my stomach, with my head off the bed."

The memory all came rushing back. How could I have forgotten the entire event? All the tissue, not only in my upper back, but in my entire body, was moving and changing. My left shoulder had gotten to the point that I couldn't hold it up, so the physiotherapist had been taping it for weeks. The rake had hit me at my left shoulder, angled slightly down to my right armpit, the knob of the rake only slightly missing my spine, hitting my back to the left of it.

There were more memories erupting: "My sister then went and told my father what had happened. He ran the family out of town." I paused for a few moments and then the tears came. "I forgot because I felt guilty, not because the stinky boy was leaving town or because I beat him—he was a menace to everyone—but I felt guilty because his older brother also had to leave. His brother was lovely. He had so many friends. I felt guilty for making his brother leave."

I remembered seeing the brother a few years back at a town function, and when I said "Hi," he snubbed me and walked away. I never understood why until now.

Then suddenly, "That stinky boy also killed my cat! He took Petite and threw her against a rock and killed her." The tears started all over again, and my body convulsed from such a deep-seated release.

I realized that moving from the outside, in wasn't only about moving my focus from constant companionship and drama to more self-awareness and enlightenment. It was also about moving in to the places of the body that were still hidden, where stories still remained silent. It would be the transition before moving outward again, but this time in a much different way.

That autumn when I started seventh grade, after the assault had always confused me. It was like I had become a different person. I had blamed it on puberty up until now. My hair went from straight to completely frizzy. Over time, as I healed, I had noticed my hair becoming straighter again. Had all that angry energy placed in me during that hit and then with my uncontrollable rage, releasing into my body and my hair follicles? The intense vibration entered my body and stay lodged. It did make sense. When I started figure skating and gymnastics that fall, I couldn't lean backward any longer, and the reason had eluded me, until now.

For the past two years in yoga class I had worked on opening my heart chakra more, worked on stretching the fascia and muscles across my back that seemed stuck, for no apparent reason. Had that process caused this to rise, inevitably, to the surface?

My behavior also changed in seventh grade. I was no longer this outgoing girl with lots of friends. I became secluded and spent hours upon hours reading. Emotionally I was a wreck and cried nearly every day. Again, I had blamed that on puberty.

Personalities change even when minor occurrences happen, so it shouldn't be a surprise that so much of me had changed as a result of this more serious trauma.

My body felt so different; I could move parts of my back that I didn't know existed. My tremor was worse—well, maybe not worse, but different. After every treatment, and there were many of them, my tremor—its frequency, pace, and depth—would change, and the answer still evaded me. What else could be locked away?

I called a good friend and breathwork classmate, who was also a licensed social worker, to book an appointment. Terry had helped our family numerous times. He and his wife lived in Yellowknife and moved the same week we did, to the same area we did, in 2004. The synchronicities were too many to ignore. We had all been to counseling with Terry at one time or another, separately and together.

Lately the tremor felt like anxiety and fear. Anxiety and fear over what? We came up with a long list of items that I had been repeating over and over in my mind for more than a year and a half. I thought it was part of resolving issues for my book, but in reality it was my ego self-sabotaging my success. Looking back, I could pinpoint the tremor to when we booked our trip to Hawaii. Too many good things were happening, and something inside of me got scared and was waiting for the other shoe to drop!

There were a few things I could finally let go of, but a few were still cycling in my brain. The boy—the "friend" who had orchestrated my rape—I still hated him because of the betrayal. I didn't want to give him any of my thoughts or energy, but now that I could put a word to how I felt, I was able to let it go. I'd let go of feeling betrayed. Knowing his personality, I knew I wasn't the only one; it was time to allow us all to heal.

My mother and sister came up again. They really had bullied me, and I had allowed it, not knowing better. That mental and emotional abuse had been the basis for letting so many after them treat me the same way—boyfriends and girlfriends alike! That had perpetuated my lack of self-love. I was now taking my power back!

On another level I knew all these events needed to happen in my life to allow me to clear karma from other lives. Somehow everything needs to be set up. It was all in our contract. Knowing that helped give me the strength to move through my stuff, to release it, no matter what it looked like. I had come so far and was so much more me than I had been twelve years before.

I was so excited about teaching a Karuna® Reiki class. I hadn't for over two years. Connecting with the archangels and the higher frequency for three days I knew would change something. It did: now I no longer could eat meat; it made me sick. The smell and taste was overwhelming, and my tremors got worse if I did. I checked my frequency chart, and, sure enough, the frequency of the meat I was eating was significantly lower than my own frequency, hence causing the disturbance in my body.

The tremor hadn't completely left, but it had lessened and was sometime barely visible. I was becoming so sensitive, I could tell when the tremor was food-related. Giving up chocolate and the occasional decaf latte would be harder. Other sugars and wheat were not as difficult. Good thing red wine hadn't shown up; that could have been devastating!

There was one more story I needed answers for.

We had been living in Bissett when I was nine. It was Easter time, and we were all outside for the morning, building ice-sculptures for the spring festival. Later that night we would have a contest and crown a king and queen.

There was still a lot of snow on the ground that year, and we were given buckets of water to help freeze our sculptures faster. I have an inkling that there was a theme, but I don't remember exactly what it was. Maybe fairy tales? I have a vague recollection of a giant cup and saucer from Alice in Wonderland.

My partner and I were hard at work when the ground shook, and there was a cloud of smoke in the distance near the mine site. There were blasts all the time, so I didn't take notice. The only thing I did notice was the boys running around yelling, "Your dad's dead, your dad's dead!" Shaking my head, I ignored this new form of name calling. They verbally abused me all the time.

The next thing I remember is eating lunch at home. When I arrived home there was a sandwich on the table for me, and Mum was in the basement doing laundry. I never mentioned to my mother what stupid stuff was being said at school. Jane was playing in her room, I suppose, waiting to attend kindergarten. The screen door at the back of the house off the kitchen made a rattling noise. Mum yelled up the stairs, "Who's at the door, Tracy-Lynn?" I jumped out of my chair to find out.

The door opened before I made it. Standing there, barely recognizable, was my dad. "I think its, Dad?"

"What? Your father wouldn't be home this … Oh my God!" as she raced up the stairs and opened the door to let my stunned father inside.

My father, who had been so handsome, with a perfect face and blond hair that swooped over like Elvis's, was covered in blood. His face was torn apart, leaving gashes everywhere. He was in shock and was not able to speak. My mother kept repeating, "Who brought you home? You need to get to a hospital!"

I don't remember the rest of that day. I imagine that Jane and I went and stayed at Grandma's. Mum, and Uncle Johnny probably drove the three hours into the city to take Dad to the hospital. I just don't recall. My next memory has Mum, Jane, and me on a train heading east to visit my mother's family just north of Toronto. It must have been May, maybe early June. I know the end of the school year hadn't arrived.

I was later told there had been an underground explosion. A man my father worked with had stood up just as my father bent down. My father felt the impact, but the man in front of him died instantly. My father had walked home after the explosion, and his own father had driven past him, never stopping to pick him up. I always found that odd, but I guess he was also in shock. My father's right eardrum had ruptured during the explosion, and he needed to get an ear drum transplant, like Jaime Sommers, who played the Bionic Woman. At least that is what we were told. Dad was already losing his hearing because of all the hours he had worked underground since the age of sixteen. The operation would help him hear even better than he had before the accident.

Sometimes we would have to drive past the house of the man who saved my father's life. His widow would be outside hanging laundry, lots of laundry, as she had five or six little children. The kids looked like they were having fun playing in the front yard. That was confusing and frustrating. Could you be happy if your father was dead? I don't think I would be. And why does one man die and another live?

Later I was told that we left Bissett to live with my mother's family in Ontario because Mum didn't want Dad to continue working in the mines. She wanted my father to return to school and get his two-year diploma as a mining engineering technologist. If he was going to stay in mining, he was going to do it in a more managerial position. They apparently didn't see eye to eye, so we left.

I don't remember there being a fight before we left or whether our departure came from years of discord. Perhaps Mum was tired of having a half marriage, which is what it was, with Dad gone all the time. Perhaps Mum was exasperated with the situation and had finally decided to walk away. I couldn't blame her. Two months later Dad came and retrieved us. He had decided to go back to school, and we moved to The Pas at the end of August 1976 to start a new chapter in all of our lives.

As I told Terry this story and he asked questions, the story changed. Then I booked a treatment with Belinda, and all the truth was revealed.

I crawled up onto her massage table and lay on my back. Belinda had her hands, front and back, on my solar plexus; something was trapped in there, and I could feel the vibration getting stronger. I now knew that I was actually eight when the tragedy of my father's accident happened. My mother had told me that there were fifteen months between the accident and leaving for Ontario, not three, like I had remembered.

I took myself back to our kitchen, eating my grilled cheese sandwich at the kitchen table. The table was white and had silver and gold sparkles embedded in the surface. Jane was playing in the living room. She didn't have kindergarten; she was still too young. The screen door just off the kitchen started to rattle. Mum was doing laundry in the basement, and I could hear the ringer washer swishing the water around as she yelled up the stairs, "Who's at the door?" I got out of my chair to find out. "I think its Dad," I yelled down to her. But suddenly I was stuck in my tracks, stunned by the image of my father.

He was covered in splatters of blood, and there seemed to be a chunk of something—flesh—on him. His face was all cut up, and his hair was all wrong. He didn't make a sound, just stood in the doorway, dumbfounded. The next thing I knew, I was flat on my back! I hadn't fainted; my eyes were wide open, and Jane was tapping my cheek. "Tracy, are you okay?" The look of concern on her face was tremendous. Was it for my father or me?

My mother stepped over me and said, "Tracy-Lynn, get off the floor. Richard, go wait in the car."

"What did your mother call you?" Belinda asked.

Pulled out of my trance, I said, "What? Oh, Tracy-Lynn."

"Did she always call you that?"

"I suppose so. Why?"

"Say 'Tracy-Lynn,' then 'Tracy,' and notice whether your body responds differently."

"Tracy." Normal. "Tracy-Lynn." Very different: there was severe pain sitting in my abdomen, between her hands.

"Notice the difference?"

"Very much so." I floated back to our kitchen in 1975. Roger was the man who had died. He had exploded into bits, and his soul, severed with shock, had entered my father's body. When my father walked through our door, Roger's soul left the discomfort of my father's body as a beam of light and entered mine, knocking me to the floor. My sister's concern was for me because she had witnessed the transference.

It had been he who was angry at his family when we passed their house, not understanding why they didn't show more grief for him. All the healing I had done had released down to this next chunk; he, perhaps was the tremor and started to appear around the time everything wonderful started to come together for me. Coincidence? Probably not. He couldn't survive if I was happy, so all the drama started making its way to the surface. All this was necessary to get me to this next step in my healing process. This, this was an unbelievable turn of events.

I had wanted to be happy that my father had lived. Roger had confused everything and made me start a continuous cycle of worry that controlled many different aspects of my life. Everything seemed to make more sense; I was no longer clouded with worry, regret, frustration, or anger. Life was meant to be lived, and I was to have fun doing it! It was a game that you played, but it wasn't about winning or losing, just being.

What a pleasant thought.

A few weeks passed, and the tremor was still present. I called my friend Susan Andrews. She and I had attended seven core CranioSacral and visceral classes together. She had also gone on and finished the brain and lymphatic curriculum. She was a few hours away in the mountains, so all winter I had waited for the weather to improve. "Susan, I need you to work on me. I think I need about three hours."

"Three hours? What's going on?"

I shared my experiences from the past year. "What I think I really need is to be put back together."

More need to release first. During the blast, Roger's soul had been blown into segments, and we found small parts of him sitting in different areas of my body. When Susan got to my sacrum, there was a huge chunk, nearly as large as the previous piece that had been found in my solar plexus by Belinda. It held so much regret—not mine, his. The remorse was overwhelming, and then I knew why, and the tears started flowing. His soul had filled me with so much masculine energy that my boys weren't able to bear it. He was sorry I'd miscarried. I grieved for my boys. Now I understood my son's comment, "Sorry. I was too scared and could not do it," and all the guilt he had felt.

I was angry with Roger. How dare he take that away from me? Then another wave of regret encased me. *Regret for what?* The memory surfaced. I couldn't connect with an age, but I remembered masturbating for a period of time in my younger years. I never understood why or where it came from. Now I knew it occurred after Rodger had taken up residence; the orgasm had made him feel more human, more normal. There was so much remorse from him and guilt released with a new awareness of what had actually gone on in my life.

What karma does a man have to clear that he is contracted to enter an eight-year-old child and grow into a woman for thirty-seven years? What karma did I have to clear? These thoughts were baffling.

I had struggled with my identity, not from the age of thirty-three, as I had thought, but from the age of eight. Ten, perhaps twenty percent of my personality had been his. He had protected me and also caused harm during my lifetime. Who would I be without him now?

I had learned how to integrate lost souls into my body, but now it was like a chunk of my soul was missing. I felt so alone. I had come to rely on Roger in many ways, had thought I was relying on myself, but now the truth had been revealed. The loss was ever present for nearly a month as I slowly found my own internal strength.

CHAPTER 18

Completion

I HAD STARTED MY BOOK, *What's Next*, nine years ago with absolutely no idea what indeed was next; hence the question. Through the years, much of life had interrupted my writing process. So it took place in chunks and spurts. Currently I was moving into an astrological one year and needed this project to be completed, mentally, emotionally, and spiritually. There was an ever present pressure to find completion. I had developed a two-day workshop called "Learn the Basics" and now was being guided to transform the workshop into a published book. My solution to publishing came in a workshop being offered by Hay House. Louise Hay was one of my idols and, although she was not instructing the workshop, I knew this was my next step.

Verbal confirmation had not been coming from my guide, Jonathan, or anyone on the other side since the shaking started nearly two years ago, but my knowing had greatly improved. Whether that meant my frequency had increased or decreased, I wasn't sure. My workshop "Learn the Basics" was all about frequencies, the chakras, and balancing all aspects of the body. I now referred to my own work. I was out of balance in several areas, specifically spiritually and physically. My mind had become consumed with my tremor and the physical ailments transforming within my body. I had continued my healing work but had not meditated in a long time because the activity in my body was so violent I couldn't concentrate on spirit. There was a part of me that was just angry and wanted answers from them.

Change occurred, but no answers were imminent. The shaking did seem to get worse when my emotions were heightened. As each day passed, more emotions seemed to rise to the surface; it had become quite overwhelming at times. I decided to let the tremor play itself out and get on with the other aspects of my life.

I flew to Denver to attend the writer's workshop. The biggest thing I took away from the weekend was how important a platform was to launch my book. I had a website and a Facebook page, and I sent out a newsletter, but more needed to be done. While I had been on my six-month hiatuses VoiceAmerica had contacted me about hosting my own Internet radio show. I had gotten nervous and more or less hung up the phone. The idea of hosting a show had lingered in my mind ever since. It was now time to call and explore that option.

My life was transforming. My book, with its new title, *Moving from the Outside, In*, was ready to be sent for its first edit. I had partially completed my *Learn the Basics* workbook, now called *Healing from the Outside, In* into a manuscript and was organizing the first thirteen episodes of my radio show, called *Healing Possibilities with Tracy Makarenko*. I would discuss my "Learn the Basics" workshop by doing seven shows, one on each of the chakras. I wasn't just sharing information; I was offering miniworkshops on the subject! I was overwhelmed with the amount of information it was possible to offer within one hour!

My guests included Dan Brulé, my Breath Master, Mia Staysko on Feng Shui, Carole M. Friesen talked about psychosomatic therapy, and Charles Virtue, son of Doreen Virtue, discussed the angels. Other shows included Suzanne Scurlock-Durana and her book *Full Body Presence* and Inna Segal, award-winning author of *The Secret Language of Your*

Body. Many others contacted me to speak about their passion and in doing so ignited mine. As they shared, I continued to heal and gain new awareness. I enjoyed interviewing guests and doing the work I loved the most, offering free healing treatments. Listeners called in, and I worked on their eyes, ears, bones, organs, heart, and many other parts of their body. So many emotions arose, so many new stories were told, so much healing occurred, not only for the callers, but for all the listeners.

All areas needed to be dealt with in order for healing to occur. A much greater understanding had entered my consciousness during this trying time in my life, with my own physical health in disarray. Looking back, I had gone through a deep emotional healing, followed by more spiritual awareness. More recently, as my physical body healed unknown areas, my memory, the mental aspect of my being, was transforming thought. I knew we healed on all four levels before we found peace: mental, emotional, physical, and spiritual.

The connection needed to be made through our feelings, our sensations, our awareness of what was inside. So many, including myself, have become detached from the self. Living outside of our body for so many years has hindered this process that was innately a part of our soul, a part of our person as a child. Doing this work allowed me to help people connect back within, and feel again!

My detachment from self had occurred without conscious thought, but because of my physical ailments. I had looked elsewhere for the answers. Perhaps unconsciously I was not ready to face those answers? Now was the time; I needed to move from the outside back in and find the next set of answers.

Over Christmas break I had become violently ill after a fifth-level visceral manipulation workshop. All my organs had responded to the work and, for nearly three weeks, had unwound. The tremor had subsided afterward, and I was pleased. Perhaps releasing the physical dysfunction in my system allowed more emotions to be dispelled. There seemed to be so many emotions trapped within my body. A lot of the emotional tension in my tissues had been released, and as it was, many more hidden traumas revealed themselves.

After Roger entered my body in March of my eighth year, many traumatic events occurred. I believe it was to help my young person displace the strangeness she felt within. In May during morning recess I was coldcocked by a swing. This memory arose while I was working on a client with the same ailment. Now my body reacted to it physically, and my left ear poured out a tremendous amount of heat. Later I called my mother, and she vaguely remembered the incident.

In June I became deaf. One day near the end of the school year I could no longer hear. I remember this being some of the best days of my life! I know that sounds strange, but my sister Jane and I spent precious time together lying in the grass watching the clouds or looking for four-leaf clover. Other moments were spent practicing lip reading. Jane would position herself so I could always count on her if I couldn't see the lips of the person talking to me. I was so at peace that summer. Why I didn't tell my parents still evades me. The jig was up by the end of summer when my mother requested I get "Grandpa ice cream" and I read, "Grandpa's boots." Off to the doctor we went, and I got my ears flushed. Life became so loud after that, but the internal unpleasantness was less noticeable or now forgotten.

I had no idea that we could lock so much away inside ourselves. As a young adult, I remembered very little of my childhood—nothing, really, before grade seven. There was no memory of my sister before she was eight. Both coincided with the rake incident; all memories had been suppressed before that point.

It was nearly four o'clock in the morning, and my organs were completely in spasm. All had been well for nearly two months, but now I could feel the shaking in every aspect of my body. I lay there and did my breathing exercises to calm my body and recognized its ability to relax. As I had taught so many of my clients, I went into my physical tissue and sat with it, looking for a story. Connecting to my emotions, I felt fear—no, it was different, deeper within me. It was more like I was scared. *What was I scared of?*

The long ago event floated into my mind. I was eight, and it must have been after the swing incident, but before my loss of hearing occurred. I was sitting at our kitchen table in Bissett across from my father, who was kneeling down in front of me, asking, "Why don't you want to go to the walk-a-thon?"

I had been adamant all week about not attending. My answer would get someone in trouble, myself or my auntie. She had told me that not even my family members would want to sponsor me. I had been slow in asking for sponsors; were they all taken?

I wasn't frightened of my father, but scared of getting into trouble. "Auntie told me that no one wants to sponsor me. That she had asked everyone first." My dad's sister was only four years older than I, but there was an eighteen-year age difference between the two of them. His sister had caused many problems for me, and my father was not pleased, so he set out the door to have a chat with her. Now I was scared what the repercussions would be when she found out I told.

Even with this partially resolved, and knowing people would sponsor me, I still had no interest in attending. The entire population, all 150 people, were present, but not me. Without my form signed, I was not allowed to walk and would miss out on the evening barbecue. That event affected many other events in my life. I would purposely leave myself out of large occasions, missing all the fun, acting like some kind of martyr. Although I didn't know for what cause.

As my mind accepted this new information and spirit melded and blended all this into my body and my emotional state, my body started to rock. Although I was still in bed it felt like I was floating on a wave. I could feel the physical compressions on the front of my body as a lengthening took place in my spine, then the compression of my spine while lengthening took place in the front of my body. Then suddenly, my entire body shuddered as different parts now softened from a huge release. So much change was taking place, and then I realized I was now lying on the ground unconscious. I was back in the school playground and had just been hit by the swing in the left side of my head, then a second time in my left upper chest.

The recess bell had rung, and whoever was on the swing jumped off to run inside, and that action had sent the swing in my direction. Only one boy noticed me and carried me into my classroom and placed me on the teacher's chair. Another student was sent to get ice and the nurse across the street at the Variety Shop. My mother was called and informed that I had a concussion and needed to be watched throughout the day. I remember none of it, but I did love having more pieces to my puzzled life.

It was then, during this healing, that a tremendous amount of grief set in. Releasing from underneath it all, underneath all the emotions that had come to the surface over the past two years. Grief for what was lost after dad's accident. Dad was not the same; Mum was not the same; I was not the same. Even Jane was probably not the same. We were all separately grieving for our old life. It had affected all of us. I can't say that my change was more dramatic than theirs, but now I understood why all the pain and suffering had occurred. Each consecutive event had allowed me to forget a little bit more of that initial trauma.

I had lost my childhood that day, the day of the accident, the day that Roger invaded my body. Then I felt arms encircling me, and I was sitting on my grandma's lap after being hit by the rake. There was uncontrollable shaking within my body that I could not stop. It reminded me of a wild animal after a traumatic event has happened in their life. That is what my body had been trying to do for the last two years—recover physically, mentally, emotionally, and spiritually from so many traumas. The grieving continued, then made room for anger to follow, which transformed into frustration and eventually left me sad and empty. The process was exhausting.

As I lay, accepting all the changes that had occurred during the last hour, there was a new emotion emerging. *What is that? Joy? Happiness?*

I started weeping. Those feelings had evaded me except in spurts since I'd been eight, trapped underneath so much suffering. They were so pure and simply beautiful. They were unconditional. My body responded like a flower opening up for a new day. My breathing, which had become so shallow for more than a year, deepened, and energy coursed through my being. I was awakening to new possibilities.

Thank you, God.

So much of me had been shared while I was venturing through the dark. What would tomorrow be like when I could offer information and healing from pure, unconditional joy and happiness?

I had done all this work not only for me and my family, but for you. To help you heal, and to help you continue your journey with as much support as you need.

Blessings to each of you.

CPSIA information can be obtained at www.ICGtesting.com
Printed in the USA
BVOW081524130713

325831BV00002B/5/P